SUETONIUS:
THE FLAVIAN EMPERORS

SUETONIUS: THE FLAVIAN EMPERORS

A Historical Commentary

Brian Jones and Robert Milns

Published by Bristol Classical Press
General Editor: John H. Betts

This impression 2003
First published in 2002 by
Bristol Classical Press
an imprint of
Gerald Duckworth & Co. Ltd.
61 Frith Street, London W1D 3JL
Tel: 020 7434 4242
Fax: 020 7434 4420
inquiries@duckworth-publishers.co.uk
www.ducknet.co.uk

A catalogue record for this book is available from the British Library

ISBN 1 85399 613 0

Printed in Great Britain by
Antony Rowe Ltd, Eastbourne

Contents

Abbreviations

The abbreviations are those of *L'Année Philologique* and *The Oxford Classical Dictionary* (3rd edn 1996), with the following additions:

AE	*L'Année Epigraphique* (Paris, 1888-)
ANRW	*Aufstieg und Niedergang der Römischen Welt*, ed. H. Temporini (De Gruyter, 1972-)
BMC	*Coins of the Roman Empire in the British Museum*, ed. H. Mattingly (Trustees of the British Museum, 1923-40)
CAH	*Cambridge Ancient History* (Cambridge University Press, 1923-)
ILS	*Inscriptiones Latinae Selectae* (Weidmann, 1882-1916)
MW	McCrum, M. and Woodhead A.G., *Select Documents of the Principates of the Flavian Emperors including the Year of Revolution* AD *68-96* (Cambridge University Press, 1966)
OCD	*Oxford Classical Dictionary*, 3rd edn (Clarendon Press, 1996)
OLD	*Oxford Latin Dictionary* (Clarendon Press, 1982)
PA	Platner, S.B. and T.A. Ashby, *A Topographical Dictionary of Ancient Rome* (Oxford University Press, 1929)
*PIR*1	*Prosopographia Imperii Romani Saec. I,II,III*, 1st edn (Reimer, 1897-8)
*PIR*2	*Prosopographia Imperii Romani Saec. I,II,III*, 2nd edn (De Gruyter, 1933-)
RE	*Realencyclopädie der Classischen Altertumswissenschaft* (Metzler and others, 1894-1980)
RP	Syme, R., *Roman Papers* (Clarendon Press, 1979-91)
StR	Mommen, Th., *Römische Staatsrecht* (Duncker and Humbolt, 1886-7)

Preface

The Translation

In preparing this translation I have used the Teubner text of Suetonius' *De Vita Caesarum* of M. Ihm, with minor variations from the printed text on six occasions. In the *Vespasian*, I have accepted Roth's conjecture of 'aut' after 'ne tribuniciam quidem potestatem' in ch. 12; Roth's conjecture of 'laetatus est et' after 'caede cuiusquam umquam' in ch. 15; and some manuscripts' reading of 'Apelli' for 'Appellari' in ch. 19. In the *Domitian*, I have accepted Ihm's own conjecture, mentioned in the *apparatus criticus*, of 'quam imperium adeptus est amisit' after 'alteroque anno' in ch. 3. In ch. 4, I have accepted Gronovius' conjecture 'Septimontiali sacro; cum quidem' in place of Ihm's 'Septimontiali sacrorum quidem' after 'largissimum epulum'. Ihm himself decribes Gronovius' conjecture as made 'probabiliter'. In ch. 12, I have accepted the reading of some manuscripts of 'conspiratione' after 'intimorum', whereas Ihm leaves a lacuna in the text between 'oppressus est' and 'amicorum etc'.

In my translation I have tried as far as possible to give what seems to me to be the precise and literal meaning of Suetonius' Latin. This has resulted at times in an English translation which is perhaps not as elegant or as 'racy' as some other modern English translations, but which, I believe, conveys accurately what Suetonius is saying. I have tried to be consistent in my translation of Roman political, administrative and military terminology; and have preferred, on the whole, to give the Latin word or words in their anglicised form rather than give what purports to be a modern equivalent. Thus I prefer to say 'legionary legate' for 'legatus legionis' rather than 'major-general' or 'brigadier'; and to say 'military tribune' for 'tribunus militum' rather than, for example, Robert Graves' misleading and anachronistic 'colonel'. The adjective 'consularis' I have translated as either 'consular' as in 'consular legate' (e.g. *Vespasian* 4) or as 'ex-consul' (e.g. *Titus* 5), as I think the one or the other more appropriate to the context. I have thought it quite proper and appropriate to translate 'cura' and 'curator' as 'commission' and 'commissioner'. With respect to the imperial titulature and designations, I have translated 'princeps' and 'principatus' as 'emperor' and 'position of emperor'; but 'imperator', when it denotes 'imperial salutations', as 'saluted victorious commander'. 'Pontifex Maximus' I prefer to leave in the Latin form, but 'Pater Patriae' I have consistently rendered as 'Father of his Country'.

Brisbane, December 2001 R.D. Milns

The Commentary

The aim of the Commentary is to assist students with little or no Latin to appreciate Suetonius as a source for the reigns of Vespasian, Titus and Domitian. References (often with translations) are given to other sources for the period, particularly Tacitus' *Histories* and the *Agricola*, the *Letters* and *Panegyricus* of the younger Pliny, his uncle's *Natural History* and the epitomes of Dio Cassius.

The debt owed to previous scholars is obvious – Birley, Eck, Syme to mention but a few. I have also found much of value in previous commentaries on the *Lives* and am indebted to the many colleagues who have helped me over the years in my work on the Flavians. They are too numerous to mention here. I need hardly add that any errors and misconceptions that remain are entirely my own. The bibliography contains only those works cited in the text: for a fuller bibliography, see Griffin (2000), Levick (1999) and Jones (1996, 2000). I have added an index of proper names occurring in the commentary and also an appendix listing (1) recent work on Suetonius, (2) other commentaries on the Flavian *Lives* and (3) articles discussing senior Flavian officials.

All dates are AD unless otherwise indicated; references to modern works are made by surname of the author(s) and date of publication. The following are cited by the author's name only – Statius (*Silvae*), Aurelius Victor (*De Caesaribus*), Orosius (*Historiae adversum Paganos*) and Eutropius (*Breviarium*).

Brisbane, December 2001 B.W. Jones

Introduction

Not so long ago Suetonius was described as being 'too keen upon petty and prurient detail to produce a scientific account of his subjects' (Duff, 1964: 508). Now he is seen as a courtier and as the author of a 'long list of scholarly, antiquarian and biographical works' (Millar, 1977: 91); and Wallace-Hadrill devotes over twenty pages to Suetonius the 'Scholarly Biographer'. This change of attitude has not occurred overnight, but the impetus for it has undoubtedly been the discovery of an inscription from Hippo Regius (= Annaba) with hitherto unknown details of Suetonius' career (*AE* 1953, 73). The result has been a fresh assessment of his value as an historical source, as is clear from the recent series of articles and monographs listed in the Appendix.

His Career

Son of Suetonius Laetus who had fought for Otho as an equestrian military tribune in Legio XIII during the civil war of 69, Suetonius Tranquillus was probably born in Hippo Regius (Annaba) in North Africa (see Birley, 1998: 203; but compare Brunt, 1990: 490) soon after the war ended and hence, so it is argued by Syme (*RP* 3.1053), acquired the *cognomen* 'Tranquillus'. On the other hand, some have suggested that he was born as early as 62, others as late as 77 (for the details, see Wallace-Hadrill, 1995: 3 n.4). Far more secure evidence shows that he was brought up in the capital and educated there. One of the teachers there was probably the aptly named Princeps (*De Gramm.* 4) and he describes himself as 'quite young' during Domitian's reign (*Dom.* 12).

A slightly older Suetonius appears in Pliny's letters. In their first exchange, from the last years of the first century AD, the theme is the effect a bad dream had on Suetonius (*Ep.* 1.18). The next (3.8: c. 101-3) clarifies their relationship: for Pliny had obtained a military tribunate for Suetonius with L. Neratius Marcellus (governor of Britain in 103: *CIL* 16.48), but Suetonius wanted to transfer it to one of his relatives. In 5.10 (?after 106), Pliny encourages him to make sure that his work (unnamed) is 'copied, read and sold'; and in 9.34 (105-8) Pliny asks him about a suitable reader for a public recitation of one of Pliny's works. By 110, Suetonius had secured the exceedingly valuable patronage of Pliny, a friend of Trajan, and influential enough to obtain for him the 'right of three children' (*Ep.* 10.94 and 95). One other letter remains (1.24; of uncertain date but probably very early), and in some ways it is the most important, for it has given rise to the belief that

Suetonius was little more than a retiring, timid scholar. Writing to Baebius Hispanus, Pliny begins 'My friend Tranquillus wishes to buy a small property', points out that amongst the property's advantages is its 'easy access to Rome' and adds that 'scholars turned landowners, like himself, need no more land than will suffice to clear their heads and refresh their eyes' (1.24.1-4). The words 'small property' and 'scholar' have been stressed rather than Pliny's comment that one of the property's advantages was the fact that it was close to Rome. The emphasis on Suetonius' desire for seclusion was misplaced. He was well aware of the real world and was seeking somewhere to relax – not peaceful retirement.

Pliny's letter to Trajan, probably written in 110 not long before his death, begins with a useful summary of Suetonius at the age of about forty:

> Suetonius Tranquillus, Sir, is not only a very fine scholar but also a man of the highest integrity and distinction. I have long admired his character and literary abilities, and since he became my close friend, and I now have the opportunity to know him intimately, I have learned to value him the more. (10.94.1)

The words 'now...intimately' could be interpreted to mean that Suetonius had accompanied Pliny to Bithynia, a not-unexpected development in view of the close relationship between literary studies and public careers in the Rome of this time. Whether or not Suetonius went to Bithynia, his reputation as a scholar was not irrelevant to his subsequent appointments and was now vouched for (in *Ep.* 10.94) by an imperial friend. Not long after the death of Pliny c. 111, Suetonius was to be found in Rome, not in search of a new patron but, rather (it may be surmised) to take up some sort of official post. Even though the preface to the *Lives of the Caesars* contained a dedication to the praetorian prefect Septicius Clarus (Lydus, *De Mag.* 2.6: see Bradley, 1998: 5), appointed to that post in 119 with Turbo (*SHA Hadr.* 9.4), such action hardly proves that Septicius replaced Pliny as a patron of Suetonius, the timid 'scholar' anxiously seeking new means of support.

More precise information is provided by the inscription from Hippo Regius (discussed most recently by Lindsay, 1993: 1-2, 15-17 and by Bradley, 1998: 4). In brief, it indicates that he held two priesthoods and was probably adlected (by Trajan) to the equestrian jury panel (if that is the correct restoration). Perhaps he maintained some of the interest in the law hinted at in *Ep.* 1.18.6, where he had appeared with Pliny in a case before the Centumviral court. The inscription finally reveals that Suetonius held three senior administrative posts within the Palace, i.e. Cultural Secretary, Director of Imperial Libraries and Chief Secretary (see Birley, 1998: 138 and 142).

As Cultural Secretary, he would have been responsible for advising and assisting the emperor on literary matters. Many of the *Lives* refer to the emperor's 'liberal studies' (e.g. *Dom.* 20), for Suetonius believed that 'an emperor ought to interest himself in literary matters...(and) the range of the literary interests he documents...is astonishing' (Wallace-Hadrill, 1995: 83-4). Subsequently, he was appointed Director of Imperial Libraries. As the Ulpian Library within Trajan's Forum was finished c. 112, this would provide a suitable moment to assign another senior administrative post to an equestrian official such as Suetonius. So, after a brief stint as Cultural Secretary, he became Director of Imperial Libraries and then Chief Secretary, presumably after the accession of Hadrian (some, however, argue that he held all his senior posts under Hadrian). This was the most prestigious post of all. It was an onerous office: the incumbent (according to Statius) had to deal with a multitude of issues, from the river heights in Egypt to candidates suitable for military appointments (*Silvae* 5.1. 95-9). For a more measured discussion of his duties, see Millar (1977) 83-110.

When he held these posts is less clear. Much depends on the date of his dismissal from the highly influential post of Chief Secretary. That he was dismissed is stated in the *Life of Hadrian*, in a passage usually assigned to the year 122 (*SHA Hadr*. 11.3). However, the *Life*'s chronological accuracy is often impugned and a case has been made for assigning this passage (and Suetonius' dismissal) to 128 (Lindsay, 1993: 4-5 and 1994: 454-68; rejected by Birley, 1998: 313; see also Birley's discussion of the dismissal, 1998: 138-40). The problem is exacerbated by the lacuna in the Hippo inscription immediately after the Trajanic adlection to the jury panel and before his three senior appointments. If he was dismissed in 122, then it is possible that some of the latter were made by Trajan; on the other hand, a date of 128 would imply that they were all Hadrianic. Scholars generally if not universally favour the earlier date.

What sort of people were appointed to these positions? Despite the *SHA*, it was not Hadrian who first appointed an equestrian to them. The innovation had occurred far earlier, possibly under Claudius (Millar, 1977: 85-6) and certainly under Vitellius (*Hist*. 1.58; *MW 338*, i.e. Sex. Caesius Propertianus). Domitian, in a sense, went further. He seems not to have looked for administrative experience in his Chief Secretary, if we are to judge by Titinius Capito. Pliny lauds Capito as 'a patron of literature and admirer of literary men, whom he helps and supports in their careers.' (*Ep*. 8.12.1). Capito, then, was a scholar, and appointed for those very qualities – an 'intellectual from the Latin world' (Millar, 1977: 89) and that is an apt description of Capito and of Suetonius as well. So, if Suetonius' 'finished work' (*Ep*. 5.10) earned for him the reputation of being a 'very fine scholar' (*Ep*. 10.94.1), it may well be that, soon after 111, he was appointed by Trajan (and promoted by Hadrian) to prestigious posts in the imperial service on the strength of his literary reputation. But these were not the sort of tasks to be assigned to a timid, retiring scholar: that image of Suetonius should be rejected. As Wallace-Hadrill has observed:

> It was his scholarship that made Suetonius and others like him useful to emperors. Because the society in which they operated placed a high value on literary culture of the hellenistic type, emperors played an important role in the world of culture.... They liked to be seen themselves as men of education, in their conversation and their public letters and pronouncements. For this reason learned men had a place in their entourage. There is no gulf between Suetonius the secretary and Tranquillus the philologist. (1995: 95-6)

His Works

Apart from the *Lives of the Caesars* and the *Lives of Illustrious Men*, he wrote in Latin and Greek on a vast range of topics. A list of them appears in the Suda and some are vouched for by Aulus Gellius, Lydus and other late writers (see Mooney, 1930: 39-44). He seems to have had a wide range of scholarly interests, for his works include *Names and Types of Clothes*, *Physical Defects*, *Insults*, *Weather-Signs*, *Names of Seas and Rivers*, *Names of Winds*, *Greek Games*, *Roman Spectacles and Games*, *The Roman Year*, *Rome and its Customs and Manners*, *The Institution of Offices*, *Famous Prostitutes*, *Kings* and *Cicero's Republic*. Unfortunately, only a few small fragments of them have survived.

His Sources

How much assistance Suetonius the Hadrianic official gave Tranquillus the biographer is still debated. Scholars have often regarded the timing of Suetonius' dismissal as relevant to the date of composition of the *Lives of the Caesars* on the assumption that the less detailed *Lives*, especially those of the Flavians, were probably written after the dismissal, because he no longer had access to the imperial archives (Wallace-Hadrill, 1995: 89-95 and Baldwin, 1983: 48). That may well be, yet, if we accept the evidence of Lydus (*De Mag.* 2.6), it is highly likely that the *Lives* as a whole were dedicated to Septicius before he and Suetonius fell from grace.

However, the archival question does not really get us very far. In the first place, it does not follow that the longer the *Life*, the greater the author's access to the archives; the more detailed treatment of Julius Caesar and Augustus can reasonably be explained by the fact that Suetonius' area of expertise was the Ciceronian and Augustan period (Wallace-Hadrill, 1995: 56-7). Again, whilst access to such evidence may well be a *sine qua non* for a modern historian, we have no reason to believe that it was so for his ancient counterpart. Suetonius is one ancient author who at least does make occasional use of archival material (see below), but does it in a way that today seems fairly casual and haphazard.

On the other hand, Suetonius obviously made a careful investigation into the family's background. Commenting on certain activities of Vespasian's grandfather (Flavius Petro), he states that 'despite my very careful investigation of this matter, I personally have not come up with any trace (of them)' (*Vesp.* 1); he probably visited the town of Vespasiae, 'where there are still very many monuments of the Vespasii' (*Vesp.* 1) and the 'humble' house where Titus was born 'in a very small bedroom which is still there to this day and on display' (*Titus* 1). He had also read of Vespasian's formidable mother who 'forced him (to seek the senatorial office) by means of abuse, (and who) continually and insultingly called him his brother's footman' (*Vesp.* 2).

There were written sources aplenty. Tacitus' *Historiae* (published at least a decade before Suetonius' *Lives*; unfortunately, the books dealing with the period after 70 have not survived) and Plutarch's *Lives of Galba and Otho* (written not long after 96) were available to him, as were various other works; but, as they have not survived, we cannot assess whether or to what extent Suetonius made use of them: no doubt they would have contained material relevant to Vespasian's early career. Apart from the writings of Tacitus and Plutarch, useful information could have been gleaned from the Elder Pliny's *Continuation of the History of Aufidius Bassus* (*Ep.* 3.5.6); and from the works of Claudius Pollio (*Ep.* 7.31.5), Fabius Rusticus (*Agr.* 10.3), Pompeius Planta (*Ep.* 9.1.1), Cluvius Rufus (*Ann.* 13.20, 14.2) and Vipstanus Messalla (*Hist.* 3.25, 28). More useful would have been the writings of Titinius Capito and, perhaps, C. Fannius *Ep.* 8.12.4; 5.5.3). Fannius was, in effect, a pre-Suetonian Suetonius, 'writing by categories' (Sherwin-White, 1966: 321). Material favourable to Helvidius Priscus could have been obtained from both Herennius Senecio's *Life of Helvidius* and from Helvidius Priscus' own diaries given to Senecio by Helvidius' widow, Fannia (*Ep.* 7.19.5-6), whilst M. Aquillius Regulus' work attacking Rusticus and Senecio (*Ep.* 1.5.2-3) would have supplied more hostile details. However, in view of the fact that Suetonius names Arulenus Rusticus rather than Senecio as Helvidius' biographer (*Dom.* 10), it is to be presumed that the role of the philosophic opposition held minimal interest for him.

Oral testimony was available in abundance. Suetonius all but ignored it. He lived in Rome during the reign of Domitian, although it is far from obvious in the Flavian *Lives* – he mentions only one incident that he witnessed personally (*Dom.* 12). Of course, it would have been unwise to refer to the activities of Flavian officials still alive in the early years of Hadrian's reign. Perhaps he had also lost interest in the entire project and was determined to complete it with all possible speed.

Lives of Vespasian, Titus and Domitian

In his *Lives of the Caesars*, Suetonius avoided an annalistic approach, preferring instead to write under various headings or categories (*per species*). So he often begins with an account of an emperor's birth and early life in chronological order until his accession, follows it with chapters on specific areas of his government (games, legislation, public works, and wars) and of his personal life and habits (including quips and artistic aspirations) and ends with the events (including omens and prodigies) leading up to his death.

Within that framework, there is a secondary theme that Wallace-Hadrill calls:

> the ethical dimension to his portrayal of a Caesar in his public capacity. Was he virtuous or vicious?.... Was he clement or cruel? Liberal, or mean and grasping? Civil or arrogant? Continent, or self-indulgent, luxurious and lustful? These are the polarities in terms of which emperor after emperor is judged.
>
> (1995: 142; see also Bradley, 1998: 18-22)

For Suetonius, then, there was an imperial 'ideal'. He had a clear image of just what constituted an emperor's obligations, duties and general behaviour, both private and public. His 'categories' are significant; they represent the criteria by which an emperor is to be assessed.

Usually, there is a definite break (*divisio*) between imperial deeds that are commendable and those that are not: in his *Life of Caligula*, Suetonius discusses that emperor's achievements (*Calig.* 1-21) and then comments 'so much for him as emperor; now to tell of Caligula the monster' (22) and the next thirty-eight chapters expand on and explain that assessment.

But the pattern varies considerably in the *Lives* of the Flavian emperors. Most of the family background is to be found in the *Vespasian*, little in the other two: Suetonius appears to have made a careful investigation into salient aspects of Vespasian's antecedents, stressing what was relevant for his assessment of the family – the financial and military activities of Petro and Sabinus as well as their knack of contracting politically valuable marriages; he even (apparently) visited the town of Vespasiae (*Vesp.* 1). As for his ethical criteria, Suetonius sees Domitian as guilty of greed, arrogance and cruelty, whereas Titus (Suetonius' ideal emperor) emerges as generous, civil and kind. In assessing Vespasian, Suetonius agreed with Tacitus' comment ('Vespasian was equal to the commanders of old, were it not for his avarice': *Hist.* 2.5).

In these *Lives*, the *divisio* is not as clearly marked as in the *Caligula*, being muted and occurring late in the *Vespasian* (16), where the brief criticism is soon followed in the main by further examples of his commendable deeds.

Similarly, in the *Titus*, the *divisio* occurs late (at Chapter 7: despite people's fears, Titus was not a 'second Nero'), the list of non-commendable deeds is brief (5-7) and even these are explained away (see below). Suetonius also varies the pattern here by providing a physical description of Titus very early in the *Life* instead of (as usual) towards the end. Quite different is the *Domitian*, with a minor *divisio* at the end of Chapter 3 (separating his early non-commendable deeds from the commendable) and the major one at 9, followed by a detailed catalogue of his vices. Thus the pattern varies considerably, according to Suetonius' view of his subject: the formulaic aspects of these *Lives* is far from intrusive.

VESPASIAN

There are only a few inaccuracies in the *Life*. Incorrect statements include his reference to Florus as having been killed (4); his figures for the military establishment in Judaea (4); the implication in (7) that there was little or no interval between the second battle of Bedriacum and Vitellius' death and his description of Commagene (8). Other misleading statements include his downplaying of Claudius' role in the invasion of Britain (4); his exaggeration of the nature of Vespasian's retirement (4); his incomplete explanation of the circumstances surrounding Nero's offer of the Judaean command to Vespasian late in 66 (4); his assessment of the attitude of the Syrian legions in 67 (4); his over-generous interpretation of the 'mud in the toga' incident (5); his explanation of just when Vespasian determined on civil war; his assessment of the reasons for army reform (8); his too brief comment on the disbanding of the Vitellian legions (8); his deficient summary of Vespasian's provincial arrangements (8) and his failure to note that Vespasian's new taxes were imposed for a limited time only (16). At times, his chronology is misleading, e.g. at 5 (tree incident, Mt Carmel and the statue).

Sometimes, and especially in reference to the events of 1 July 69 and to Vespasian's performance in Alexandria, it is clear that Suetonius used the same source as Tacitus; but, on at least six occasions they differ on matters of some importance. Suetonius' assessment of Vespasian's proconsular performance in Africa (4) contradicts Tacitus at Hist. 2.97; Tacitus at Ann. 16.5 assigns Vespasian's famous 'lapse' (4) to a different time and place; they differ on the date when the Judaean legions swore allegiance to Vespasian (6 but Hist. 2.79); they disagree on the timing of Vespasian's visit to the Serapeum (7); and Suetonius' reference to Helvidius Priscus (15) is at considerable variance with Tacitus' praise of him at Hist. 4.5. Finally, there is Suetonius' claim at 6 that a number of Danubian vexillations declared for Vespasian well before 1 July – contradicted by Tacitus at Hist. 2.46 and 2.85.

The only substantial account of the reign itself apart from Suetonius' is that provided by Dio Cassius (or, rather, his epitomators). Whilst it seems that he and Suetonius had access to a common source, the few additional pieces of information to be found in Dio suggest that either he included items from Tacitus that did not fit into a Suetonian category (e.g. the reference to Vespasian's astrologer Barbillus in 66.9.2) or else that he had access to a source other than Tacitus. Dio's additional items include Vespasian's problems with the people of Alexandria including the tax of six obols and the fact that some of their taunts were addressed to Titus (66.8.4-7); his banishment of the astrologers, even though he consulted one himself, i.e. Barbillus (66.9.2); an anecdote illustrating his greed, not included in Suetonius' extensive list (66.10.3a: the people laughed 'at him every time he used to say, when spending money "I am paying for this out of my own purse"'); his preference for the Gardens of Sallust over the palace (9.4); his reply to Vologaesus, omitting the royal titles as Vologaesus had addressed him simply as 'Flavius Vespasianus' (10.3); Mucianus' attacks on the Stoics and the subsequent expulsion of philosophers apart from Musonius (10.1-11.2); the fact that the temple of Peace was dedicated in 75 (15.1); and the fate of Julius Sabinus and his family (16.1-2). The only significant difference is Suetonius' omission of the last item.

Aurelius Victor and his epitomator usually repeat Suetonius' version of events precisely, but in this *Life* they occasionally provide extra information, e.g. on Vespasian's policy towards the Parthians (though the details are inconsistent; see 6); on the number of new senators enrolled by Vespasian (9); on Suetonius' use of the word 'greed' to describe Vespasian's financial policy (which Victor virtually rejects, referring to it as 'wisdom rather than greed'; 16); on the fact that some of Vespasian's 'new' taxes were imposed for a limited time only (16); on work connected with the Via Flaminia (17); and, in the epitome alone, on the reason for Titus' execution of Caecina Alienus (25).

TITUS

Apart from Julius Caesar, Augustus and Claudius, only Vespasian and Titus (out of Suetonius' twelve Caesars) were deified, and, in this élite company, Suetonius obviously favoured Augustus and Titus. That emerges from his treatment of Titus' vices – other emperors were 'savage' and 'greedy'; Titus was merely suspected (the word occurs twice in *Titus* 7) of such behaviour.

Dio's account of Titus' activities also provides details not mentioned by Suetonius. Dio has a detailed account of Caenis' activities, including the fact that, as Antonia's secretary, she wrote out her 'secret' letter to Tiberius denouncing Sejanus (66.14.1-4). There is also Titus' sham fight with Caecina Alienus (15.2); Berenice's arrival in Rome after 75 when she 'behaved as Titus' wife' (15.4); the beheading of Heras and the flogging of Diogenes for 'denouncing' Berenice and Titus (15.5); the involvement of Eprius Marcellus in the Caecina affair (16.4); the rumour that Titus poisoned Vespasian (17.1); the rise of Terentius Maximus, another false Nero, and the fact that the Parthian leader Artabanus granted him refuge (19.3b); Agricola's activities in Britain (20.1-2) and the useful information that Titus received his fifteenth imperial salutation for the victories in Britain (20.3); the unusual phenomena (giants, droughts and earthquakes) preceding the eruption of Vesuvius (22.1-13.3); a list of the buildings ruined by the fire of 80 in Rome (24.2); and a detailed account of the beast hunts, sea-fights and gladiatorial exhibitions following the opening of the Flavian amphitheatre (25.1-5).

DOMITIAN

As with the other Flavian *Lives*, a number of Dio's observations about military matters, senators and various other items and individuals are unique to him.

In the first category, we have (all examples from Dio's Book 67) the causes of the revolt by the Nasamones and their defeat by Flaccus (4.6); the character of the Dacians and Decebalus (6.1-2, 5); the war in 89 against the Marcomanni and Quadi (7.1-2); Julianus' victory at Tapae (10.1-3); Chariomerus of the Cherusci financed by Rome (10.5); Lucius Maximus defeats Saturninus and burns incriminating papers (11.1-2); the Lygians' request for aid from Rome, resulting in the Suebi seeking an alliance with the Iazyges (12.5) and finally (12.5), Domitian's visit to Masyus of the Semnones. Dio (but not Suetonius) refers to the following senators, viz. Julius Ursus (3.1; 4.2); Helvius Agrippa (3.3); Lusianus Proclus (11.5); Maternus (12.4); Juventius Celsus (13.3-4); Acilius Glabrio (14.3); Manlius Valens (14.5) and Nerva (role in Domitian's murder: 15.5-6). Finally, various items and individuals appear in Dio but not in Suetonius, e.g. Domitian's eunuch Earinus (2.3); Domitian's ten-year consulship and perpetual censorship (4.3); his macabre dinner party (9.1-5), and Apollonius of Tyana's reaction on hearing of Domitian's death (18.1).

This catalogue need not be as depressing as appears at first sight. Suetonius automatically excluded military matters not involving the emperor personally; not every senator was relevant to the Suetonian schema and it would have been unwise to mention the role Hadrianic ancestors (Nerva and Ursus) played during Domitian's reign. Furthermore, even a brief glimpse at the *Domitian* reveals a number of gems. Chapters seven to nine contain a wealth of detail about a variety of legal and other reforms, whilst eighteen to twenty-two give an indication (available nowhere else) of his private life, i.e. physical description, meals, recreation and so on. Suetonius' account of the Games (4), a special field of interest to him, is particularly valuable. Unforgettable, too, are the anecdotes, e.g. the spectator who, in effect, questioned the referee who happened to be Domitian or the sense of humour shown by Aelius Lamia (10).

But Suetonius' hostility to the last Flavian is quite clear. His statement that Domitian was awarded an ordinary consulship in 73 only because Titus ceded it to him is wrong. Favourable references (in 8) provide but a veneer of neutrality and are set in a hostile context – the fate of the errant Vestals and their lovers. Further bias is apparent in the arrangement of certain items: some that could well have been included amongst Domitian's commendable deeds are located elsewhere. Participating in drinking bouts is used in other *Lives* to illustrate imperial vices, but Domitian's rejection of such behaviour is not regarded as commendable (see 21). One of Domitian's most impressive buildings, the massive palace complex on the Palatine, is excluded from the relevant section of his commendable deeds (5) and relegated to the non-commendable (15), whilst the numerous arches (13) he erected in Rome are cited not as examples of his works but of his arrogance. As Bradley has pointed out, 'the construction of the *Domitian* leaves no doubt about the bias of the biography and Suetonius' opinion of Domitian' (1981: 133).

Suetonius had a favourable opinion of Vespasian. The negative aspects of his character are mentioned but suitably disguised (*Vesp.* 15) – merged in a clever series of amusing anecdotes (a device not paralleled in the other *Lives*). He rated Titus even more highly. Introducing him as the 'darling of the human race', Suetonius quickly detailed his remarkable physical and mental gifts as evidence of that statement, since to have left them to the 'usual' place would have been both illogical and artistically damaging. But Domitian's cruelty and greed were real: his achievements could not save his reputation. That said, credit must be given to Suetonius for producing a readable, entertaining and mainly reliable account of the Flavian emperors.

Translation

THE DEIFIED VESPASIAN

1. Because of the revolt and deaths of three emperors, the empire had been long unsure and, as it were, wandering without direction. It was the Flavian family that finally picked it up and consolidated it – a family which, to be sure, was obscure and without any ancestral images, but nevertheless in no way to be regretted by the state, even though it is agreed that Domitian deservedly paid the price of his greed and savagery.

Titus Flavius Petro, a citizen of Reate, was either a centurion or a volunteer veteran on the Pompeian side in the civil war. He ran away from the battle of Pharsalus and took himself home; and here, after he had secured a pardon and his discharge, he henceforth practised the trade of money-collector. His son, who had the surname Sabinus, had no experience of soldiering, even though certain persons relate that he was released from his oath on account of illness when he was senior centurion or, as some relate, when he was still in command of companies. He farmed the 2.5% tax in Asia; and there remained statues set up to him by the citizens with this inscription: 'To a man who collected the taxes honestly.' Afterwards, he practised money-lending among the Helvetii and there he met his death, leaving behind his wife, Vespasia Polla, and two children by her, of whom the elder, Sabinus, advanced to the Prefecture of the City, while the younger, Vespasian, progressed right up to the position of emperor. Polla, who was born at Nursia of an honourable family, had as her father Vespasius Pollio, three times military tribune and Prefect of the Camp, and as her brother a senator of praetorian rank. There is even a place at the sixth milestone, when one is going from the district of Nursia to Spoletium, at the top of the mountain, which is called Vespasiae, where there are still very many monuments of the Vespasii – a great testimony of the distinction and antiquity of the family. I would not deny that it has been suggested by certain persons that the father of Petro was from the Transpadane area and had been a contractor of the sort of labourers who are in the habit of migrating annually from Umbria to Sabine territory for the cultivation of the fields; and that he had settled in the township of Reate after marrying a local girl. Despite my very careful investigation of this matter, I personally have not come up with any trace of it.

2. Vespasian was born among the Sabines, on the other side of Reate, in a smallish village named Falacrinae, on the fifteenth day before the Kalends of December, in the evening, when Q. Sulpicius Camerinus and C. Poppaeus

Sabinus were consuls, five years before Augustus died. He was brought up under the control of his paternal grandmother, Tertulla, on her estate at Cosa. This is why, even as emperor, he constantly visited the place of his childhood, with the villa being kept as it had formerly been, evidently in order that nothing might be lost from what he had always seen. Moreover, he honoured the memory of his grandmother so greatly that on regular religious and festal days he also persisted in drinking from a silver cup of hers.

After he had assumed the toga of manhood, he shunned the broad stripe for a long time, even though his brother had obtained it, and it was only his mother who was at last able to make him seek it. She indeed forced him to it by means of abuse rather than entreaties or authority, since she continually and insultingly called him his brother's footman.

He served his military tribunate in Thrace; as quaestor he obtained Crete and Cyrene by lot as his province; as a candidate for the aedileship and afterwards the praetorship, he gained the former after a defeat and then only just, in sixth place, but the latter straightway, at his first attempt and among the highest. As praetor, in order that there might be no way in which he was not obliging to Gaius, who was hostile to the Senate, he demanded extraordinary games for his German victory and proposed that it should be added to the punishment of the conspirators that they should be cast forth unburied. He also gave thanks to him before that most distinguished body because, as he said, Gaius had deemed him worthy of the honour of a dinner.

3. Amidst all this, he married Flavia Domitilla. She had formerly been the mistress of Statilius Capella, a Roman knight from Sabrata in Africa, and of Latin status, but afterwards pronounced freeborn and a Roman citizen by the court of the Recoverers, with her father Flavius Liberalis, who was born at Ferentium and was nothing more than a quaestor's clerk, giving her her freedom. From her he had as children Titus, Domitian and Domitilla. He outlived his wife and daughter, losing both of them when he was still a private citizen. After the death of his wife he renewed his relationship with Caenis, who was the freedwoman and private secretary of Antonia and with whom he had once had an affair; and even when he became emperor, he regarded her as virtually his lawful wife.

4. When Claudius was emperor, he was sent to Germany as a legionary legate, thanks to the influence of Narcissus. From there, he was transferred to Britain and engaged the enemy on thirty occasions. He brought under our authority two very strong tribes, more than twenty townships and the Isle of Wight, which is next to Britain, partly under the command of the consular legate, Aulus Plautius, and partly under that of Claudius himself. As a result, he received triumphal decorations and after a brief interval a double priesthood, not to mention the consulship, which he held for the last two months of the year. The time between this and the proconsulship he spent wholly in inactivity and retirement, because he was afraid of Agrippina, who was still influential with her son and who hated a friend of Narcissus, even after his death.

Afterwards, he gained Africa by lot and governed it most honourably and with great respect, except for the fact that in a civil disturbance at Hadrumetum turnips were thrown at him. To be sure, he returned no richer, since with his credit now almost destroyed, he mortgaged all his estates to his brother and was forced to stoop to retail trading in order to maintain his rank; and for this reason he was popularly called 'the muleteer.' It is also said that he was convicted of having extorted 200,000 sestertii from a young man for whom he had obtained the broad stripe contrary to the wishes of his father, and for that reason was given a stern rebuke.

He was one of Nero's Companions on the latter's Greek trip, where he fell into the deepest disgrace because he used either to leave too often when Nero was singing or to fall asleep if he stayed. He was therefore banned not only from Nero's company but also from his public receptions; and he retired to a small out-of-the-way town until a province, together with an army, was offered to him as he was hiding away and even fearing the worst.

There had spread throughout the whole East an ancient and firm belief that it was ordained in the Fates that men setting out at that time from Judaea would become masters of the world. As became clear afterwards from the outcome, this was foretold about a Roman emperor. The Jews, however, referred it to themselves and rose in rebellion. They slew their governor and on top of this routed the consular legate of Syria as he was bringing aid, seizing a legionary eagle. To suppress this disturbance there was needed a larger army and an energetic commander – though one to whom so great a matter could be entrusted with safety. Thus Vespasian was chosen above all others as being a person both of approved industry and one who was in no way to be feared because of the lowliness of his birth and name. Two legions, therefore, eight cavalry squadrons and ten infantry cohorts were added to the existing forces and Vespasian's older son was appointed as one of the legates. As soon as he reached his province, he turned the attentions of the neighbouring provinces also upon himself because he immediately corrected the discipline of the camp, and because he engaged in one or two battles with such resolution that he received a blow on his knee from a stone and several arrows in his shield during the storming of a fortress.

5. When, after Nero and Galba, Otho and Vitellius were fighting for the position of emperor, he formed a hope for the imperial position which he had long ago conceived because of the following portents.

In the suburban villa of the Flavii, an ancient oak-tree, which was sacred to Mars suddenly put forth from the trunk a single branch at the occasion of each of the three births of Vespasia – indubitable indicators of the future destiny of each one. The first was thin and quickly dried up and hence the girl who was born did not live a year; the second was very strong and broad and such as to foretell great happiness; but the third was like a tree. For this reason they say that the father Sabinus, encouraged moreover by the inspections of entrails, reported to his mother that a Caesar had been born to her as a grandson; and that she did nothing but burst into laughter, because she was amazed, as she said, that while she was still sound of mind, her son was already talking like a dotard.

Later, when he was aedile and Gaius Caesar, angry that attention had not been given to sweeping the streets, had ordered him to be loaded up with mud, which was heaped by soldiers in the fold of his official toga, there were not lacking people to interpret this that at some future time the state, trampled down and deserted in some civil disturbance, would come into his protection and, as it were, into his bosom.

On one occasion, when he was eating his lunch, a strange dog brought in a human hand from the crossroads and dropped it under the table. On another occasion when he was at dinner, a plough-ox, which had shaken off its yoke, burst into the dining room and put the servants to flight. Then, as though it had suddenly become weary, it fell forwards at the very feet of the reclining Verpasian and lowered its neck in submission. A cypress tree, too, on his ancestral farm, was torn out roots and all, and thrown down without any violence of a storm; and on the following day it rose up again greener and stronger.

Moreover, in Achaea he dreamt that there would be the beginning of happiness for himself and his family as soon as a tooth had been extracted from Nero; and it so happened that on the following day, the doctor came into the entrance-room and showed him a tooth which had just been extracted.

In Judaea, when he was consulting the oracle of the god of Carmel, the responses were so encouraging that they promised that whatever he was planning or turning over in his mind, be it ever so great, would come to pass; and one of the aristocratic captives, Josephus, asserted with great resolution, as he was being cast into chains, that it would come about that he would be freed in a short while by the same Vespasian, but now as emperor. Prophetic signs were also being reported from Rome: that Nero during his last days had been warned in a dream to bring the carriage of Jupiter Best and Greatest from its sanctuary to Vespasian's house and from there into the Circus; and that as Galba was entering office, not long after the electoral meeting for his second consulship, the statue of Julius Caesar had of its own account turned towards the East; and that at the battle of Bedriacum, before the battle was joined, two eagles had fought in the sight of everybody and that when one had been defeated, a third had supervened from the rising of the sun and had driven away the victorious bird.

6. Nevertheless, he made no attempt, even though his own followers were most ready and even pressing, until he was assured by the chance support of some men who were both unknown to him and not present with him.

Two thousand men had been sent to help Otho from each of the three legions of the Moesian army. It was reported to them after they had commenced their journey that Otho had been defeated and had committed suicide. Nonetheless, they pressed on as far as Aquileia, since they gave little credence to the story. There they behaved with violence and engaged in every kind of rapine, taking advantage of the opportunity and the absence of discipline; but since they became afraid that, on their return, they would have to give an account of their behaviour and submit to punishment, they formed the plan of choosing and making an emperor. For they claimed that they were inferior neither to the Spanish army, which had made Galba emperor, nor to the Praetorians, who had made Otho, nor to the German army, which had made Vitellius. And so they put forward the names of all the consular legates, wherever they might be. When they were rejecting all the others – one for one reason, another for another reason – and when certain men from the Third legion, which had been transferred from Syria to Moesia just before Nero's death, began heaping praises on Vespasian, everybody agreed and without delay inscribed his name on all their pennants. At that time the matter was checked, since the units were recalled to their duty for a while. But when the news of their actions had become widespread, Tiberius Alexander, the Prefect of Egypt, was the first to administer the oath of loyalty to Vespasian and his legions on the Kalends of July; and in the future this was observed as the day on which he received the position of emperor. Then the Judaean army swore in his presence on the fifth day before the Ides of July.

The things which made the biggest contributions to his undertaking were: the circulation of a copy of a letter – either genuine or forged – of the dead Otho to Vespasian, which demanded vengeance in an appeal at the end and begged him to aid the state; the spreading at the same time of a rumour that the victorious Vitellius had decided to change the winter quarters of the legions and to transfer the German legions to the East to a safer and easier service; and moreover Licinius Mucianus from amongst the provincial governors and the Parthian Vologaesus from among the kings. Mucianus put aside the jealousy which he was bearing without concealing it up to that time because of rivalry and promised the Syrian army, while Vologaesus promised 40,000 archers.

7. Having therefore undertaken civil war and having sent leaders and troops in advance to Italy, he crossed over to Alexandria in the meantime in order to gain control of the stronghold of Egypt. It was here that he entered the temple of Serapis alone, after removing everybody else, in order to get a sign about the stability of his rule. After he had offered much propitiation to the god, he at length turned round and thought that he saw the freedman Basilides offering him the sacred foliage, crown and bread-cakes, as is the custom there. Yet there was agreement that Basilides had not been admitted by anybody and that for a long time now he hardly ever entered because of a muscular illness, and was then a long way away. Then straightway there arrived a dispatch reporting that the forces of Vitellius had been routed at Cremona and that Vitellius himself had been killed in Rome.

Because he was, so to speak, an unexpected and still new emperor, he was lacking in authority and a certain majesty. This too he acquired. A certain man from the ordinary people who had lost his sight and likewise another with a crippled leg approached him together while he was sitting in front of the tribunal, begging him for the help for their infirmity that had been shown to them in a dream by Serapis. He would, they had been told, make the eyes better if he spat on them and would heal the leg if he deigned to touch it with his heel. He could hardly believe that the business would in any way be successful and for that reason he did not even dare to attempt it. But finally, when his friends were openly urging him on in front of the crowd, he attempted both; and the outcome did not let him down. At about the same time, on the instigation of people prophesying, there were dug up in a consecrated place at Tegea in Arcadia vessels of ancient workmanship and there was on them a face that looked like Vespasian.

8. Such was his stature and so great was his reputation when he returned to Rome, where he celebrated a triumph and then added eight consulships to his original one. He also undertook the censorship and throughout the whole period of his rule he regarded nothing as having higher priority than first of all to stabilise and then also to beautify the virtually shattered and tottering state.

Some of the soldiery had progressed to every form of licence and audacity because of confidence caused by their victory and others because of the resentment caused by their disgrace. Moreover, provinces and free states, not to mention certain kingdoms, were behaving in a rather turbulent manner. He therefore both cashiered and restrained very many of the troops of Vitellius, whilst to those who shared in his victory he made no extraordinary indulgence, to such an extent that he paid late even their legitimate rewards. And lest he should let pass any opportunity for correcting discipline, he rejected with a toss of his head a young man who smelled of perfume, when the man was giving thanks to him for a prefecture which he had gained, and also rebuked him with the very stern statement that 'I would have preferred you to smell of garlic'; and he revoked the commission. Indeed, when the marines, who pass on foot in turn from Ostia and Puteoli to Rome, were requesting that something should be established for them under the heading of 'shoe money', he sent them away without a reply and, as if this were not enough, he ordered that henceforth they should run barefoot; and from that time that is how they run.

He deprived Achaea, Lycia, Rhodes, Byzantium and Samos of their liberty and reduced them to provincial status; and he did the same with Rough Cilicia and Commagene, which up to that time had been under royal jurisdiction. He put legions into Cappadocia because of the constant incursions of barbarians and gave it a consular governor in place of a Roman knight.

Rome was unsightly because of earlier fires and collapsed buildings. He allowed anybody to occupy the empty areas and put up buildings, if the owners did nothing. Having undertaken the restoration of the Capitol, he himself was the first to set his hands to clearing away the rubble and carried some of it off on his own shoulders. He also undertook the restoration of 3,000 bronze tablets which had all been destroyed by fire at the same time, after he had tracked down copies from everywhere. These were a most handsome and ancient record of empire, in which were contained from almost the beginnings of the city decrees of the Senate and resolutions of the plebs dealing with the granting to anyone of alliance, treaty and special conditions.

9. He also built as new works the temple of Peace next to the Forum and the temple of the Deified Claudius on the Caelian Hill, which had been begun by Agrippina but had been almost totally destroyed by Nero. He also built the amphitheatre in the middle of the city, after he had found out that this is what Augustus had intended.

The most distinguished social classes had been both depleted by various kinds of slaughter and contaminated by longstanding neglect. He both cleansed them and filled them up after holding a revision of the Senate and of the equestrians in which the most unworthy were removed and all the most honourable of the Italians and provincials were enrolled. And in order that it might be made known that the two classes differed not so much in freedom of speech as in social standing, he made a pronouncement concerning a quarrel between a senator and a Roman knight to the effect that 'senators should not be abused, but it was in accordance with their citizen status and morally correct that they should be abused in return for abuse'.

10. The number of law-court cases had everywhere grown to an excessive size because old cases still remained on account of the interruption of the administration of justice, whilst new cases were being added as a result of the circumstances and disturbances of the time. He therefore chose by lot men through whom things that had been seized in the war could be restored and who could give extraordinary judgements on cases in the court of the Hundred, for the settling of which it seemed that the lifetime of the litigants would hardly suffice, and thus reduce them to a very small number.

11. With nobody to restrain them, licentiousness and luxury had increased. Vespasian was responsible for the Senate's resolving that if a woman had taken as a sexual partner another person's slave, she should be regarded as a slave; and that those people who lent money on interest to sons who were under their father's control should never have the legal right of demanding back their money – that is to say, not even after the death of the father.

12. In all other matters he behaved like a citizen amongst citizens and with mercy right from the start of his time as emperor up to his death; and he never tried to hide his former modest background and he often even flaunted it. Indeed, when certain people were trying to trace back the origin of the Flavian clan to the founders of Reate and a companion of Hercules, whose tomb still stands on the Salarian Way, he made fun of them of his own accord. To such an extent did he not seek eagerly after any external distinctions that on the day of his triumph, being wearied by the slowness and boredom of the procession, he could not refrain from saying that he deserved his punishment because, in his old age, he had been so absurdly eager for a triumph, as though it was either owed to his ancestors or had ever been hoped for by himself. He did not even accept the tribunician power <or> the designation of Father of his Country until late. For he had dropped the practice of searching those who came to greet him whilst the civil war was still going on.

13. He tolerated in a most lenient manner the free speech of his friends, the innuendos of the barristers and the obstinacy of the philosophers. Licinius Mucianus was a man of notorious lewdness who showed too little respect for Vespasian, because of his confidence in his services rendered. Vespasian never brought himself to rebuke him except in private and to the extent that he added, when complaining to a common friend, the rider 'I, however, am a man'. When Salvius Liberalis dared to say, in the course of his defence of a rich man who was on trial, 'What does it matter to Caesar if Hipparchus has a hundred million sestertii?', Vespasian himself also applauded him. When Demetrius the Cynic came across him on the road after his condemnation and did not deign either to stand up or to greet him, but even barked out something or other, Vespasian regarded it as quite sufficient to address him as 'Dog'.

14. Being very little inclined to remember or to seek vengeance for insults and enmities, he gave the daughter of his foe Vitellius in marriage with great magnificence and he also gave her a dowry and fitted her out. When he was in a state of anxiety after his banishment from court under Nero and was asking what he should do and where he should go, someone from the office of the chamberlain had, at the moment he was driving Vespasian out, ordered him to go to hell. When this man was later begging forgiveness, Vespasian did not let his anger go beyond words – and, indeed, in almost as many and identical words. For he was so far from being driven to destroy anybody because of some suspicion or fear that when his friends warned him to be on his guard against Mettius Pompusianus because he was popularly believed to have a horoscope of the emperor, he actually made him consul, thereby guaranteeing that at some time he would be mindful of the kindness received.

15. It would not be easy to find any innocent person who was punished unless Vespasian was not present and in ignorance, or at any rate unless he did not wish it and had been misled. Although Helvidius Priscus had been the only person to greet him by his private name of Vespasian after his return from Syria and, as praetor, had passed over him in all his edicts without any mark of respect or any mention of him, Vespasian did not become angry with him until he had been almost brought down to the level of an ordinary citizen by Priscus' extremely insolent arguments. He put a great a great value on saving Priscus by any way whatever, even though he had firstly been banished and then had been ordered to be executed, and he sent men to recall the executioners; and he would have saved him, had it not been falsely reported that he had already perished. Be that as it may, he never rejoiced at the death of any person; <and> he even wept and groaned over just punishments.

16. The only thing in which he can deservedly be reproved is his greed for money. For he was not contented with reimposing the taxes which had been dropped under Galba and with adding new and burdensome ones nor with increasing the tribute for the provinces and in some cases even doubling it; but he also openly practised business activities that would have been shameful even for a private citizen, buying certain things only in order to retail them later at a higher price. He did not even hesitate to sell public offices to candidates or acquittal to innocent and guilty defendants alike. It is also believed that he deliberately made a practice of promoting all his most rapacious procurators to higher offices in order that he might afterwards condemn them when they were richer; and it used to be popularly said that he used them like sponges because he would, as it were, both soak them when they were dry and squeeze them when they were wet.

Some people relate that he was naturally very greedy and that he was reproached with that by an old ploughman, who shouted out that a fox changes its fur but not its ways, after Vespasian had refused to give him for nothing the freedom for which he was humbly begging Vespasian, after he had gained the imperial position. On the other hand there are those who believe that he was driven by necessity to looting and plundering because of the extreme poverty of the Treasury and the Privy Purse. They say that he gave proof of this right at the start of his time as emperor, when he professed that for the state to be able to stand firm there was a need of forty billion sestertii. And this seems to be closer to the truth, since he made excellent use even of his ill-gotten gains.

17. Being very generous to every class of person, he topped up the property requirement for admission to the Senate; he supported needy men of consular rank by annual grants of 500,000 sestertii; he restored to a better condition very many states throughout the whole world that had been afflicted by earthquake or fire; and he supported very strongly indeed men of talent and the arts.

18. He was the first to establish an annual salary of 100,000 sestertii for Latin and Greek teachers of rhetoric. He presented outstanding poets, not to mention artists and likewise the restorer of the Coan Venus and the Colossus, with a splendid largess and a large payment. When an engineer promised to transport great columns to the Capitol at a very small cost, he gave him a far from modest reward for his invention but rejected the work after first saying that the man should allow him to feed his poor plebs.

19. At the plays by means of which the restored stage of the Theatre of Marcellus was being dedicated, he brought back the old entertainments too. He gave to the tragic actor Apelles 400,000 sestertii, to the cithara players Terpnus and Diodorus 200,000 sestertii, to some 100,000 sestertii and 40,000 sestertii as a minimum amount, in addition to very many gold crowns. Moreover he held dinner parties constantly and more often in formal style and sumptuously in order that he might help the food sellers. Just as he used to give take-home presents to the men at the Saturnalia, so he gave them to the women on the Kalends of March. Nevertheless, not even in this way could he get rid of his former reputation for greed. The people of Alexandria persisted in calling him Herring-Stuffer, using the nickname of one of their kings, who was a man of the most unseemly stinginess. At his funeral, the leading mime actor, Favor, was carrying the mask of Vespasian and, in accordance with custom, was imitating the deeds and works of the man when alive. He openly quizzed the procurators on the cost of the funeral and procession; and hearing that it was ten million sestertii, exclaimed, 'Give me a hundred thousand sestertii and you can even throw me into the Tiber'.

20. He was of a square build, with stout and strong limbs and a face like somebody straining to relieve himself. One of the men-about-town spoke about this feature in a very witty manner, when he said in response to Vespasian's request that he should make a jest about him too, 'I shall, as soon as you have finished emptying your bowels'. He enjoyed excellent health even though the only things that he did to preserve it were to have his throat and the other parts of his body rubbed down rhythmically in the ball courts and have a day of fasting each month.

21. He maintained in general the following ordering of his life. Whilst emperor, he always used to wake up quite early and whilst it was still night. Then after reading his correspondence and the minutes from all branches of government, he would admit his friends; and while he was being greeted, he would both put on his shoes himself and get dressed. When all the business that had come to him had been settled, he used to have time for being carried in his litter and then for sleep, where one of the concubines, whom he had set up in great numbers in place of the deceased Caenis, would lie next to him. Then he would pass from his private retreat into the bath and the dining room. It is said that at no other time was he more affable and indulgent; and the servants would eagerly lie in wait for those moments in order to ask for something.

22. Indeed, he was most genial both over dinner and always on other occasions; and he used to transact much business by means of a joke. For he was a man very much given to witticisms, even though scurrilous and vulgar, so that he did not even refrain from obscene innuendos. Nevertheless, several very witty sayings of his are extant, amongst them the following. When he had been advised by Mestrius Florus, a former consul, that he should say 'wains' not 'woins', he greeted him the following day as 'Flayrus'. He was overcome by a women who claimed that she was dying of love for him. When he had taken her to bed and had given her 400,000 sestertii in return for her sexual favours, he was asked by his treasurer how he wanted the amount to be entered in the accounts: 'To Vespasian, object of a passion', he replied.

23. He could also use verses in Greek in a most timely manner; and of a certain person who was very tall and rather well endowed by nature he said (Homer, *Iliad* 7.213): 'Striding out greatly, brandishing his long-shadowing spear'. The freedman Cerylus had become extremely rich and had begun to pass himself off as freeborn and, by a change of name, as Laches in order to evade the claim of the imperial purse in the future. Of him Vespasian said (Menander, frg. 223,2: Kock): 'Laches, Laches,/When you do die, back to your roots once more will you/Cerylus be'. However, he especially made use of witticisms in the case of unseemly profits, in order that he might dilute the animosity by means of some joke and turn it into a witty saying.

After he had put off one of his close servants who was seeking a managerial post for somebody who was supposed to be his brother, he summoned the actual candidate into his presence. He then demanded the amount of money which the man had agreed with his sponsor and gave him the job without delay. When the servant later accosted him, he said, 'Get yourself another brother. The one you think is yours is mine'. Suspecting whilst on a journey that the mule driver had got down to put shoes on the mules in order to create time and delay for a litigant who approached him, he asked the mule driver how much the shoeing had cost and made a deal for a part of the money. When his son Titus was finding fault with him on the ground that he had devised a tax even on urine, he put money from the first payment to Titus' nose and asked whether he was offended by the smell; and when Titus said 'No', Vespasian said, 'and yet it comes from urine!' When envoys reported that a colossal statue costing no small sum had been decreed to him at public expense, he bade them to set it up right there and then, displaying his empty hand and saying that 'The base is ready'. Not even amidst the fear and extreme danger of death did he refrain from jokes. For when, among all the other prodigies, the Mausoleum had suddenly opened and a comet had appeared in the sky, he kept on saying that the former concerned Junia Calvina from the clan of Augustus, while the latter referred to the Parthian King who had a thick head of hair; and also at the final onset of his illness, he said, 'Oh, dear, I think I'm becoming a god'.

24. In his ninth consulship he was assailed in Campania by light attacks of fever. He straightway went back to Rome and then made for Cutiliae and the countryside around Reate, where he used to spend the summer each year. Here, when on top of his pressing illness he had also damaged his intestines by a very frequent use of cold water, but was nonetheless performing as usual his imperial tasks, so that he even listened to embassies whilst lying down, he was brought to the point of fainting by a sudden relaxation of the bowels and said that an emperor ought to die standing up. While he was getting up and straining, he died in the hands of those who were supporting him on the ninth day before the Kalends of July, aged sixty-nine years, seven months and seven days.

25. It is generally agreed that he had always been so sure about his and his children's natal star that he ventured to state to the Senate, after incessant conspiracies against him, that either his sons would succeed him or nobody would. It is also said that once, in a dream, he saw a balance placed in the middle of the forecourt of his house on the Palatine, with the tongue equally poised, since in the one pan stood Claudius and Nero and in the other himself and his sons. Nor was he deceived by this, since each of the two groups ruled for the same number of years and for an equal length of time.

THE DEIFIED TITUS

1. Titus, of the same surname as his father, the beloved and darling of the human race – he had such an abundance whether of talent or of art or of fortune for winning the goodwill of all and that too (which is most difficult) whilst emperor, since as a private citizen and even when his father was emperor he was the object of hatred, not to mention popular vituperation – Titus was born on the third day before the Kalends of January, in the year made famous by the assassination of Gaius, in a humble house near the Septizonium, in a very small and dark bedroom, which is still there to this day and on display.

2. He was brought up at court along with Britannicus and was educated in the same subjects and with the same teachers. The story goes that it was at this time that a forehead-diviner was brought in by Narcissus, the freedman of Claudius, to examine Britannicus and that he asserted most emphatically that Britannicus would never become emperor, but that Titus, who was standing close by, certainly would. They were, however, such close friends that it is believed that Titus, who was reclining next to Britannicus, tasted the potion from which Britannicus died after he had drunk it, and was troubled for a long time by a serious illness. It was in memory of all these things that he later set up a golden statue to Britannicus in the Palace and he dedicated and accompanied a second, an equestrian statue made of ivory, which is still to this day carried in the processions at the Circus games.

3. In his boyhood his gifts of body and of mind straightway shone forth and then increasingly throughout the stages of his life. He had a distinguished appearance, which was such that there was no less authority in it than charm; he had exceptional strength, even though he was not tall and had a stomach that was a little too prominent; and he had a unique memory and an ability to learn virtually all the arts of war and peace. He was very skilful in the use of weapons and in riding; at pleading or in composing poetry in Latin and in Greek he was sharp and fluent, even to the point of composing on the spot; nor was he without knowledge of music, since he sang and played the lyre in a pleasing and skilful manner. I have heard from many people that he was in the habit of taking things down very rapidly in shorthand also, as he competed for a game and fun with his secretaries, and that he used to imitate whatever handwriting he saw and that he often claimed that he could have been an excellent forger.

4. He served in Germany and Britain as a military tribune, gaining the highest reputation for his industry and no less for his unassuming behaviour, as is obvious from the large number of statues and pictures of him and of inscriptions to him throughout each of the two provinces.

After his military service he gave an attention to the forum which was honourable rather than assiduous; and at the same time he married Arrecina Tertulla, whose father, though of equestrian rank, had at one time been prefect of the Praetorian cohorts. After her death, he married Marcia Furnilla, a woman of illustrious family, and divorced her after she had produced a daughter.

Next, after holding the office of quaestor, he was put in charge of a legion and brought into his power the very strong Judaean cities of Tarichaeae and Gamala, after losing his horse from between his legs in one battle and mounting another whose rider had died fighting near him.

5. Soon afterwards, when Galba was in control of the state, he was sent to congratulate him and wherever he went he turned men's attention to him in the belief that he was being summoned for the purpose of adoption. But when he perceived that once again the whole situation was in confusion, he returned from his journey; and having approached the oracle of Paphian Venus, whilst he was consulting it about his sea voyage he was also confirmed in his hope of the imperial position. Having soon obtained this and having been left to subdue Judaea, in the final assault on Jerusalem he slew twelve defenders with the same number of arrow shots and captured it on the birthday of his daughter. The soldiers were so joyful and full of goodwill that in their congratulations they saluted him as victorious commander and held him back when he was soon afterwards leaving the province, demanding with prayers – and also with threats – that he should either remain there or lead them all away at the same time with himself. This was the origin of the suspicion that he had tried to rebel from his father and to claim for himself a kingdom in the East. He increased this suspicion when, en route to Alexandria, he wore a diadem while consecrating the Apis bull at Memphis. This was indeed in accordance with the practice and ritual of the ancient religion, but there was no lack of people to interpret it in a bad sense. For that reason he hurried to Italy; and after putting in first at Rhegium and then at Puteoli in a transport ship, he hastened thence to Rome with all speed; and, as though trying to show the baseless nature of the rumours about him, said to his father, who was not expecting him, 'Here I am, father, here I am'.

6. Nor from that time on did he ever cease to play the role of partner in and even protector of the imperial position.

He triumphed together with his father, conducted the census with him, and was his colleague both in the tribunician power and in seven consulships. He also took upon himself the management of almost all official duties, since in person he both dictated letters and drew up edicts in his father's name and even read out his speeches in the Senate in place of the quaestor. He also took on the prefecture of the Praetorian guard, which had hitherto never been held except by a Roman knight; and he acted in a somewhat uncivil and violent manner, since he executed without hesitation all whom he most suspected, after suborning men to demand them for punishment, as though with general agreement, throughout the theatres and the camps. Among these was Aulus Caecina, a man of consular rank, whom he invited to dinner and then ordered to be stabbed when he had scarcely left the dining room. To be sure, there was a pressing danger, since he had also seized a copy of an address to the soldiers that Caecina had prepared. By means of such actions he did indeed provide well for security in the future, but he also won for the present an extremely great amount of ill will, so that hardly anybody ever passed to the position of emperor with such adverse talk about him and with more general lack of support.

7. As well as his brutality, he was also suspected of a riotous lifestyle, since, it was said, he used to extend his revels to the middle of the night along with all his most extravagant friends. Nor was he less suspected of having a libidinous nature on account of his troops of lecherous young men and eunuchs and on account of his famous passion for queen Berenice, to whom he was even said to have promised marriage. He was also suspected of rapacity because it was agreed that he was in the habit of selling favours and doing deals in his father's judicial decisions. Finally, people openly opined and predicted that he would be another Nero. But that reputation turned out for his good and was changed into the greatest praises when no vice was discovered in him, but on the contrary the highest virtues.

The dinner parties which he held were pleasant rather than lavish. He chose friends in whom the emperors after him also acquiesced as being essential to themselves and to the state and made especial use of them. He immediately sent Berenice away from the city, though he did not want it and neither did she. He ceased not only from favouring too lavishly certain of his most pleasing young men, even though they were such artists in dancing that they later dominated the stage, but desisted altogether from watching them in a public gathering.

He took nothing away from any citizen; he refrained from the property of others as nobody had ever done before; and he did not accept even the contributions that were permitted and customary. Nevertheless, he was inferior to none of his predecessors in munificence, since he put on a most magnificent and sumptuous gladiator show after he had dedicated the amphitheatre and had quickly built up hot baths close by. He also put on a naval battle in the old enclosure for naval battles, and gladiators in the same place, and on one day five thousand wild beasts of every kind.

8. Because, however, he was naturally most generous, he was the first to confirm all past benefits by means of a single edict and to forbid their being sought from him, even though in accordance with the practice of Tiberius all succeeding Caesars had refused to regard benefits conferred by previous emperors as valid unless they gave these same benefits in person and to the same people. In fact, in all the other requests that people made, he maintained as his most inflexible policy not to send anyone away without hope. Indeed, even when his servants kept on warning him that he was promising more than he could fulfil, he said that nobody should depart unhappy from a conversation with the emperor. Moreover, having on one occasion remembered over dinner that he had given nothing to anybody during the whole day, he produced that memorable and deservedly praised saying: 'Friends, I have lost a day'.

He particularly treated the whole populace at every opportunity with such geniality that on promising a gladiatorial show he stated that he would give it not in accordance with his own wish but that of the spectators; and he clearly did so. For he neither refused anything when people asked and urged them to take the initiative in asking for what they wanted. Indeed he openly flaunted his predilections for the armour of the Thracians and often joked with the populace in word and gesture, like a supporter, though keeping his dignity safe and no less his impartial behaviour. In order that he might not pass over anything that would win him popular favour, he frequently admitted the ordinary people while he bathed in his hot baths.

Under him there occurred some chance and unhappy events, such as the eruption of Mount Vesuvius in Campania; the fire at Rome, which lasted for three days and as many nights; and likewise a plague of unprecedented magnitude. In those adversities, being many in number and of such a nature, he showed not only the concern of an emperor but also the unparalleled love of a parent – now offering consolation by means of edicts, now offering help as far as his property sufficed. He drew by lot from the ranks of the ex-consuls commissioners for the restoration of Campania; and he assigned the property of those who had been destroyed by Vesuvius and who had no surviving heirs to the restoration of the afflicted communities. At the burning of the city, after he had sworn publicly that he was the only one to have lost property, he allocated out all the adornments of his villas to public works and temples, and put several members of the equestrian class in charge, in order that each individual task might be carried out the swifter. There was no divine or human aid that he did not apply to healing sickness and easing illnesses, since he sought out every kind of sacrifice and cure.

Amongst the evils of those times there were also informers and accusers as the result of a long-standing freedom from restraint. He ordered that they should be soundly beaten in the Forum with whips and clubs and that finally, after they had been paraded though the arena of the amphitheatre, some should be put up for purchase and sold and others should be taken away to the harshest islands. Moreover, in order to put a permanent curb on people who were likely at some time to attempt similar practices, he forbade, amongst other things, actions to be taken about the same matter under several laws or for an investigation to be held about the status of any of the dead beyond a certain number of years.

9. Having stated that he was accepting the office of Pontifex Maximus in order to keep his hands clean, he kept his word and from that time he was neither the instigator of nor an accessory to the death of anybody, even though at times there was not lacking a reason for taking revenge; and he swore that he would rather die than destroy anybody. When two men of patrician family had been convicted of aspiring to the position of emperor, he did nothing other than warn them to desist, telling them that the imperial position was given by fate and promising that if they had any other desire, he would grant it to them. And immediately he sent his own runners to the mother of one of them, who was far away, to tell the worried woman that her son was safe. The men themselves he not only invited to an intimate dinner party but on the following day, at a gladiatorial show, he also deliberately seated them on either side of himself and handed over to them the swords of the fighters, which had been offered to him, for them to inspect. It is also said that after he had learned the birth star of each of them, he asserted that danger was threatening them both, but at some future time and from someone else; and so it turned out.

Although his brother did not cease plotting against him, but was almost openly seeking the support of the army and contemplating flight, he could not bring himself either to kill him or to remove him or even to hold him in less regard. Instead, he continued to swear that he was his colleague and successor, just as he had done from the first day of his reign, often begging him in private with entreaties and tears to be willing at last to reciprocate his brother's feelings towards him.

10. In the midst of these events, he was cut short by death, with humanity rather than himself being the greater loser.

After bringing to completion the games, at the end of which he wept copiously in front of the people, he made for the Sabines, being very sad because the victim had escaped whilst he was sacrificing and because there had been thunder, though the weather was clear. Then having immediately caught a fever at his first lodging place, he is said to have pulled back the curtains when he was being conveyed from there in a litter, to have looked up at the sky and to have complained strongly that life was being snatched away from him, though he did not deserve it. For, he said, there was no deed of his that needed repentance with one and only one exception. What sort of a deed that was neither he himself revealed at that time nor could anyone easily conjecture. Some people believed that he recalled the sexual relationship which he had with the wife of his brother; but Domitia swore most solemnly that she had had no relationship; and she would not have denied it if there had been any relationship at all – indeed, she would rather have boasted about it – a thing which came very readily to her in all her unchaste activities.

11. He died in the same country house as his father, on the Ides of September, two years, two months and twenty days after he had succeeded his father, in the forty-second year of his life. When it became openly known and everybody was mourning publicly no differently than they would in a private grief, the Senate rushed to the Senate House before it could be convened by edict; and opening the doors, which hitherto had been closed, it gave such great thanks and heaped such great praises on him dead as it had never done to him when he was alive and present.

DOMITIAN

1. Domitian was born on the ninth day before the Kalends of November, when his father was consul-designate and about to enter office in the following month, in the sixth region of the city 'At The Pomegranate', in a house which he later turned into a temple of the Flavian clan. It is said that he passed the time of his youth and early manhood in such poverty and such disrepute that he had no silver vessel in use. It is also sufficiently agreed that Claudius Pollio, a man of praetorian status against whom there is the poem of Nero entitled 'Luscio', kept and sometimes produced a hand-written note of his promising him a night. Nor were there lacking people to assert that Domitian had also been debauched by Nerva, soon to become his successor. In the war against Vitellius, he fled for refuge into the Capitol along with his uncle Sabinus and a part of the forces who were present. When, however, the enemy burst in and the temple was ablaze, he secretly spent the night at the house of a sacristan. In the morning, concealed in the dress of a devotee of Isis and among the sacrificing priests of an untrustworthy religion, he made his way across the Tiber, with one companion, to the mother of a fellow-student of his and hid so well that he could not be detected despite the searching of those who had followed closely on his footsteps. He only came forward after the victory and having been saluted as Caesar, he took on the office of urban praetor with consular power, but in a purely formal manner, since he handed over the administration of justice to his closest colleague, while he himself exercised the whole power of absolute rule in such an unrestrained manner that he already showed what he would be like. Without going into every detail, he had sex with the wives of many men and even forcibly took in marriage Domitia Longina, who was married to Aelius Lamia; and in one day he handed out more than twenty city or provincial offices, so that Vespasian kept on saying that he was amazed that Domitian was not sending a successor for him also.

2. He also began a campaign against Gaul and the Germanies, which was not necessary and which was contrary to the advice of his father's friends. His motive was merely to put himself on an equality with his brother both in riches and in honour.

Having been rebuked for these things, he lived with his father in order that he might be made more aware both of his age and of his station, and he used to follow in a litter the sedan chair of his father and of his brother, whenever they went out; and he accompanied the Jewish triumph of each of them on a white horse. Moreover, he held only one of his six consulships as 'ordinary', and this was because his brother gave way to him and gave him his support.

He himself also made an amazing pretence of moderation and especially of enthusiasm for poetry which had previously been as unusual to him as it was afterwards despised and rejected; and he even gave public recitals. Nor, when Vologaesus, the Parthian king, had asked for help against the Alani and one of Vespasian's sons as the leader, did he any the less strive with all his strength for himself to be sent in preference to all others; and because the matter was brought to nought, he tried to seduce other kings of the Orient by means of gifts and promises to make the same demand.

After the death of his father, he hesitated for a long time whether he should offer the soldiery a double bounty and he never had any hesitation in stating that he had been left as a partner in the imperial position but that fraud had been applied to the will. Nor did he cease, from that time on, to make plots against his brother, both secretly and openly, until he ordered him, after he had been attacked by a serious illness, to be left as though dead, before he could completely breathe out his spirit; and after his death, he deemed him worthy of no honour except deification, but often even slandered him by means of indirect speeches and edicts.

3. At the beginning of his time as emperor, he was in the habit of taking for himself daily a solitary retreat of some hours and of doing nothing other than capturing flies and piercing them with a very sharp pen. When, therefore, somebody asked if there was anybody inside with Caesar, Vibius Crispus made the witty reply, 'Not even a fly'. He then gave the title of Augusta to his wife Domitia, by whom he had had a son in his second consulship, whom he lost in the second year after he gained the imperial position. When she had been ruined by her passion for the actor Paris, he divorced her and then, being unable to endure the separation, he brought her back alleging that the people demanded it.

With respect, however, to the government of the empire, for some time he presented a varied picture, with an equable blending also of vices and virtues until he turned his virtues also into vices: as far as one can conjecture, in addition to his natural disposition he was rapacious because of indigence and cruel because of fear.

4. He continuously put on magnificent and sumptuous shows, not only in the amphitheatre but also in the circus, where in addition to the usual races of two- and four-horse chariots he also organised a double battle consisting of both cavalry and infantry; and in the amphitheatre a naval battle as well. For <he put on> beast hunts and gladiators even at night time at the lamp stands; and not only fights between men but also between women. Moreover he was present so consistently at the quaestorian games, which he had had brought back after they had formerly been dropped, that he gave the people the right to demand two pairs of gladiators from his own school and brought them in at the very end in splendour appropriate to the court. At every show of gladiators there stood in front of his feet a small boy, clothed in scarlet, with a small and hideous head, with whom he used to converse very much – sometimes seriously. He was certainly heard to enquire, when Domitian was asking him if he knew anything, why Domitian had decided to put Mettius Rufus in charge of Egypt at the next appointment of officers. He put on naval battles between virtually standard-sized fleets after a lake had been dug out and surrounded with seats next to the Tiber; and he watched the battles amidst torrential downpours of rain.

He also put on Secular Games, making his chronological calculations to the year, not in which Claudius most recently, but in which August formerly had put them on. At these Games, on the day of the Circus games, he reduced the individual races from seven to five laps each in order that a hundred races might more easily be completed.

He also established a three-fold five-yearly contest to Capitoline Jupiter, consisting of music, horse racing and gymnastics; and it had considerably more victors than it has now. For they used to compete in speeches in prose, in Greek and Latin; and as well as singers who accompanied themselves on the cithara, there also competed cithara-players who accompanied the chorus and straight cithara-players, while in the stadium young girls also competed in running. He presided over the contest wearing sandals and clad in a purple toga in the Greek fashion. On his head he wore a golden crown with images of Jupiter and Juno and of Minerva, while the priest of Jupiter and the college of the Flavian priests sat beside him in identical dress, except that on their crowns there was also an image of Domitian himself. He also celebrated each year on the Alban Mount the festival of Minerva which fell on the fifth day after the Ides of March. He had established a priestly college to Minerva, from which men chosen by lot were to act as master and were to put on outstanding beast hunts and stage plays and, in addition, contests of orators and poets. He gave on three occasions a gift of three hundred sestertii to the people and a very lavish feast among the spectacles of a gladiator show. This was at the festival of the Seven Hills where, after distributing to the Senate and equestrian order hampers of bread and meat and little baskets of the same to the plebs, he was the first to begin eating. On the next day he scattered all sorts of things as presents; and because the greater part had fallen among the ordinary people, he proclaimed fifty tickets for each block of seats of the senatorial and equestrian orders.

5. He restored very many extremely magnificent buildings which had been destroyed by fire, amongst them the Capitol which had been burned down again; but all of them under his name alone and without any mention of their original builder. Moreover he erected a new temple on the Capitol to Jupiter the Guardian; a forum which is now called 'Nerva's'; likewise a temple of the Flavian clan; and a stadium, odeum and a basin for naval battles. It was from the stonework of this latter that the Circus Maximus was constructed after both of its sides had been burnt up.

6. He undertook campaigns partly of his own free will and partly of necessity: of his own free will against the Chatti, of necessity the one against the Sarmatians after a legion had been cut down, together with its legate. He made two campaigns against the Dacians – the first after the consular governor, Oppius Sabinus, had been killed and the second after the killing of Cornelius Fuscus, the Prefect of the Praetorian cohorts, to whom he had entrusted the whole war. He held a double triumph over the Chatti and the Dacians after battles of varying outcome; from the Sarmatians he only brought back a laurel wreath for Jupiter Capitolinus.

He ended a civil war that had been stirred up by L.Antonius, the governor of Upper Germany, in his absence and by means of a marvellous piece of good luck, since the Rhine had suddenly thawed at the actual hour of the battle and had checked the forces of barbarians who were about to cross over to Antonius. He learned about this victory by presages before messages, since a large eagle had embraced with its wing a statue of him at Rome, on the very day when the action took place, and had given out most propitious clatterings with its wings; and a little after the death of Antonius, the story was spread abroad to such an extent that several people maintained that they had also seen his head brought there.

7. He also made many changes in the routine practice of things: after bringing back the custom of formal dinners, he did away with food parcels to the people. At the circus games he added two factions of charioteers – those of the gold and the purple clothing – to the four original ones. He banned actors from the stage, though he granted them the right of practising their art indoors. He forbade the castration of males. He regulated the prices of the eunuchs who were still remaining with the dealers. On one occasion, when there was the greatest abundance of wine but the greatest scarcity of grain, because he thought that the fields were being neglected by an excessive enthusiasm for vines, he made an edict that nobody should plant new vines in Italy and that vineyards in the provinces should be cut down, leaving a half at the most. He did not, however, persist in carrying the matter to completion. He shared certain of the most important offices amongst freedmen and Roman knights. He forbade the encamping of two legions together and the deposition by anybody of more than a thousand sestertii at the standards because it seemed that L.Antonius, when stirring up his revolt at the winter quarters of two legions, had also taken security from the amount of the deposits. He also added a fourth payment of three gold pieces to the soldiers.

8. He dispensed justice with diligence and industry, very often even in the forum, in front of the tribunal, outside the normal procedure. He rescinded the decisions of the members of the Centemviral Court that had been made on a basis of self-interest. In like manner, he warned the Recoverers not to indulge in improper declarations of freedom. He censured venal judges, along with the council of each one. He was also responsible for the tribunes of the plebs accusing a despicable aedile of extortion and seeking judges for him from the Senate. He also gave such attention to controlling the urban magistrates and provincial governors that they never were seen to be more modest or just; we saw many of these, after Domitian, charged with all kinds of crime. After he undertook the improvement of morality, he ended the liberty that prevailed at the theatre of viewing amongst the knights regardless of rank. Writings which were libellous and which had been made public, in which leading men and women were marked out, he abolished – and not without disgracing the authors. He removed from the senate a man of quaestorian rank on the ground that he was gripped by a passion for making theatrical gestures and for dancing. He deprived women of ill-fame of the use of the litter and of the right of receiving legacies and inheritances. He struck off the list of judges a Roman knight because he had taken back in marriage his wife against whom he had levelled the accusation of adultery when he divorced her. He condemned certain men of each of the two orders under the Scantinian law. He curbed the unchaste actions of the Vestal Virgins, which had been overlooked by his father also and his brother, in various ways and sternly – early acts by means of capital punishment, later ones in the ancient manner. For although he had permitted the Oculatae sisters and Varronilla a free choice of death and had relegated their seducers, he later ordered Cornelia, the Chief Virgin, who had formerly been acquitted but then after a long interval had been charged again and convicted, to be buried and her debaucher to be flogged to death with rods in the Comitium; though he made an exception of a man of praetorian rank, to whom he conceded exile because he had made a confession about himself, when his case was still in doubt and the interrogations and tortures had produced nothing certain. Moreover, to prevent any aspect of the worship of the gods from being defiled with impunity, he had soldiers demolish a memorial which a freedman of his had erected to his son from stones destined for the temple of Jupiter Capitolinus, and sank in the sea the bones and remains which were in it.

9. In the early stages, he so shrank away from any kind of slaughter that while his father was still absent and after recalling the verse of Virgil <*Georgics* 2.538>:

> 'Before an impious race did feast on slaughtered bullocks'

he intended to issue an edict that oxen should not be sacrificed. As a private citizen he also showed scarcely any indications of greed and avarice nor for a considerable time as emperor; indeed, on the contrary he often gave great proofs not only of self-restraint but even of generosity. He treated all around him most generously and there was nothing that he urged on them with greater importance and vehemence than that they should do nothing in a mean fashion. He did not accept inheritances that were left to him by those who had children. He even voided a legacy in the will of Rustus Caepio, who had stipulated that his heir should present a certain sum of money to each senator as they entered the Senate House. He freed from danger all defendants whose names had been publicly posted at the Treasury before the last five years and he did not allow them to be prosecuted again unless within a year and under the condition that exile should be the penalty for an accuser who did not win his case. He granted pardon for the past to quaestors' clerks who were trafficking according to custom but contrary to the Claudian law. The pieces of land which were left over after the fields had been divided into portions among the veteran soldiers he granted to their former occupiers as having been acquired by long usage. He suppressed false charges concerning the Privy Purse by means of the heavy punishment of those bringing false charges; and a saying of his was reported that 'an emperor who does not chastise informers encourages them'.

10. But he did not remain in a constant course either of clemency or of self-restraint, though he degenerated somewhat more quickly into cruelty than into cupidity. He killed a pupil of the pantomime Paris, who was still a youth and at that time sick, because he seemed in his art and his appearance not unlike his master. He likewise killed Hermogenes of Tarsus because of certain allusions in his History, while he crucified the scribes who had copied it. He had a head of a household dragged down at the games into the arena and thrown to the dogs because he had said that a 'Thracian' was the equal of a net-fighter but was not a match for the giver of the gladiatorial show. On him was a placard: 'A Thracian fan who spoke impiously'.

He put to death very many senators, amongst them several men of consular rank. Of these, he killed Civica Cerealis whilst actually in his proconsulship of Asia; Salvidienus Orfitus and Acilius Glabrio in exile, on the ground that they were plotting revolution; and the rest individually for the most insubstantial reasons. He put Aelius Lamia to death because of jokes that were indeed suspicious but old and harmless: after the abduction of his wife he had said to Domitian, who was praising his voice, 'I keep it under control'; and to Titus, who was encouraging him to another marriage he had replied, 'You don't want to get married as well, do you?' He killed Salvius Cocceianus because he had celebrated the birthday of the emperor Otho, his paternal uncle; Mettius Pompusianus because he was generally reported to have an horoscope of the emperor and because, it was alleged, he used to carry around a map of the world painted on parchment and speeches from Titus Livius of kings and leaders and because he had given his slaves the names of Mago and Hannibal. He killed Sallustius Lucullus, the governor of Britain, on the ground that he had allowed lances of a novel shape to be called 'Lucullan'; and Junius Rusticus on the ground that he had published praises of Paetus Thrasea and Helvidicus Priscus and had called them 'most holy men'. Using the opportunity offered by this charge, he removed all philosophers from Rome and Italy. He also killed Helvidius, the son, on the ground that he had satirised his divorce from his wife in a comic piece on the stage under the guise of Paris and Oenone; and Flavius Sabinus, another of his cousins, on the ground that the herald had wrongly proclaimed him to the people on the day of the consular elections not as consul-elect but as emperor.

However, becoming considerably more cruel after his victory in the civil war, he tortured many of the opposing side, even while he was trying to track down conspirators who were in hiding, by means of a novel kind of interrogation – by applying fire to the genitals; he also amputated the hands of not a few. There is sufficient agreement that only two of the more important persons were granted pardon – a broad-stripe tribune and a centurion, who, in order that they might the more easily show themselves free of guilt, had demonstrated that they were homosexuals, and for that reason they could not have been of any importance either with the leader or with the soldiers.

11. He was however endowed with a cruelty that was not only great but also artful and unexpected. He invited an accountant into his bed chamber on the day before he crucified him, bade him sit on the couch next to him, sent him away carefree and happy and even honoured him with portions from his dinner. When he was on the point of condemning Arrecinus Clemens, one of his close friends and spies, on a capital charge, he held him in the same or even greater favour until he said to Clemens, who was driving with him for the last time, after seeing the man who had informed against Clemens, 'Do you want us to listen to this vile slave tomorrow?'

In order, also, to abuse the more despicably the endurance of people, he never delivered a gloomier verdict without a preface of clemency, so that there was no surer sign of a cruel death than the mildness of the emperor. He had brought into the Senate House certain men on a charge of treason; and after he had announced that he would on that day find out how dear he was to the Senate, he had easily brought it about that they were condemned to be punished even in the ancestral manner. Then, being alarmed at the savagery of the punishment, he interceded with these words in order to reduce the ill-will created – for it would not be inappropriate to get to know the very words: 'Members of the Senate, allow to be obtained from your sense of loyalty that which I know that I shall obtain with difficulty – that you should grant a free choice of death to the condemned. For you will spare your own eyes and all will understand that I was present in the Senate'.

12. Financially drained by his spending on buildings and shows and by the pay which he had added, he tried to reduce the numbers of soldiers in order to lighten military expenditure. But since he perceived that he thereby became exposed to the barbarians and since nonetheless he persisted in extending his expenses, he had no concern about plundering in every way. The property of the living and the dead were seized everywhere on the accusations of anybody at all and on any charge at all. It was enough that any deed or word against the majesty of the emperor should be produced. The inheritances of totally unrelated people were confiscated if even one person came forth to say that he had heard from the dead man, when he was alive, that Caesar was his heir. The Jewish privy purse was managed most rigorously, beyond all the rest. To it were reported all those who were living a Jewish life, even without professing it, or who had not paid the tributes imposed upon the race by concealing their origin. I remember that, as a young man, I was present when a ninety year old man was being examined by a procurator, in a very crowded council, to see whether he had been circumcised.

Being from his youth of a character that was not at all civil and being also impudent and immoderate both in word and in deed, he held out his hand to Caenis, the mistress of his father, who had returned from Istria and was offering him a kiss, as was her practice. Taking it ill that the son-in-law of his brother had also himself servants dressed in white, he exclaimed (Homer *Iliad* 2.204):

> 'A multiplicity of kings is not a good thing'.

13. Indeed, after he had gained the position of emperor, he neither hesitated to boast in the Senate that he had given the imperial position to both his father and his brother and they had given it back to him, nor to issue an edict, when he was bringing back his wife after divorcing her, saying that she had been recalled to his divine bed. He also heard with pleasure people shouting, 'Good luck to our Lord and Lady!' on a feast day in the amphitheatre. But, when everybody was begging him in great concord at a competition on the Capitol to restore Palfurius Sura, who had formerly been expelled from the Senate and had just then won the crown of victory over the orators, he even deemed them worthy of no answer and merely ordered them, by means of the herald's voice, to shut up. With like arrogance, when he was dictating a circular letter in the name of his procurators, he began thus: 'Our Lord and God orders this to be done'. From this came the practice henceforth that he should not be called otherwise even in the writing and conversation of anyone. He did not allow statues to be set up to him on the Capitol unless they were golden and silver and of a certain weight. The arcades and arches with four-horse chariots and the insignia of triumphs which he erected through the regions of the city were so large and so many that on one of them was inscribed in Greek: *arci* [= enough!]. He held seventeen consulships, more than anybody before him. Of these he took the seven middle ones in successive years, but he held all of them almost purely for the title and none beyond the Kalends of May and the majority only up to the Ides of January. Moreover, when he had assumed the name Germanicus after his two triumphs, he changed the names of the months of September and October to Germanicus and Domitianus, after his own names, on the ground that in the one month he had taken on the imperial position and in the other he had been born.

14. Through these deeds he became an object of fear and hatred to all; and he was at length killed <by a conspiracy> of friends and close freedmen, together with his wife. He had long suspected the year and last day of his life – and even the hour as well as the manner of his death. The Chaldeans had foretold everything to him as a youth and his father too had on one occasion at dinner openly laughed at him when he was refraining from mushrooms as being ignorant of his fate because he did not rather fear steel. Being therefore always timid and nervous, he used to be immoderately disturbed by even the smallest suspicions. It is believed that he was driven to give up the decree which he had put forward about cutting down vines especially by the fact that pamphlets had been scattered about containing this verse <*Anth.* Pal. IX.75>:

> 'Even if you cut me down to the root, I shall still bear fruit, sufficient to pour in libation over you, goat, when you are sacrificed'.

Because of that same fear, he refused a novel and carefully thought out honour offered by the Senate, even though he was especially eager for all such things. In the honour it had been decreed that whenever he held the consulship, Roman knights, who had been chosen by lot, should go before him amongst the lictors and attendants, wearing the official robe and with military spears.

Becoming more anxious by the day as the time of the suspected danger drew near, he decorated with phengite the walls of his porticos in which he habitually walked in order that he might foresee whatever was happening behind his back by means of the reflections on its shiny surface. Nor would he listen to the majority of prisoners unless in seclusion and by himself and after taking their chains into his hand. In order to persuade his household slaves that the killing of a patron should not be dared even with a good precedent, he condemned to death Epaphroditus, the petitions' officer, because it was believed that Nero, after he had been deserted, had been aided by his hand in attaining his death.

15. Finally, he suddenly killed his cousin, Flavius Clemens, a man of the most contemptible inactivity, on the slenderest of suspicions and almost in his very consulship. He had even at that time publicly designated Clemens' small sons as his successors and, after abolishing their former names, had ordered that the one should be called Vespasian, the other Domitian. It was above all by this deed that he hastened on his death.

For eight months in a row there had occurred or been reported so many lightning strikes that he exclaimed, 'Let him now strike whom he wants'. The Capitol and the Temple of the Flavian clan, likewise his Palatine house and even his bed chamber were hit from the sky; and even the inscription was struck from the base of a triumphal statue by the force of a whirlwind and fell onto the adjacent monument. The tree which, when Vespasian was still a private citizen, had been overturned and had then risen up, now once again suddenly fell down. The Fortuna of Praeneste, which throughout the whole time he was emperor had habitually given a happy and virtually the same answer to him whenever he entrusted the new year to her care, finally gave a most gloomy answer – and not without the mention of blood.

He dreamt that Minerva, whom he worshipped superstitiously, was departing from her chapel and saying that she could no longer protect him because she had been disarmed by Jupiter. He was, however, upset by nothing as much as by the reply and fate of the astrologer Ascletarion. Domitian asked him, after he had been informed against and was not denying that he had mentioned what he had seen by means of his art, what death awaited him. When he asserted that in a brief while he would be torn apart by dogs, Domitian ordered him to be killed without delay, but to be burned as carefully as possible in order to demonstrate the foolhardiness of his art. When this was being done, it happened that, the funeral pyre having been demolished by a sudden storm, dogs began to tear the half-burnt corpse apart and that this was related amongst other gossip of the day to Domitian, while he was dining, by Latinus, the actor of mime, who had by chance noticed it whilst passing by.

16. On the day before he died, after he had ordered that apples which had been offered to him should be kept until tomorrow, he added: 'If only I may be permitted to enjoy them'; and turning to his neighbours, stated that on the following day the moon would be spotted with blood in Aquarius and some deed would take place about which men would talk throughout the whole world. At about midnight he was so terrified that he leaped out of bed. Then in the morning he listened to a diviner who had been sent from Germany and who, when consulted about the lightning flash, had predicted a change in the state – and condemned him to death. Whilst he was rather violently scratching a festering wart on his forehead, he said, as the blood flowed forth, 'May it be only this far'. Then when he was asking the time, the sixth hour was deliberately reported to him instead of the fifth, of which he was afraid. When he was happy with these things, as though the danger had now been brought to an end and he was hurrying to his bodily care, the chamberlain Parthenius turned him back by stating that there was someone who was bringing something of importance and that it should not be put off. He therefore removed everybody and took himself to his bedroom; and there he was killed.

17. On the manner of the plot and his death the following details have generally been made public. When the conspirators were hesitating as to when and how they should attack him (that is, whether when he was bathing or dining), Stephanus, the procurator of Domitilla and at that time on a charge of embezzlement, offered his advice and help. He wrapped his left arm, as though it were injured, in wool and bandages for several days in order to avert suspicion; and then, just before the actual hour, he inserted a dagger. Claiming to have information about a conspiracy and hence being admitted, he stabbed Domitian in the groin while he was reading the pamphlet which had been handed to him and was in a state of astonishment. Wounded and fighting back, there attacked him Clodianus, an adjutant, Maximus, a freedman of Parthenius, Satur, the head of the servants of the bedchamber and certain men from the gladiator school; and they slew him with seven wounds. A boy who was as usual assisting with the care of the Lares of the bedchamber and hence was present at the killing, used to give this further piece of information: that he had been ordered by Domitian straightway at the first wound to pass him a dagger that was hidden under the pillow and to summon the servants; that he had found nothing at the bedhead except a sword-hilt and furthermore that everything was shut up; and that Domitian meanwhile, after seizing Stephanus and bringing him to the floor, struggled with him for a long time, trying now to wrench the knife from him and now to dig his eyes out with his fingers, mangled though they were.

He was slain on the fourteenth day before the Kalends of October, in the forty-fifth year of his life and in the fifteenth of his rule as emperor. His nurse Phyllis buried with due ritual his body, which had been carried out by corpse-bearers on a common bier, in her suburban mansion on the Latin Way, but she secretly brought his remains into the temple of the Flavian clan and mingled them with the ashes of Julia, the daughter of Titus, whom she had also brought up.

18. He was tall in stature, with a countenance that was modest and full of the redness of blushing, with large eyes, though their vision was somewhat dull; moreover, he was handsome and well shaped, especially in his youth, and indeed in his whole body with the exception of his feet, where the toes were rather short. Later he also became unsightly because of baldness, the obesity of his stomach and the thinness of his legs which, however, had grown very lean as the result of a lengthy illness. He felt so much that he was recommended by the modesty of his face that on one occasion he vaunted as follows in the Senate: 'Up to this point, to be sure, you have approved of both my mind and my face.' He was so vexed by his baldness that he interpreted it as an insult to himself if anyone else was charged with baldness either as a joke or in a quarrel. Nevertheless, he inserted even the following in a booklet which he addressed to a friend on the care of the hair, consoling both him and himself:

> '"Do you not see how I too am handsome and great?"
> <Homer *Iliad* 21.108>
>
> And yet the same destiny of my hair awaits me, and I shall endure with a brave spirit my hair growing old in my youth. I would have you know that there is nothing more pleasing than beauty and nothing more short-lived.'

19. Being intolerant of toil, he did not walk casually though the city; and when on campaign and on the march, he rarely rode on horseback but was constantly carried in a litter. He was gripped by no enthusiasm for arms, but by a very special one for archery. Very many people often viewed him in his Alban retreat killing a hundred wild animals of different kinds and even deliberately shooting the heads of certain ones in such a way that by means of two hits he produced the effect of horns. Sometimes he aimed his arrows with such skill at the hand of a boy, who was standing at a distance and showing the spread-out palm of his right hand as a mark, that all passed through gaps between his fingers without doing any harm.

20. At the beginning of his time as emperor he neglected the humane studies, even though he had had the libraries that had been destroyed by fire rebuilt at a very great expense, with copies of texts being sought from everywhere and people sent to Alexandria to transcribe and correct them. Nevertheless, he never gave any attention to history or to learning poetry or even to essential composition. He used to read nothing except the Memoirs and Acts of Tiberius Caesar; and he used to prepare his letters and speeches by means of somebody else's talent. Nevertheless, he was a person of not inelegant speech and occasionally even of noteworthy sayings: 'I would wish' he said, 'to be as handsome as Maecius thinks he is'; and he described the head of a certain person that was reddish and hoary because of the diversity of his hair as 'snow sprinkled with honeyed wine'.

21. He used to say that 'the lot of princes is most wretched since they are only believed about the discovery of a conspiracy after they have been killed'.

Whenever there was the time, he would amuse himself with dice, even on working days and during the morning hours; and he used to bathe during the day and he would lunch to satiety, so that he did not easily take anything at dinner time except a Matian apple and a modest drink in a flask. He used to give dinner parties frequently and abundantly, but virtually on the run; certainly, they did not go beyond sunset nor were they such that he held a drinking party afterwards. For he did nothing until bedtime except walk up and down by himself in seclusion.

22. Being an excessively lustful person, he used to call his frequently occurring sexual intercourse 'bed wrestling' as though it were a kind of exercise; and there was a rumour that he used personally to depilate his mistresses and to swim among the commonest prostitutes. Although he had most firmly refused his brother's daughter who had been offered to him in marriage while still a virgin, because he was bound by his marriage to Domitia, he actually seduced her not long after, when she had been betrothed to another – and this was even when Titus was still alive. Then, when she had been deprived of her father and husband, he loved her most passionately and openly, so that he even became the cause of her death when she was compelled to abort the foetus conceived by him.

23. The people accepted with indifference the fact that he had been slain, but the soldiers took it very badly and immediately tried to call him 'the Deified'. They were also ready to avenge him, had not leaders been lacking; and this they did do a little later, demanding most persistently for punishment the instigators of the murder. The Senate, on the other hand, was so overjoyed that after eagerly filling the senate house, it did not refrain from abusing the dead man with the most insulting and bitter kind of shouting, nor from also ordering ladders to be brought and shields and statues of him to be pulled down forthwith and dashed to the ground there and then, nor finally from decreeing that his inscriptions should everywhere be erased and all memory of him should be abolished.

A few months before he was killed, a crow spoke on the Capitol: 'All will be well', nor did there fail to be someone to interpret the portent thus <*FPR* p. 370>:

> The crow which sat on the Tarpeian roof but lately
> Could not say 'all's well', but did say 'all will be'.

They also say that Domitian himself dreamed that a golden hump grew out from behind his neck and that he was certain that there was being portended a happier and more joyful condition for the state after him, as indeed happened soon, thanks to the self-restraint and moderation of the succeeding emperors.

Commentary

THE DEIFIED VESPASIAN

1 *[page 11]*

Because...savagery: The biographies of Vespasian, Titus and Domitian form the eighth and last book of Suetonius' *Lives of the Caesars*, introduced by a concise and not inaccurate summary of the family's historical significance.

three: Galba, Otho and Vitellius.

Flavian family: The name was not rare. During the Republic, Flavians could be found not only in the Sabine territory but elsewhere as well.

without...images: So none of Vespasian's ancestors in the male line (or female: Badian, *OCD* 749) had held a curule office; but see Hopkins, 1983: 255-6.

greed and savagery: Suetonius maintains and develops the theme in *Dom.* 3, 9 and 10.

Petro: Vespasian's paternal grandfather is mentioned only here.

Reate: Reate (Rieti) was a Sabine town on the Avens (Velino), where the Salarian Way crossed the river.

volunteer veteran: They were usually former praetorians retained for further service under improved conditions, often as centurions (Maxfield, 1981: 210).

Pharsalus: Caesar defeated Pompey at Pharsalus in Thessaly (48 BC).

discharge: There were three categories of discharge, i.e. honourable (after the appropriate term of service was completed), through illness, and dishonourable. So Petro must have gained an honourable discharge unless he had retired through ill health.

money-collector: Petro collected debts on commission.

Sabinus: Four Flavians named Titus Flavius Sabinus are known to us: Vespasian's father, brother (City Prefect in 69), the latter's son (consul 72) and grandson (ordinary consul 82). This is Vespasian's father.

senior centurion: If Sabinus really was a former senior centurion, the consequences are important: he would have received a substantial gratuity as well as considerable social prestige.

command of companies: i.e. He had been a centurion. Some idea of the relative importance of the posts Sabinus may have held emerges from their pay scales. Under Augustus, the annual pay was 900 sestertii for an ordinary soldier, 9,000 for a volunteer veteran, 13,500 for a centurion (M.A. Speidel, 1992: 102, 106) and 60,000 (Duncan-Jones, 1974: 3) for a senior centurion.

tax in Asia: Import duty was levied at varying rates – at 2.5% in Asia and Gaul, 2% in Spain and 5% in Sicily. So Sabinus was a senior tax-collecting agent stationed at Ephesus (van Berchem, 1978: 269).

money-lending: Sabinus had moved from Asia to Switzerland in order to become a banker or moneylender (van Berchem, 1978: 269-70). He must have been remarkably successful as he was able to provide both his sons with the senatorial census.

Helvetii: Their territory, more or less equivalent to Switzerland, formed part of Gallia Belgica under Augustus and of Upper Germany under Domitian. Their capital was Aventicum (Avenches).

Vespasia Polla: Vespasian's mother came from an equestrian family that was wealthy enough to ensure that her brother could attain senatorial status.

Sabinus: Before Vespasian's accession to the Empire, Sabinus was the senior Flavian in age, status and reputation. His was a very distinguished career (*MW* 97), set out in (often disputed) detail by Tacitus in *Hist.* 3.75. The likeliest interpretation is that of A.R. Birley (1981: 224-5): he served as legionary legate in Britain, became consul probably in 47 and governed Moesia. He then became City Prefect on two occasions, from 61 to 68 and again in 69. For a hostile account of his actions in December 69 (as well as those of his son, later consul in 72), see Wallace, 1987: 357.

Prefecture of the City: The City Prefect was a senior senator with *imperium*; he commanded the urban cohorts and was responsible for maintaining law and order in the city, presiding over his own court of justice. OCD 1131, 1239.

Nursia: Nursia (Norcia) was a Sabine mountain-town at the foot of the Apennines.

Pollio: Nothing else is known of him.

military tribune: In the Republic, the tribunes were senior officers of a legion with previous military experience, but, during the Empire, their significance diminished with the creation of the post of legionary legate and the tribunate was held early in one's career (*Vesp.* 2).

Prefect of the Camp: His role was administrative (transport, garrison duties etc) and was ranked next in seniority after the senatorial legionary legate and the laticlave tribune. So, apart from the centurions, he was the only officer with any real military experience.

senator of praetorian rank: Vespasian's maternal uncle (Vespasius) was the first of his ancestors to attain senatorial rank and would have done so in Augustus' reign: the shrewd Sabinus married well.

Spoletium: Spoleto is some 30 km from Nursia. *OCD* 1436.

Transpadane area: It was not granted the citizenship until 49 BC. Consequently, some said that Vespasian's great-grandfather was not even an 'Italian'. However, Suetonius' careful investigation revealed that the rumour had no apparent foundation.

contractor...labourers: i.e. he imported labourers and then hired them out to local farmers, probably another unfounded rumour. Perhaps the efforts of the pro-Flavian historians to stress (i.e. invent) the Flavians' loss of influence under the 'bad' Julio-Claudian emperors inspired even greater inventiveness.

very careful investigation: Apparently, Suetonius was capable of careful, independent research.

2 *[pages 11-12]*

Falacrinae: Situated some 30 km from Reate on the Salarian Way.

fifteenth day before the Kalends of December: November 14. The Kalends was the first of December and the Romans counted inclusively.

Camerinus...Sabinus: They were ordinary consuls in AD 9.

five years: Augustus died on 19 August 14.

Tertulla: Petro's wife.

estate at Cosa: Vespasian was brought up in the Etrurian coastal town of Cosa whilst Sabinus was in Ephesus, not (as Braithwaite, 1927: 23) when he was in Aventicum.

toga of manhood: As he was born in 9, he probably assumed this toga on 17 March c. 27 (Millar, 1977: 291).

shunned the broad stripe: The senatorial 'broad stripe' has to be distinguished from the narrow one assigned to members of the equestrian order. It is usually accepted that, once this was conferred on Vespasian in his late teens, he became eligible to hold one of the minor, pre-quaestorian offices (the vigintivirate), a view rejected by Chastagnol (1976: 253-6; but compare Barrett, 1989: 312) who argues that Vespasian must have remained an equestrian until he was of an age to sue for the quaestorship (at least twenty-five) and so he could never have held a post in the vigintivirate and would have served in Thrace as an equestrian tribune. Chastagnol accepts the statement of Dio (59.9.5) that, until the accession of Gaius in 37, only the sons of senators could receive the 'broad stripe' when they 'assumed the toga of manhood' (*Aug*. 38.2).

long time: Perhaps Sabinus had insisted that he would try for senatorial status once this was legally possible, whereas Vespasian, with his well-attested interest in monetary matters (*Vesp*. 16), may have repeatedly taken the opposite point of view, preferring to emulate his father and grandfather.

brother obtained it: According to Chastagnol (see above), Sabinus was granted the senatorial broad purple stripe on his toga at the time of his quaestorship in 34, and not before.

mother: Vespasian's change of heart may have been due to the formidable Vespasia, but Morgan (1996: 47) has suggested that it was linked to the omen of the cypress (*Vesp*. 5).

footman: He was a slave who walked in front of his master to clear the way; the term then came to be used of a client who performed a similar service for his patron.

military tribunate in Thrace: This post was held before the quaestorship, with one senatorial and (in theory) five equestrian tribunes assigned to each legion. It was perhaps c. 29-31 that Vespasian served in Thrace as equestrian tribune (see above) in either the IV Scythica or V Macedonica. There had been problems in Thrace before and during this period (Ann. 2.64-7, 3.38, 4.46-51).

Crete and Cyrene: He was probably there from July 35 until June 36. As he became aedile in 38 at his second attempt, he must have tried first in 36 – and his brother Sabinus was quaestor in 34 (A.R. Birley, 1981: 227). Cyrene became a province c. 75 BC, was united with Crete a few years later and, having become a senatorial province under Augustus, was entitled to a quaestor who usually helped with financial matters.

by lot: Every year, quaestors selected by lot were sent to each of the senatorial provinces.

aedileship: Vespasian held the post in 38 (A.R. Birley, 1981: 226). For Gaius' reaction to Vespasian's neglect of his duties, see *Vesp.* 5.

afterwards the praetorship: Vespasian was not necessarily aedile and praetor in successive years.

defeat: Vespasian's defeat may have been due to the lack of time to campaign between his return from Crete and the elections.

sixth place: Last.

praetor: Almost certainly, he was praetor in 40 (Nicols, 1978: 4-7; Levick, 1999: 11).

obliging to Gaius: Vespasian's speeches imply that he never let slip an opportunity to curry favour with Gaius.

extraordinary games: As well as those regularly celebrated each year.

German victory: The reference is to Gaius' so-called 'German' campaign (described as 'ridiculous' by Tacitus, *Hist.* 4.15) that began in September 39. See Barrett, 1989: 132-9 and Lindsay, 1993: 138-44.

conspirators: Gaetulicus (commander of the Upper German legions) and Lepidus (married to Drusilla, Gaius' sister) were implicated in a conspiracy, if such it was, to kill Gaius and seize the throne; see Simpson (1980: 347-66), Barrett (1989: 105-13) and Lindsay (1993: 110-11). Apparently, the emperor's other sisters (Julia and Agrippina) were also involved. It was suppressed in person by Gaius at Mogontiacum and word of what had happened reached Rome by 27 October 39 (*CIL* 6.2029). Gaetulicus and Lepidus were executed, Julia and Agrippina exiled (Dio 59.22.5-6; *Claud.* 9.1, *Calig.* 24.3).

unburied: This was part of the standard penalty for treason. If Vespasian's proposal coincided with Agrippina's return to Rome with Lepidus' ashes, then the hostility she showed towards him (*Vesp.* 4) may well have had its origins at this time (Jones, 1984a: 581-3). Moreover, if she left

Mogontiacum in October 39, she would have arrived back in January 40, when the new praetors (Vespasian included) had just taken up office. Her welcome was Vespasian's speech – no wonder she hated him.

gave thanks: Vespasian's speech of thanks in the Senate to Gaius was his third as praetor: the invitation to dinner was probably a reward for the first two.

honour of a dinner: A wealthy provincial paid 200,000 sestertii for an invitation to dine with Gaius (*Calig.*39) and a similar invitation issued by Domitian was much prized by Statius (4.2) and by Martial (8.39.1-2). Not everyone enjoyed dining with Titus, however (*Titus* 6), nor did those invited to Domitian's macabre dinner when he alone spoke and then only on 'topics relating to death and slaughter', where the name tags were gravestones...' (Dio 67.9.1-5).

3 *[page 12]*

amidst all this: In Gaius' reign.

Flavia Domitilla: Vespasian's wife, so it seems, was not deified, and it is usually assumed that she did not receive the title *Augusta* either (Castritius, 1969: 492-502; but see Kienast, 1989: 141-47).

Roman knight: During the early Empire, there were many provincials in the equestrian order, and Vespasian adlected more (*Vesp.* 9).

Sabrata: Lying to the west of modern Tripoli, Sabratha (Sabart or Tripoli Vecchio) was probably founded by the Phoenicians; later, it became a Roman colony. *OCD* 1342.

Latin status but afterwards pronounced freeborn: So she had been a Junian Latin (*OCD* 78). Suetonius' choice of words may well explain the use of 'freedwoman' in the *Epit. de Caes.* 10.1 and 11.1 to describe her. Levick argues that 'she either was or had been deemed an ex-slave' and believes that, probably, 'her mother was (Liberalis') freedwoman and concubine, freed without good cause shown, contrary to the lex Aelia Sentia, so acquiring only Latin status' (1999: 12; but see also 212). Her much disputed status is discussed by Ritter, 1972: 759-61; Kienast, 1989: 141-7 and Weaver, 1990: 275-305.

Recoverers: Usually three or five in number, they were appointed by the praetor and were employed instead of a single judge in certain cases, e.g. (as here) of disputed legal status, debt or extortion. See *Dom.* 8 and *OCD* 1296.

father...giving her her freedom: In cases of disputed legal status, those under investigation could not act for themselves but only through an agent.

Flavius Liberalis: Just possibly, Flavia Domitilla was related to Vespasian by blood; one is also reminded of the eminent Flavian senators, *Flavius* Silva Nonius Bassus (ordinary consul 81) and Salvius *Liberalis* Nonius Bassus (*Vesp.* 13). See Salomies, 1992: 132-3.

Ferentium: On Ferentium (Ferento), in southern Etruria, see Murison,

1992: 89 and *OCD* 592.

quaestor's clerk: There were thirty-six quaestors' clerks, some of whom were freedmen. Suetonius' scornful tone derives from the fact that they were paid a salary.

Titus, Domitian: Both were born in Rome, Titus on 30 December 39, Domitian on 24 October 51.

Domitilla: This Domitilla (*PIR*2 F 417), Domitian's sister, is the 'deified Domitilla' appearing on coins and inscriptions, as is clear from Statius (1.1.97-8; compare Kienast, 1989: 141-7). Born after 51 (Nicols, 1978: 8-9; but compare Townend, 1961: 62), she was married, so it seems, to Petillius Cerialis (consul II in 74). Her daughter, presumably by Petillius, was also called Domitilla and she married Flavius Clemens, grandson of Vespasian's brother; in 95, Clemens was executed and his wife banished. But Domitilla's relationship with Clemens (wife or niece?) and her place of exile have provoked much discussion. In brief, Dio (67.14.1-2) claims that she (Clemens' wife) was banished to Pandateria. In the Acts of Saints Nereus and Achilleus, she (now Clemens' niece) was exiled to Terracina, whereas Eusebius claims that 'Clemens' niece was banished to Pontia' (*Hist. Eccl.* 3.17). Finally, Cardinal Caesar Baronius (c. 1600) was the first to 'discover' two Domitianic victims named Domitilla (*Annales Ecclesiastici* 4.586), a version still accepted by Sordi, 1994: 50-1.

still a private citizen: Before 1 July 69.

Caenis: (Antonia) Caenis (*PIR*2 A 888) was the secretary and freedwoman of Antonia (see below), thereby giving Vespasian a direct link with the imperial family when she became his mistress. She was eminently capable and trustworthy; it was to her that Antonia dictated the letter to Tiberius about Sejanus (Dio 60.14.1-2). After Vespasian's accession, she amassed great wealth by selling 'procuratorships, generalships, priesthoods and, in some instances, even imperial decisions' (Dio 67.14.3). Domitian's attitude towards her is revealed in *Dom.* 12. She died in the early seventies (Dio 67.14.1).

Antonia: Daughter of Marcus Antonius, Antonia (36 BC-AD 37) married Tiberius' brother Drusus and bore him three children, Germanicus, Claudius and Livia Julia (Livilla). She exerted considerable influence through her circle whose members included not only such eminent senatorial families as the Vitellii, Plautii and Petronii but also wealthy and influential Jews (Agrippa I, Agrippa II and Tiberius Julius Alexander's family). See Kokkinos, 1992.

4 *[pages 12-13]*

Germany: Soon after January 41, he was sent to Strasburg as legionary legate of the II Augusta (*Hist.* 3.44), no doubt to prepare the legion for its part in the invasion of Britain. According to Josephus, Vespasian 'restored peace to the West when convulsed by the Germans': *BJ* 3.4). For a more sober assessment, see Levick, 1999: 16.

legionary legate: Suetonius fails to mention the fact that Vespasian's older brother Sabinus also commanded one of Claudius' legions (either IX Hispana, XIV Gemina or XX Valeria Victrix).

Narcissus: The power and influence of the imperial freedman Narcissus (*PIR2* N 23), Claudius' Chief Secretary, were legendary (*AJ* 18.182; *Claud.* 28; *Vit.* 2.5; Dio 60.19.2-3;). He may even have been responsible for having Titus admitted to court as a companion for Claudius' son, Britannicus; but for opposing Claudius' marriage to Agrippina and favouring Britannicus rather than Nero, he was forced to commit suicide (*Ann.* 13.1). Vespasian's other 'allies' at court were L. Vitellius (below) and Caenis (*Vesp.* 3).

Britain: Pro-Flavian writers (Josephus, *BJ* 3.5-6; Valerius Flaccus, *Argon.* 1. 7-11; Silius Italicus, *Pun.* 3.597-8) exaggerated Vespasian's role in the Claudian invasion. A more realistic account is provided by Tacitus (*Agr.* 13.3; *Hist.* 3.44). Before the emperor's arrival, Vespasian and his elder brother Sabinus had 'crossed the river [? Medway]...and killed many of the foe' (Dio 60.20.3). By 47, Vespasian had probably advanced as far as the Fosse Way, somewhat to the north of Cirencester. See Frere (1987: 48-69), Salway (1993: 49-72) and Levick (1999: 16-20).

thirty occasions: Eutropius (7.19.1) repeats Suetonius' account (as usual) but gives the number as thirty-two.

two very strong tribes: The Durotriges were probably one of them, the other being either the Belgae (Nicols, 1978: 8), the Dumnonii (Frere, 1987: 58) or the Dobunni (Salway, 1993: 70); but that they were the Belgae and the Atrebates (Mooney, 1930: 387) is unlikely.

twenty townships: Possible candidates include Maiden Castle, Hod Hill, South Cadbury, Waddon Hill, Ham Hill, Wiveliscombe, Hembury, Tiverton, Okehampton, Cullompton, Bury Barton, Killerton and North Tawton (Frere, 1987: 58-9). The experience in siege-warfare served him well in Judaea two decades later.

consular legate Aulus Plautius: Suffect consul in 29, Plautius (*PIR2* P 457) governed Pannonia from 41 to 43 and then became Britain's first consular governor (from 43 to 47). He established Roman ascendancy over the area south of the Exe/Humber line (Dio 60.30.2; *Claud.* 24.3; *Agr.* 14.1). His political influence was enormous: his mother was a Vitellia, his wife a Pomponia and his sister had married P. Petronius, an old friend of Claudius (Seneca, *Apoc.* 14.2); these families, forming part of Antonia's circle, were closely linked to the eminent L. Vitellius – and Vespasian was a 'client of Vitellius' (*Hist.* 3.66). See Birley, 1981: 37-40 and Hind, 1989: 1-21.

command...of Claudius himself: Attested also by Dio 60.21.2-5, 23.1; but Suetonius saw Vespasian as one of the greatest emperors and so deliberately downplayed Claudius' role as well as that of Sabinus.

triumphal decorations: After 19 BC, only members of the imperial family could receive a triumph, since a general in the field was regarded as the emperor's representative. He could, however, still receive the appropriate insignia (Maxfield, 1981: 105-9). Usually, these were awarded only to a general of consular rank – but Claudius' generosity was notorious.

double priesthood: The reward was (probably) a priesthood in a major college and membership in a sodaliity.

consulship last two months: Vespasian was suffect consul with Claudius in November and December 51, despite Suetonius' statement in *Claud.* 14 that, in 51, the emperor relinquished his office after six months. So Vespasian was consul at the minimum age, but had received no remission for his children.

inactivity and retirement: Suetonius exaggerates the extent of Vespasian's 'retirement'. After all, Titus was still being educated at court with Britannicus and he himself would have been required to attend the two regular Senate meetings per month (Dio 55.3.1) and to observe his normal priestly duties – whilst (unlike his son) not being welcome at court.

afraid of Agrippina: Vespasian had reason to fear her (*Vesp.* 2). However, at a time when she exercised real power (*Ann.* 12.7), he became consul and his son's education at court continued.

influential with her son: Tacitus refers twice to her power (*Ann.* 13.12; 14.1), greatest in the first years of Nero's reign.

Africa: He was proconsul there c. 62.

honourably...great respect: Suetonius' assessment (shared by Silius Italicus, *Pun.* 3.599) is seemingly at odds with *Hist.* 2.97 and 4.49. But, if he had returned home no richer (see below), then it was his severity and parsimony that earned him his unfavourable reputation.

Hadrumetum: Hadrumetum (modern Sousse) is a city of Phoenician origin south of Carthage. *OCD* 663-4.

turnips: Similarly, Claudius had pieces of bread thrown at him in the Forum because of a grain shortage.

returned no richer: This is consistent with Suetonius' reference to the 'poverty' experienced by Domitian in his youth (*Dom.* 1).

mortgaged...to his brother: On Vespasian's brother Sabinus, see Vesp. 1. Tacitus introduces his account of the mortgage with the words 'it is believed' (*Hist.* 3.65), apparently doubting the accuracy of the rumour (Nicols, 1978: 30).

retail trading...muleteer: As Reate was known for its mules (*NH* 8.167), Vespasian may have supplied the famous mules of Nero's court (Dio 62.28.1; *NH* 33.140; *Nero* 30.3) – though selling mules was inappropriate behaviour for a senator.

broad stripe: See *Vesp.* 2.

stern rebuke: He must have been rebuked (by Nero) presumably just after his return from Africa, when he was 'no richer'.

Nero's Companions: Emperors travelling beyond Rome and Italy were accompanied by selected friends who were usually assigned specific tasks and paid a salary (*OCD* 372). For Nero's enormous entourage (his cheerleaders were said to number five thousand), see Dio 63.8.3 and Bradley, 1979: 152-7.

Greek trip: During the tour (September 66 to early 68: Smallwood, 1967: 26), Nero sang publicly at all the musical contests (*Nero* 22.3-24), returning in triumph to Rome with 1808 victorious crowns (Dio 63.20.1-21.1). See further Bradley, 1978: 61-72.

leave too often: Nero was seriously offended by such behaviour (*Nero* 23.2); even those showing 'less vigorous applause or the silence of indifference...were often struck by soldiers' (*Ann.* 16.5). Nonetheless, Vespasian – apparently – dared to repeat the offence.

fall asleep: The sources differ in their accounts of Vespasian's lapse. Tacitus sets it during the Quinquennial Games of 65 in Rome (*Ann.* 16.5). Dio agrees with Suetonius and places it in Greece, with Vespasian being reprimanded (? once again) by Phoebus, not for sleeping, but for frowning at Nero's behaviour (66.11.2). Later (*Vesp.* 14), Suetonius reports the reprimand but with no indication of the setting. Possibly, Vespasian erred once and once only. However, if we accept a major lapse on his part in 65 (as Tacitus), then he may have been considered guilty of a less serious offence in Greece that resulted in a brief estrangement, 'enhanced' by pro-Flavian historians. Still, would someone as sycophantic as Vespasian have risked offending Nero twice?

banned: Thrasea Paetus took such a prohibition as a forewarning of imminent execution (*Ann.* 15.23).

public receptions: Vespasian was banned 'not only from the inner circle but even from the general audience' (Wallace-Hadrill, 1996: 283). See further *OCD* 1350.

retired: The estrangement must have been of extremely short duration, since Nero left Rome for Greece late in September 66 (above) and Vespasian was fighting in Judaea early the following year.

province together with an army: Judaea and three legions (see below). At first, however, Vespasian's base was not in Judaea, but in the Syrian city of Ptolemais (Nicols, 1978: 48, 114). His official province, then, possibly included Syria. So Josephus' comment that Nero sent Vespasian 'to take command of the armies in Syria' (*BJ* 3.7) should not be rejected outright.

hiding away and even fearing the worst: Suetonius fails to explain fully the unusual circumstances surrounding Nero's offer. At one moment, Vespasian was in hiding and in fear of his life, at the next, Nero was 'lavishing soothing and flattering compliments' (*BJ* 3.7) on him and he was being offered command of three legions with, so it seems, the unprecedented privilege of choosing his legionary commanders (see below). But it could be argued that both the seriousness and the effect of Vespasian's 'offence' has been grossly exaggerated. Once again, the Flavian historians on whom Suetonius relied strained the truth to and beyond its limits in disguising the slavish adulation lavished by Vespasian on the emperor of the day and exaggerated (or invented) any loss of influence the family suffered. One thinks of Pliny ('in the last years of Domitian, Pliny bounded forward in his official career': Syme, 1958: 77) and the version he presented of his relationship with Domitian.

ancient and firm belief: The prediction is also reported in *Hist.* 5.13, *BJ* 6.312 and Orosius 7.9.2.

men...from Judaea: Tacitus uses the same words, but, unlike Suetonius and Orosius (7.9.2), explains that the plural 'men' (*Hist.* 5.13) refers to both Vespasian and Titus. Josephus, however, prefers the singular, i.e. 'the oracle... signified Vespasian' (*BJ* 6.312).

Roman emperor: This explanation, accepted by Josephus (*BJ* 6.312), was rejected by Eusebius (*Hist. Eccl.* 3.8) and other Christian writers.

Jews referred it to themselves: This error was also noted by Josephus ('many wise men went astray': *BJ* 6.312). Orosius (7.9.2) wrongly assigns the prediction to the occasion when Vespasian visited Mt Carmel (*Vesp.* 5).

slew their governor: He was Gessius Florus (Goodman, 1987: 152-5), a Greek from Clazomenae, appointed procurator of Judaea in 64. His repressive régime (*BJ* 2.277-8) led to the outbreak of insurrection in 66. Despite Suetonius, Florus was not killed; he withdrew to Caesarea (*BJ* 2.331) and was still alive when Cestius Gallus later lay siege to Jerusalem (*BJ* 2.531). The error was noted by Orosius who, though usually copying Suetonius precisely, states that the 'Roman garrison was wiped out' (7.9.2).

consular legate of Syria: This was Cestius Gallus, a man who had already 'passed his prime' (*RP* 3.1382), being suffect consul in 42 and appointed to Syria twenty-four years later. Tacitus dismisses him as being 'often defeated in battle' (*Hist.* 5.10). Leaving Antioch with a large force (XII Fulminata, vexillations from the IV Scythica, VI Ferrata, III Gallica and X Fretensis, six auxiliary cohorts and four *alae*: *BJ* 2.500), he took Joppa, marched on Jerusalem but, presumably because it was late in the season (November), abandoned the siege and was defeated at Beth Horon with the loss of nearly 6,000 men (*BJ* 2.513-56). Soon after, he died (*Hist.* 5.10).

legionary eagle: The legion must have been the XII Fulminata as only vexillations of the others were present. It was certainly humiliated (*BJ* 5.41), but probably did not lose its eagle (Ritterling, *RE* 12.1706); it was not used by Vespasian, but was assigned to Titus for the assault on Jerusalem. Later, it was sent to Melitene (*BJ* 7.18).

larger army: It consisted of three complete legions (V Macedonica, X Fretensis and XV Apollinaris: *BJ* 3.65) and other forces amounting to some 60,000 men (*BJ* 3.69).

energetic commander: Tacitus uses similar language (*Hist.* 2.5, 4.8).

entrusted with safety: Even at the end, Nero seems to have regarded Vespasian as 'safe' – and correctly so.

approved industry: Josephus (*BJ* 3.3) not unexpectedly agrees with Suetonius' assessment ('a man with the steadiness resulting from years and experience'), as does Aurelius Victor 8.4.

no way to be feared...lowliness of birth and name: This was not the whole story. The urgency of the situation (the loss of 6,000 men) and the time of year (mid-winter) would have reduced the number of acceptable candidates present in Greece with Nero. Another factor may have been Vespasian's connections with prominent members of Jewish nobility. Thanks to his mistress Caenis and his powerful supporters L. Vitellius (*Hist* 3.66) and Narcissus (*Vesp.* 4), he had been involved with Antonia's circle which included the families of the Jewish king Julius Agrippa I and Ti. Julius Alexander (appointed prefect of Egypt in 66).

two legions added to the existing forces: It is not easy to make sense of this statement since, in the winter of 66/67, there were practically no Roman forces in Judaea and Vespasian was assigned not two, but three legions. Presumably, Suetonius regards Vespasian's 'province' as both Syria and Judaea – yet, in the next sentence, he refers to the 'neighbouring provinces' one of which is clearly Syria. Here, though, he must mean that, when Vespasian arrived in Ptolemais, he was in effective command of the forces in Syria until Mucianus arrived later in the year: the X Fretensis was a Syrian legion, whereas the V Macedonica (from Moesia) and the XV Apollinaris (from Pannonia) were still in Asia after Corbulo's Armenian campaign and so were 'added' to the X Fretensis.

eight cavalry squadrons and ten infantry cohorts: Josephus states that Vespasian added five squadrons and eighteen cohorts to the one squadron and five cohorts already in Judaea (*BJ* 3.66) – and Josephus is more likely to be correct. In addition, the client kings provided a further 18,000 men (*BJ* 3.68), making a total of 60,000 (*BJ* 3.69).

older son...one of the legates: Titus' appointment was unusual. Aged about 27, he was not yet of praetorian rank; moreover, this was the only recorded occasion when the leader of an expeditionary force had his own son in control of one of his legions. Nero must have given Vespasian a completely free hand in choosing the commanders of his three legions, viz. XV Apollinaris (Titus), X Fretensis (Trajan's father; he and Titus may well have married sisters or half-sisters (Champlin, 1983: 257-64; Bennett, 1997: 11-12) and V Macedonica (Sex. Vettulenus Cerialis, almost certainly from Reate).

his province: Judaea (so *Hist.* 2.5), even though Vespasian based himself for a time at Ptolemais (in Syria: 4.4).

neighbouring provinces: Egypt and Syria.

corrected discipline: Suetonius implies that the standard of discipline among the Syrian legions was low – hardly likely in the brief interval between

Corbulo's death (mid 66) and Vespasian's arrival (early 67). The real problem was the loss of the patronage that Corbulo had been expected to provide. What Vespasian (or Mucianus) had to 'correct' was the soldiers' hostility, for Vespasian, after all, was Nero's representative. Moreover, apart from their annoyance at the loss of their prospects, they had to face a commander who had just severed his own friendship (*Hist.* 4.7) and his son's marital connection (*Titus* 4) with the group to which Corbulo himself had been aligned.

one or two battles: Vespasian's first victories in June 67 were at Japha, Garizim and Jotapata (*BJ* 3.306-39).

such resolution: In his account of the Jewish campaign, Josephus tends to portray a somewhat different Vespasian from Suetonius' and to stress the bravery of his hero, Titus.

several arrows...fortress: The reference is to Jotapata in Galilee, where the defenders were led by Josephus – who claimed that Vespasian received a 'slight wound in his foot' (*BJ* 3.236).

5 *[pages 13-15]*

hope...long ago conceived: Presumably, Suetonius means that Vespasian had long ago conceived the hope of becoming emperor and was now determined to bring it to fruition. On this basis, some (listed in Jones, 1984: 63) have (unconvincingly) dated Vespasian's imperial aspirations to the occasion of Josephus' prediction (*BJ* 3.399-403) and of Titus' visit (October 67) to Mucianus in Syria (*BJ* 4.32).

portents: Of the eleven portents listed here, all apart from two (the oak tree and the eagles at Bedriacum) are found in other authors: Dio has seven of them, Tacitus three and Plutarch and Orosius one each. The prophecy of *BJ* 3.399-403 appears in Suetonius (below), Dio and Orosius – but not in Tacitus who refers to the prophecies on three occasions (*Hist.* 1.10, 2.1 and 2.78) and dismisses them (*Hist.* 1.10). In fact, they were intended to advance Vespasian's claim to the throne (particularly amongst the members of the eastern legions) and to disguise the family's obscure origins (*Vesp.* 4) and Vespasian's lack of prestige (*Vesp.* 7).

oak-tree sacred to Mars: Usually, the oak was regarded as sacred to Jupiter, as in Ovid, *Met.* 7.623.

three births of Vespasia: Vespasia's three children by Flavius Sabinus were an unnamed daughter, Flavius Sabinus (*Vesp.* 1) and Vespasian.

inspections of entrails: The 'entrail-observer' (*haruspex*) claimed to reveal the future by the appearance of the victim's entrails. *OCD* 667-8.

aedile: Vespasian was aedile in 38 (*Vesp.* 2).

sweeping the streets: During the Empire, the aediles were still responsible for this and similar tasks. *OCD* 15-16.

mud...official toga: Dio 59.12.3 repeats the story, explaining that 'it signified that Gaius had entrusted the city to him outright for its improvement'. The interpretation provided by Suetonius and Dio is a fine example of how the Flavian historians they consulted had dealt with certain aspects of Vespasian's career under the Julio-Claudians: having one's toga filled with what, perhaps euphemistically, is described as mud was (with an over-generous interpretation) not the low point in a senator's career, but rather an omen of future greatness. Suetonius' sources tried to downplay the family's successes under the Julio-Claudians and emphasise their misfortunes: so Vespasian was (?twice) officially rebuked by Nero (*Vesp.* 4) and Domitian was brought up in poverty (*Dom.* 1).

official toga: This was the *toga praetexta*, white with a purple border, that could be worn only by curule aediles, praetors, consuls and senior priests. Vespasian must have been a curule aedile (a post open to both patricians and plebeians) since plebeian aediles were ineligible to wear this type of toga.

strange dog: A similar report appears in Dio 66.1.2. The appearance of a strange dog was regarded as an omen.

human hand: A sign of imperial power.

crossroads: Rubbish and even human bodies were often left at the crossroads; hence the presence of the dog.

plough-ox...dining room: Dio (66.1.2) also reports this portent.

lowered its neck: The most obvious sign of Vespasian's future position.

his ancestral farm: The estate of Vespasian's grandmother Tertulla at Cosa; but, in *Hist.* 2.78, the tree is located on Vespasian's property.

without..storm: So, too, *Hist.* 2.78 – but, according to Dio, it was 'uprooted and overthrown by a violent wind' (66.1.1).

rose up again: So, too, Dio 66.1.3 and Tacitus, who describes Vespasian as then 'quite young' (*Hist.* 2.78). Suetonius, on the other hand, who apparently arranged his omens chronologically (the oak in *Vesp.* 5 is assigned to Augustus' reign, the next group to Gaius' and the later ones to Nero's), would have him in his late twenties at the time of cypress tree-omen and so some years older than Tacitus states (Morgan, 1996: 43-4). See also *Dom.* 15.

tooth extracted from Nero: So, too, Dio 66.1.3.

oracle of the god of Carmel: Carmel (a mountain in the north-west of Israel with the city of Haifa on its slopes) was also the name of the god (*Hist.* 2.78). When Vespasian was sacrificing there late in May 69, its priest Basilides predicted success in whatever he planned (*Hist.* 2.78). This was part of the Flavians' plan of action. The soldiers of the eastern legions had to be convinced that Vespasian's success was predetermined, a conviction later strengthened by the miracles ascribed to him when he visited Alexandria (*Vesp.* 7). Apparently, Suetonius arranged the omens in chronological order (see above), but he places the visit to Mt Carmel before Josephus' prophecy (of c. July 67). So, as with the omen of the cypress (above), Suetonius is in error.

one of the aristocratic captives, Josephus: This is the historian (Flavius) Josephus (Cohen, 1979; Rajak, 1983; Goodman, 1995), a Jewish priest with Hasmonaean connections – hence 'aristocratic'. Born in 37 or 38, he led the Jewish forces against Vespasian but surrendered on the fall of Jotapata in 67. He assigns his prophecy to this period, immediately after his capture. When interviewed by Vespasian, he addressed him as follows: 'You will be Caesar, Vespasian, you will be emperor, you and your son here' (*BJ* 3.401). Thanks to Titus, so Josephus claims, his life was spared; he was with Titus during the siege of Jerusalem and was later given Roman citizenship and an annual allowance. He remained in Rome for the rest of his life. Josephus' motives in claiming to have made this prophecy have been questioned, but it must have been intended to justify his personal conduct, as with the similar prediction ascribed to Rabban Johanan ben Zakkai – see further Rajak, 1983: 188-9 and Price, 1992: 264-70. Vespasian encouraged the story for other reasons, not least because of his family's lack of status (*Vesp*. 4).

freed by Vespasian now as emperor: Dio 66.1.4 reports the same prophecy, but with minor differences (details in Rajak, 1983: 191). Presumably, Suetonius had no knowledge of the *BJ*, given the discrepancies in this section (the fate of Florus, the loss of the eagle, the composition of Vespasian's legionary and auxiliary forces, and the details of Vespasian's wound at Jotapata).

Nero...warned in a dream: Also in Dio 66.1.3.

carriage of Jupiter: This was the sacred chariot bearing the statues of the gods in a solemn procession that opened the games in the Circus. Senior senators provided an escort, led by the emperor who, according to Nero's dream, would soon be Vespasian.

electoral meeting for his second consulship: Galba held his second consulship in 69. During the Empire, what passed for consular elections were held in March and October, and Galba reached Rome in the first days of October 68. So, if we accept Suetonius' chronology (see below), the reference is to the occasion when the people were assembled in the Campus Martius to hear the result announced – and the statue of Caesar on the island on the Tiber would be visible from there.

statue turned towards the East: It predicted the transfer of imperial power from the West to the East. Suetonius assigns the portent to the last months of 68, Plutarch (*Otho* 4.5) and Tacitus (*Hist*. 1.86) to the next year, after Galba's death on 15 January.

Bedriacum: Bedriacum lies midway between Verona and Cremona, probably near the modern village of Tornata. The reference is to the first of two battles of 69, between the armies of Otho and Vitellius; the second, between Vitellius' and Vespasian's forces, was fought some months later. See further Wellesley, 1975: 75 and 146.

two eagles: Otho and Vitellius, the third being Vespasian. A simpler version of the story appears in *Hist*. 2.50, Dio 63.10.3 and *NH* 10.135.

6 *[page 15]*

his own followers...pressing: Tacitus (*Hist.* 2.76-7) and Josephus have a similar theme: 'He was now (May/June 69) urged by Mucianus and the other generals to act as emperor and the rest of the army clamoured to be led against all opponents' (*BJ* 4.605).

chance support...men not present: The reference is to the Danubian vexillations mentioned below and in no other ancient source. In *Hist.* 2.85 and *BJ* 4.619, the Moesian legions (still in Moesia) act only after hearing of Vespasian's proclamation in Egypt.

two thousand from each of the three legions: Suetonius' account differs from Tacitus' (*Hist.* 2.46 and 2.85). According to Suetonius, the soldiers, in vexillations, rioted after Otho's death and were the first to declare for Vespasian. In Tacitus, it appears that complete legions were involved, that the rioting occurred before Otho died and that the Moesian army declared for Vespasian only after those in the east. For a more detailed discussion of the two versions, see Chilver, 1979: 210-11.

Otho...had committed suicide: Tacitus just as clearly assigns the incident to Otho's lifetime (*Hist.* 2.46).

Aquileia: Aquileia was in Venetia, a few kilometres from the head of the Adriatic. *OCD* 133.

Spanish army: The VI Victrix.

praetorians: Otho had seized power thanks to their 'affection and loyalty' (*Otho* 8.1). See *Hist.* 1.23-7 and Wellesley, 1975: 20-7.

German army: Vitellius had been proclaimed emperor by the armies of Upper and Lower Germany on 3 January.

names...consular legates: The candidates would have been Pompeius Silvanus (in Dalmatia), Aponius Saturninus (Moesia), Tampius Flavianus (Pannonia), Licinius Mucianus (Syria), and, in theory, Vettius Bolanus (Britain) and Cluvius Rufus (Spain); see Eck, 1982: 284-6.

men from the Third legion: Ordered to Moesia in 68 from service under Corbulo, the Syrian III Gallica declared first for Otho, then played a decisive role in Vespasian's elevation, being the first in Moesia to declare for him (*Hist.* 2.74, 85). In the seventies, its commander Aurelius Fulvus, grandfather of the emperor Antoninus Pius, was granted the consulship and patrician status by Vespasian and, in 85 a second (ordinary) consulship by Domitian.

inscribed his name...pennants: These pennants would hang from a crossbar attached to a staff; according to Dio, they 'resembled sails, with purple letters upon them to distinguish the army and its commander-in-chief' (40.10.3).

news...widespread: Suetonius' version of events is given greater credibility by the details he provides in this section and by the link with the July proclamation.

Tiberius Alexander: Prefect of Egypt in 69, Tiberius Julius Alexander (*PIR*2 J 139) was the first military governor to declare for Vespasian (1 July) who dated his reign from Alexander's proclamation in Egypt. An apostate Jew, he became procurator of Judaea (c. 46-48) and, later, prefect of Egypt. Alexander, Agrippa II and Berenice formed part of the 'oriental group' that supported the Flavians in 69 (*Hist.* 2.74). Moreover, his father had very close connections with Claudius' mother Antonia (*AJ* 19.276). Alexander later served as Titus' chief of staff during the siege of Jerusalem (*MW* 329), and may even have become praetorian prefect (Griffin, 2000: 10). See also Titus 6.

Prefect of Egypt: Egypt was the only major province under the control of an equestrian governor (*Hist.* 1.11).

first to administer the oath of loyalty: Tacitus (*Hist.* 2.79) agrees with Suetonius' statement that Vespasian was first proclaimed Emperor in Egypt and not in Judaea as Josephus states (*BJ* 4.592-620). Alexander's legions were the III Cyrenaica and the XXII Deiotariana.

Kalends of July: 1 July.

observed as the day...emperor: So, too, *Hist.* 2.79; numerous coins and inscriptions consistently date Vespasian's tribunician power from 1 July 69. See *Vesp.* 12.

then the Judaean army: Josephus reverses the order (*BJ* 4.592-620) in an attempt to disguise what had happened, an emperor proclaimed in Egypt with 'oriental' support (including the 'little Cleopatra', Berenice) that recalled events of a century before. The Judaean legions involved were the V Macedonica, X Fretensis and XV Apollinaris.

in his presence: The same phrase occurs in *Hist.* 2.79; Tacitus possibly used the same source.

fifth day before the Ides: 11 July. Tacitus, however, has 3 July (*Hist.* 2.79). See Chilver, 1979: 240.

copy of a letter...genuine or forged: In favour of the second alternative is Suetonius' claim that, just before he committed suicide, Otho 'burned all his papers' (*Otho* 10.2). One is almost tempted to see here the 'hand' of the Flavian expert in such matters, the master forger Titus (*Titus* 3).

rumour...to transfer the German legions: According to Tacitus, the rumour was spread by Mucianus (*Hist.* 2.80).

Licinius Mucianus: Gaius Licinius Mucianus (*PIR*2 L 216) was suffect consul on three occasions: c. 64, 70 and 72. On his early career, see *OCD* 859. Appointed to Syria late in Nero's reign, he came into dispute with Vespasian, his neighbour in Judaea (see below). With this settled, he encouraged Vespasian's imperial ambitions and was instrumental in persuading the Syrian legions to support the Flavians, a far from easy task (*Vesp.* 4). According to Dio, Mucianus' plan was that, 'while Vespasian should have the name of emperor, he himself as a result of the other's good nature might enjoy an equal share of power' (65.8.4). In the latter, he was to be disappointed – for his subsequent activities, see *Vesp.* 7 and 13.

Vologaesus: Vologaesus I was king of Parthia from 51 to 79. For a discussion of his (somewhat belated) offer of support – it reached Vespasian after the news of Vitellius' death (*Hist.* 4.51) – see Dabrowa, 1981: 187-204.

Mucianus put aside the jealousy: Vespasian would have reached Ptolemais early in 67, some months before Mucianus whose arrival (to take up his Syrian command) could, perhaps, be assigned to early August. Their relationship rapidly worsened, possibly because Vespasian had set up his base camp in Syria (at Ptolemais) and maintained it there (*Vesp.* 4). Some of their friends tried to reconcile the pair, but it was Titus who acted as mediator, perhaps as early as September 67, during his absence from the siege of Gamala, 'having been sent off to Syria to Mucianus' (*BJ* 4.32).

Syrian army: Syria originally had four legions (III Gallica, IV Scythica, VI Ferrata and XII Fulminata) but the III Gallica was transferred to Moesia (*Vesp.* 6). In all, then, Vespasian had nine legions (three from Judaea and two from Egypt: *Hist.* 2.76).

40,000 archers: Tacitus refers to them as 'cavalry' (*Hist.* 4.51). Presumably, they were mounted archers.

7 *[page 16]*

undertaken civil war: Suetonius is imprecise. For Vespasian, the civil war had already begun on 1 July 69, when 'Tiberius Alexander (administered) the oath of loyalty to Vespasian' (*Vesp.* 6), and not with activities described subsequently.

leaders and troops...to Italy: Mucianus and Antonius Primus were sent. The former set out for Italy (*Hist.* 2.83; Dio 65.9.2), but, without waiting for him to arrive, Antonius Primus moved against Vitellius with the Dalmatian, Pannonian and Moesian armies and defeated him.

crossed over to Alexandria: Similarly Dio 65.9.2 and Orosius 7.9.3. Whilst Mucianus marched against the Vitellians, Titus remained in Judaea and Vespasian crossed to Alexandria (*Hist.* 2.82) where he would have arrived c. November 69. The visit was important for a number of reasons. Apart from Alexandria's strategic position, Vespasian needed to be seen as remote from the pillaging and slaughter inevitable in a civil war. Furthermore, his representatives, including Tiberius Julius Alexander, needed time to strengthen his support in those legions who had to be assured that Vespasian's success was predetermined. Henrichs (1968: 55) argues that, in their accounts of what happened in Alexandria, both Suetonius and Tacitus relied on a common source that was derived from an account of Alexander the Great's visit some four hundred years before. Nonetheless, their accounts differ in certain vital details. Tacitus assigns Vespasian's visit to the Serapeum after, and as a result of, his miraculous cures (*Hist.* 4.82) and, unlike Suetonius, assigns both events to 70 (*Hist.* 4.81). See also Scott, 1936: 9-13, Henrichs, 1968: 54-72 and Levick, 1999: 68-9.

stronghold of Egypt: Suetonius probably means Alexandria and Pelusium (as in *B. Alex.* 26.2). For the strategic significance of Egypt, see *Ann.* 2.59 and *Hist.* 3.8.

temple of Serapis: The Serapeum at Alexandria was described by Ammianus Marcellinus (22.16.12). On its location, see Henrichs, 1968: 55 and, for Serapis in general, Takacs, 1995 and *OCD* 1355-6.

removing everybody...sign about stability of his rule: Both these details appear in Tacitus (*Hist.* 4.81, 82).

freedman Basilides: He has been identified (Scott, 1936: 11-13) with the Egyptian noble (*Hist.* 4.82) of the same name consulted by Vespasian at Mt Carmel (*Vesp.* 5), named by Tacitus at *Hist.* 2.78 but not by S; there is also another Basilides, the procurator in Egypt in 49 (*PIR*2 B 60 and 61). Basilides' name was in itself an omen ('basileus' in Greek means 'king'), a point stressed by Tacitus at *Hist.* 4.82 but not by Suetonius.

sacred foliage...bread-cakes: In a number of Ptolemaic documents, these items appear as symbols of kingship. For more detail, see Henrichs, 1968: 61.

straightway: Again, Tacitus has the same word (*Hist.* 4.81). It is worth noting that swiftness is a standard feature in the terminology of ancient thaumaturgical literature.

dispatch...Cremona...Vitellius killed: Tacitus' account differs from that of Suetonius and Josephus. The latter states that he accompanied Vespasian to Alexandria (*Vita* 415; *Ap.* 1.48), and that, once there, Vespasian heard of both the victory at Cremona and the death of Vitellius (*BJ* 4.656). Suetonius agrees. There was, however, an interval of some eight weeks between the two events. So Tacitus' version is obviously correct: Vespasian probably heard of Cremona in the middle of November before reaching Alexandria, whereas news of Vitellius' death (December 20) came later (*Hist.* 3.48: cf. 4.51). See Nicols, 1978: 84-5.

Cremona: After this, the second battle of Bedriacum (October 24/25), Antonius Primus' forces sacked Cremona.

forces routed...Vitellius killed: See *Hist.* 3.1-36 and Wellesley, 1975: 128-50 (Cremona); and *Hist.* 3.83-5 and Wellesley, 1975: 188-203 (Vitellius).

unexpected...emperor: That was indeed Nero's (correct) assessment. Hence he had entrusted Vespasian with the Judaean command and even given him *carte blanche* in the selection of his three legionary commanders (*Vesp.* 4), all this despite the fact that Titus' marriage to Marcia Furnilla (Barea Soranus' niece) and Vespasian's friendship with Thrasea Paetus (Hist. 4.7) – before the Pisonian conspiracy – were well known. Both relationships must have been severed precisely at the right time.

lacking in authority...acquired: Much the same point is made in *Hist.* 4.81.

Portents indicating support from the gods helped to supply the authority and prestige he lacked, for they enabled his agents to convince the credulous, ordinary soldiers that his success was in fact predetermined. Note how the various portents were deliberately designed to appeal to the prejudices, or beliefs, of each particular group of likely supporters, in Italy (*Vesp.* 5), in Greece (*Vesp.* 7) and in the East (5 and 7). Vespasian's wonder-working abilities have been discussed by a number of scholars – see the bibliography in Garzetti, 1974: 631-2 and in Benediktson, 1993: 325-7.

a certain man from the ordinary people: Tacitus' version begins with the same phrase (*Hist.* 4.81).

lost his sight...crippled leg: The same story appears in both Tacitus (*Hist.* 4.81) and Dio (66.8.2).

make the eyes better if he spat: For the use of saliva in such cases, see *NH* 28.7 and the gospel of *John* 9.6-7 and *Mark* 8.23.

touch it with his heel: The presumed magical power of Serapis' feet is indicated by the votive offerings to the god consisting of a marble foot together with part of the ankle as a base for the god's head; there are also gems and coins inscribed with Serapis-headed feet. So, for the Alexandrians, Vespasian was indeed Serapis and, on what seems to be a contemporary papyrus fragment, he was addressed as 'Serapis, Son of Ammon, Saviour and Benefactor' (*MW* 41; see *Vesp.* 19).

did not even dare: Tacitus (*Hist.* 4.81) discusses Vespasian's reluctance in more detail.

friends openly urging him: Yet another detail that appears in *Hist.* 4.81. Presumably, Tacitus and Suetonius used a common source.

Tegea in Arcadia: Tegea (in south east Arcadia) was one of the oldest towns in the Peloponnesus with an important cult centre of Athena Alea outside it. *OCD* 1478-9.

8 *[pages 16-17]*

returned to Rome: Josephus (*BJ* 7.39) has Titus celebrating Vespasian's birthday (Nov. 17) in Berytus and, soon after (*BJ* 7.63), receiving news of Vespasian's arrival in Italy. So it could be suggested that Vespasian, travelling via Asia Minor and Greece, probably reached Rome early in October 70.

celebrated a triumph: For the details, see *Titus* 6.

added eight consulships to...original: His first ('original') consulship was suffect, held with Claudius in 51; the other eight were ordinary. In 70 came his second, with Titus as colleague (both *in absentia*), the third in 71 with (the future emperor) Nerva and then six more (in 72, 74, 75, 76, 77 and 79), all with Titus. His continuous tenure of the office, though derided by Pliny (*Pan.* 58.4), was intended to supply the prestige the new emperor lacked (*Vesp.* 7).

censorship: Both Augustus and, more importantly, Claudius tried to revive this Republican magistracy. The latter had assumed it in 47 with A. Vitellius, performing a number of censorial functions. With this precedent, Vespasian and Titus assumed the ofice in April (presumably) 73, as was the practice in the Republic, and relinquished it in 74 (Censorinus, *De Die Natali* 18.14). However, the widely-accepted theory that they were designated to the censorship as early as 71 should be rejected (Buttrey, 1980: 15, 23). As far as Vespasian was concerned, there were sound reasons (not the least of them financial) for assuming the office. Apart from revising the membership of the Senate and the equestrian order (*Vesp*. 9), exercising a general supervision over the community's morals and conducting the census, the censors saw to the leasing of revenue-producing state property (e.g. mines) and to the letting out contracts for new buildings and for restoring those that were old or damaged (*Vesp*. 8 and 9). According to Dio, the emperors as censors could 'investigate our lives and morals as well as take the census, enrolling some in the equestrian and senatorial classes and erasing the names of others from these classes' (53.17.7).

licence and audacity: Suetonius could have added that more pressing reasons for army reform included the rebellion on the Rhine (*Hist*. 4 *passim*) and the surrender to (or collusion with) the Batavian Julius Civilis and the pro-Vitellian legions.

disgrace: The Vitellians' defeat at Cremona (Wellesley, 1975: 128-50).

provinces: His policy towards the provinces and the free states was, in the main, based on the need to increase taxation revenue and to reorganise and strengthen the eastern frontier: internal dissensions may have provided the official excuse for intervention – if one was felt necessary. See the changes in status noted below.

free states: These were communities which, by special agreement, had local autonomy and, sometimes, immunity from taxation.

certain kingdoms...turbulent manner: Commagene and Lesser Armenia, for example (see below), were not acting 'in a turbulent manner' – though that may well have been Vespasian's excuse to justify annexing them.

cashiered...troops of Vitellius: Suetonius' statement needs emendation. Three of the four Vitellian legions present at the second battle of Cremona (I Italica, XXI Rapax and XXII Primigenia) were not disbanded; the other (the V Alaudae) may have suffered that fate or else it was transferred to Moesia. Those disbanded (I Germanica, IV Macedonica, XVI Gallica and, probably, XV Primigenia) had only vexillations fighting for Vitellius at the second battle of Cremona, but the legions themselves were punished for either colluding with or surrendering to Civilis and were replaced by the II Adiutrix, IV Flavia Felix and XVI Flavia Firma. Another serious problem was the sixteen praetorian cohorts raised by Vitellius. Before Vespasian reached Rome, Mucianus had begun to reduce their number (*Hist*. 4.46).

indulgence: By the time of Claudius, it was customary for an incoming emperor to give his troops a special sum of money or donative (*donativum*) with the intention or hope of ensuring their support. The amounts paid by each ruler varied considerably: Augustus gave the praetorians 1,000 sestertii each (but in his will), Claudius and Nero made an annual grant of 15,000 per man, Galba refused to pay any and Mucianus offered them 100 sestertii each (Dio 65.22.2).

paid late...legitimate rewards: Those veterans granted honourable discharge (*Vesp.* 1) were entitled to certain 'bounties' – the soldiers of Caesar's tenth legion demanded 'discharge and bounties' (*Iul.* 70). The praetorians received 20,000 sestertii in Augustus' reign and the legionaries 12,000 (Dio 55.23.1). By 'late', Suetonius presumably means a payment by Vespasian to supplement the one hundred sestertii previously paid by Mucianus (Dio 65.22.2).

correcting discipline: Vespasian was a noted disciplinarian (*Hist.* 2.5).

prefecture: i.e. the command of an auxiliary cavalry squadron.

smell of garlic: Braithwaite's comment is worth citing: 'I suppose the point of Vespasian's remark was that he would rather have a boorish, manly *praefectus* than a cultured effeminate one (to smell of garlic being the mark of the yokel' (1927: 44).

marines: The marines at Ostia (25 km. from Rome at mouth of the Tiber) and Puteoli (12 km. west of Naples) belonged to the naval base of Misenum on the bay of Naples. The other major base was at Ravenna. A member of the latter fleet was issued with the first extant diploma of Vespasian's principate (dated 26 February 70: Roxan, 1996: 248-54).

pass on foot: Apparently, the marines were acting as couriers; the cohorts 'stationed at Ostia and Puteoli (by Claudius) to deal with fires' (*Claud.* 25.2) were probably also marines.

Achaea...Roman knight: It is incorrect to allocate the same date (1 Oct. 73/30 Sept. 74, according to Garzetti, 1974: 641) to all the changes – Achaea lost its liberty in 70; Commagene was annexed in 72 whilst the Cappadocia-Galatia complex was not created before 75 and Byzantium was still a free city in 77. In addition, Suetonius does not even mention the annexation of Emesa, Palmyra or of Lesser Armenia (in 71/2: Kokkinos, 1992: 312; Millar, 1993: 83-4), even though the latter entailed the removal of Aristobulus, Rome's consistent ally. On the other hand, his inclusion of Lycia has been challenged (see below) as has his exclusion of Cos (Magie, 1950: 1428-9). Some of the extensive changes were made early in the reign for reasons both financial (increasing sources of taxation) and strategic (strengthening the eastern frontier) – but the official excuse was the need to settle internal dissensions (see below). It was for the first of these reasons that the next five places lost their liberty, Achaea well before the others.

Achaea: Assigned to the Senate by Augustus (Dio 53.12.40), Achaea was made an imperial province by Tiberius (*Ann.* 1.76), was returned to the Senate by Claudius (*Claud.* 25.3) and granted its freedom by Nero (*Nero* 24.2). When Vespasian arrived in 70 (see above), he deprived it of its liberty (Philostratus, *V. Apoll.* 5.41) since 'the Hellenes had forgotten the meaning of freedom' (Pausanias 7.17.2), and it became a senatorial province once more, governed by a proconsul of praetorian rank.

Lycia: As the Lycians lost their liberty under Claudius (*Claud.* 25.3), it must have been restored at some point by Nero. Suetonius' testimony that Lycia had lost it again under Vespasian has been rejected by Eck (1982: 285-6), a view accepted (with hesitation) by Syme, 1995: 275) but rejected by Bosworth, 1976: 65. Vespasian's first governor of Lycia-Pamphylia may have been Hirrius Fronto Neratius Pansa (Strobel, 1985: 173-80).

Rhodes: Rhodes' freedom had been lost in 44 ('because the Rhodians... had impaled some Romans': Dio 60.24.4) and restored in 53 (*Claud.* 25.3). Presumably, Rhodes lost it again at the time of Vespasian's visit (see *BJ* 7.21) in 70 and was included in the province of Asia. See Magie, 1950: 1427-8 and Jones, 1971: 76-7.

Byzantium: Its freedom, like that of Rhodes, was frequently lost and restored. A free city in Cicero's time (*Prov. Cons.* 4.7), it was controlled by the Senate in 53 (*Ann.* 12.62-3). Since the Elder Pliny described it as a free city (*NH* 4.46), it presumably did not lose its freedom until quite late in Vespasian's reign and was incorporated into the senatorial province of Pontus-Bithynia (Pliny, *Ep.* 10.43.1).

Samos: Part of the province of Asia since 129 BC, Samos was granted its freedom by Augustus (Dio 54.9.7) and was described as a free city by the Elder Pliny (*NH* 5.135). Presumably, it was during the latter part of Vespasian's reign that it was, once again, incorporated into the province of Asia.

reduced to provincial status: This is technical language, implying the imposition of a governor.

Rough Cilicia: On his accession, Gaius had given Rough Cilicia to Antiochus IV (hence 'under royal jurisdiction') together with Commagene (Dio 59.8.2); previously, it had been ruled by Cleopatra (a gift from Antony) and then by Amyntas (King of Galatia). Vespasian now detached Plainland Cilicia from Syria and added it to Rough Cilicia to form the new province, probably in 72 (Gwatkin, 1930: 60). Its first governor seems to have been (P. Nonius) Asprenas Caesius Cassianus (Eck, 1982: 291-2). See Magie, 1950: 266-77: Jones, 1971: 191-214 and Mitford, 1980: 1230-61.

Commagene up to that time under royal jurisdiction: Situated to the south of Cappadocia, to the north of Syria, the east of Cilicia and the west of the Parthian empire, Commagene together with its capital Samosata was of considerable strategic significance. But Suetonius is wrong: it was Rough Cilicia and not Commagene that was 'up to that time under royal jurisdiction'. In 18, after the death of Antiochus III, it was governed by Q. Servaeus (*Ann.*

2.56); under Gaius, Commagene was restored to Antiochus IV and then taken back again (Dio 59.8.2). On his accession, Claudius returned it to Antiochus (Dio 60.8.1). In 72, however, Caesennius Paetus was authorised to invade the country (*BJ* 7.219-243), even though Antiochus had been consistently loyal to Rome (*Ann.* 13.7; *Hist.* 2.81, 5.1). The pretext was his alleged Parthian sympathies. Brief resistance was offered by his sons (Epiphanes and Callinicus) but they were obliged to flee to the Parthian king who surrended them to a Roman force led by Velius Rufus (see *MW* 372 and Jones/Milns, 1984: 101-5). However, the outcome was not unfavourable for Antiochus and his family – they all 'took up abode in Rome and were treated with honour' (*BJ* 7.243), and, in 109, Antiochus' grandson (son of Epiphanes and so suitably named C. Julius Antiochus Epiphanes Philopappus (Philopappus = 'lover of his grandfather') became consul (Birley, 1998: 62-4). It is, of course, just possible, that Antiochus and Vespasian had met three or four decades previously as members of Antonia's court (*Vesp.* 4), as Antiochus was there, serving as Gaius' 'tyrant-trainer' (Dio 59.24.1). Commagene now became part of Syria, its capital being renamed Flavia Samosata.

Cappadocia: With the death of Archelaus in 17, Cappadocia had become a procuratorial province (Dio 57.17.3-7) and remained so until Vespasian's reign. Until recently, scholars believed that, between 71 and 72, Cappadocia became the centre of the new (consular) Cappadocia-Galatia complex, with Trajan's father (*Vesp.* 4) as its first governor (Dabrowa, 1980: 382; Sherk, 1980: 996-7). Now, of its two legions, the first to move eastwards was the XII Fulminata, sent by Vespasian to Melitene (in Cappadocia) c. September 70 (*BJ* 7.18) and it was generally assumed that the second was the XVI Flavia Felix, raised 'by Vespasian in Syria' (Dio 55.24.2-3). However, it is now clear that as late as 75 the XVI Flavia was still in Syria (van Berchem, 1983: 186 and 1985: 85-7). So the new Cappadocia-Galatia complex was not a sudden Vespasianic creation.

legions: At the time of Vespasian's acclamation in July 69, no legions were stationed there (*Hist.* 2.81). Suetonius means that the new province was to have more than one legion and thus a governor of consular rank. For the first few years, presumably, the legate of the XII Fulminata at Melitene could act as governor. Consular status came after the incorporation of Lesser Armenia and the transfer of the XVI Flavia Firma from Antioch to Satala.

constant incursions of barbarians: Sherk (1980: 997) and others have assumed that Suetonius' 'barbarians' were the Alani, a theory rejected by Bosworth, 1976: 67. Suetonius was probably referring to the Heniochi, Colchians and other tribes of the Pontic coast who had posed problems previously. In the summer of 69, one group massacred a cohort stationed at Trapezus, forcing Vespasian to send several vexillations from Judaea to deal with the problem (*Hist.* 3.47-8); and the same Pontic coast 'barbarians' had already caused Caesennius Paetus concern (*Ann.* 15.9). What Vespasian needed before his series of annexations was a plausible excuse and the Pontic 'barbarians' provided it.

consular governor: On the possibility that the first governor was of praetorian rank (the legate of the XII Fulminata), see above. The earliest known consular governor of the enlarged province was Cn. Pompeius Collega (*PIR2* P 600), attested in 76 (*MW* 86).

Rome unsightly: In this section and the next, Suetonius provides examples from within Rome of Vespasian's attempts to restore the city (also *Epit. de Caes*. 9.8 and Dio 66.10.1a). Inscriptions attest to his restoration, at his own expense, of Rome's streets (*MW* 412) and aqueducts (*MW* 408 a). In discussing the implications of Vespasian's action in being the first to move the debris in the area of the old temple, both Casson (1978: 43-50) and Brunt (1980: 81-100) attempt to link the restoration of the Temple of Jupiter on the Capitol with the rebuilding of Rome. There is no support whatever for this in Suetonius (or, for that matter in Dio 66.10.2); these are completely separate activities that are being credited to Vespasian. See Wardle, 1996: 208 and Keaveney, 1987: 213-16.

earlier fires: The reference is to the fire of June 64 (*Nero* 38.1-3) and the burning of the Capitol in December 69 (*Vit*. 15.3).

restoration of the Capitol: Before Vespasian reached Rome, the Senate had voted (*Hist*. 4.4) for the restoration of the Capitoline temple that had been destroyed in December 69 (*Vit*. 15.3; Dio 65.17.3). Vespasian's role is described by Suetonius (here) and Dio (66.10.2), but their versions seem to be at variance with *Hist*. 4.53, where control of the rebuilding was assigned by the absent emperor to Julius Vestinus, with proceedings beginning on 21 June 70, well before Vespasian's return. However, two quite separate activities are being described – the moving of the cult-stone of the god Terminus whose presence guaranteed the permanence of Roman power (Tacitus) and the actual preparations for the rebuilding (Suetonius and Dio); see Townend, 1987: 243-8. Vespasian regarded the restoration of the Capitol and the worship of Jupiter as vital, not least in providing the new dynasty with some sort of legitimacy. Now whilst the temple of Jupiter on the Capitol was Rome's most significant religious building throughout the Republic, it lost status under the immediate successors of Augustus; it was Vespasian who employed every means of demonstrating his connection with Jupiter. The restored temple in particular was intended to show that he now had divine approval of all his actions: on this, see especially Wardle, 1996: 221-2. In 80, the temple was again destroyed (Dio 66.24.2), but almost immediately partly restored. On the temple itself, see Steinby, 1996: 144-53.

clearing away the rubble: These preliminaries to the rebuilding were undertaken soon after Vespasian reached Rome in October 70.

restoration of 3,000 bronze tablets: All official arrangements between Rome and foreigners were engraved on bronze tablets and attached to the walls of public buildings and temples. Recorded also were the original notifications of the awards of citizenship made to former soldiers in the form of the so-called military diplomas. Tacitus also refers to the renewal of the tablets. According to him, however, before Vespasian reached Rome in 70, the Senate had appointed a commission 'to determine and replace the bronze tablets of the laws that had fallen down from age' (*Hist.* 4.40). This could perhaps be another version of what Suetonius says but 'bronze tablets of the laws' is more general than the items listed by Suetonius; 'fallen down from age' is vastly different from 'destroyed by fire' and Suetonius has no reference to a commission (see Bauman, 1982: 116).

tracked down copies: Domitian acted in similar fashion when restoring the libraries destroyed by fire (*Dom.* 20).

decrees of the Senate: During the Republic, they represented the advice or recommendation of the Senate to the magistrates. In the Empire, they were implemented by a clause in the praetor's edict and, after Hadrian, they usually had the force of law. A most interesting example is the recently-discovered decree (Eck, 1996) concerning Gnaeus Calpurnius Piso, prosecuted in the Senate following the death of Germanicus in 19; he had committed suicide before the trial ended. See also the decrees in *Vesp.* 11.

resolutions of the plebs: These were resolutions of the plebeian tribal assembly that, by the Hortensian Law of 287 BC, gained the force of law. *OCD* 1389.

9 *[page 17]*

new works: Apart from the new works he mentions in this section, Suetonius elsewhere notes Vespasian's restoration of the temple of Jupiter (*Vesp.* 8) and of the stage-buildings of Marcellus' theatre (*Vesp.* 19). There was also his extension of the city boundary (*PA* 395), his restoration of the temple of Honour and Virtue (*NH* 35.120), the erection of the Vespasianic Granaries (Jones, 1992: 85) and of the shrine to Jupiter the Preserver. For the triumphal arches assigned to his reign (Dio 65.7.2), see Kleiner, 1989: 85-91 and 1990: 127-36. In addition, there is considerable epigraphic evidence of his building activity in Rome, Italy and the provinces (*MW* 79, 86, 151, 317, 339, 413-6, 418-19, 421, 424-6, 433-5, 443-4, 448-9 and 468; Castagnoli, 1981: 261-74.

temple of Peace: It also appears in Aurelius Victor's list (9.7). Work on it started soon after the triumph of 71 (*BJ* 7.158) to celebrate the return of peace and the closing of the gates of the temple of Janus (Orosius 7.9.9); it was quickly completed, with the dedication taking place in 75 (Dio 66.15.1). Some fifteen to twenty years later, however, it seems that Domitian altered it radically (Anderson, 1983: 110). Josephus provides more details of Vespasian's work:

> (The temple) was very speedily completed and in a style surpassing all human conception. For, besides having prodigious resources of wealth on which to draw, Vespasian also embellished it with ancient masterpieces of painting and sculpture; indeed, into that shrine were accumulated and stored all objects for the sight of which men had once wandered over the whole world, eager to see them severally while they lay in various countries. Here, too, he laid up the vessels of gold from the temple of the Jews.
> (*BJ* 7.158-61)

In general, see *PA* 386-8 and Blake, 1959: 89-90.

Forum: i.e. the *Forum Romanum*, to the south of the temple.

temple of the Deified Claudius: The temple had been almost destroyed by Nero to enable him to erect a huge nymphaeum as part of the Golden House. Vespasian's action in rebuilding it was consistent with his efforts to distance the new dynasty from Nero's policies, and probably coincided with the dedication of the temple of the Deified Claudius in Britain (Fishwick, 1987: 297). See Steinby, 1993: 277-8 and the illustrations in Barrett, 1996: 148-51.

Caelian Hill: Situated south of the Esquiline, it was the most south-easterly of the seven hills of Rome. Its chief buildings included Claudius' temple and the barracks for various military units. See Steinby, 1993: 208-11.

Agrippina: Claudius' wife (*Vesp.* 2).

almost totally destroyed by Nero: Nero needed to make room for his Golden House and for work on the Claudian Aqueduct (Frontinus, *Aq.*1.20, 2.76). See *PA* 120.

amphitheatre: Built on the site previously occupied by the lake of Nero's Golden House, the monumental Flavian Amphitheatre (not known as the Colosseum until the middle ages) was begun by Vespasian, enlarged and dedicated by Titus in 80, with games lasting 100 days (*Titus* 7; Dio 66.25.1-5 and *BMC* 2: 190-1, 270) and completed by Domitian who added the fourth level and was probably responsible for the amphitheatre's subterranean rooms and equipment (Anderson, 1983: 95). The building held some 45,000 spectators, with standing-room for another 5,000. See Steinby, 1993: 30-5 and Auguet, 1994: 34-42.

Augustus had intended: This is the only reference to Augustus' intention to build an amphitheatre in the centre of Rome; but both Suetonius (*Aug.* 29.5) and Dio (51.23.1) do mention a stone amphitheatre built 'in the Campus Martius' by Statilius Taurus in 29 BC. See Steinby, 1993: 36-7.

most distinguished: The senatorial and equestrian orders.

cleansed: Senators could be expelled from the Senate either by the emperor (acting as censor) or by a vote of the Senate itself; for examples, see *Dom.* 8.

filled them up: According to Aurelius Victor (9.9) and his epitomator (9.11), Vespasian increased the Senate's numbers from 200 to 1,000. For an analysis of the composition of Vespasian's Senate, see Devreker, 1980a: 257-68.

revision of the Senate and...equestrians: The precedent was established by Augustus (Dio 55.31.2) and followed by Gaius and Claudius (*Calig.* 16.2; *Claud.* 16.1).

most unworthy removed: One of these was M. Palfurius Sura (*PIR*2 P 63). See *Dom.* 13. According to the Scholiast on Juvenal (4.53):

> He was expelled from the Senate by Vespasian and became a Stoic. After Domitian was killed, he was accused and condemned by the Senate as being one of Domitian's powerful informers.

He may be 'Seras', a Domitianic informer executed by Nerva (Dio 68.1.2).

most honourable...enrolled: Tacitus also refers to the adlections of this period (*Hist* 2.82). Most occurred during the censorship of 73/4 but a number of Vespasian's supporters were so honoured during the civil war as a reward for the stance adopted at that time. There were also two types of adlection, one enabling a member of the equestrian order to enter the Senate and the other promoting senators to a higher senatorial rank. We know of twenty-eight in the first category (seven promoted before 73) and six in the second (Devreker, 1980: 70-87). Of the twenty-eight, three were of unknown origin, six were Italians, nineteen provincials (and thirteen of these came from the western provinces) whereas the Senate as a whole was 63.2% Italian against 33.6% provincial (Devreker, 1980: 86). Finally, it is worth noting that adlection to the Senate in 73/74 or in the preceding years did not automatically mean that subsequent favours could be expected, as the belated consulships of C. Antius A. Julius Quadratus (in 94), Ti. Julius Celsus Polemaeanus (92) and C. Caristanius Fronto (90) indicate. A number of senators were also adlected into the patriciate including Agricola, Trajan's father and both the father and grandfather of Antoninus Pius (for a list, see Eck, 1970: 108-9). See further Eck, 1970: 103-5; Millar, 1977: 293-6 and Devreker, 1980: 70-87.

Italians and provincials: We have a fair amount of information about Vespasian's senatorial appointments, two of the more interesting being M. Cornelius Nigrinus (from Spain: he governed Moesia, Lower Moesia and Syria in the eighties and nineties) and C. Antius A. Julius Quadratus (from Ephesus: under Trajan, he governed Syria and was proconsul of Asia). Of the Italians, the best known is the conqueror of Masada, L. Flavius Silva Nonius Bassus (from Urbisaglia in Picenum), who was one of the very few non-Flavians to receive an ordinary consulship in the period 70-81. See also Devreker, 1980a: 257-68 and 1982: 492-516.

differed...social standing: This was the theoretical distinction between the orders, i.e. one of rank rather than privilege. The (equestrian) Suetonius observes the distinction – Vespasian's father married into 'an honourable family', i.e. *honestum genus* (*Vesp.* 1: equestrian), whereas Titus' second wife was 'of a very distinguished family', i.e. *splendidum genus* (*Titus* 4: senatorial).

10 *[pages 17-18]*

The number...of the time: The theme of repairing the losses caused by the civil war is continued. The interruption of jurisdiction in 68/69 had resulted in a vast build-up of cases, and the violation of property rights at that time had exacerbated the situation.

He chose by lot...could be restored: Suetonius states that special commissioners were chosen by lot to restore property seized illegally. Tacitus' version is different; according to him, this took place under the aegis of the Senate and before Vespasian returned to Rome (*Hist.* 4.40).

men...who could give extraordinary judgements: The commissioners were empowered to give preference to the most urgent cases and may even have been authorised to sit on special occasions, such as days exempt from legal business.

court of the Hundred: It dealt with civil cases, problems of status (*Dom.* 8), inheritance, right of way etc. The panel, originally of 100 members was increased to 180 (four courts of forty-five members each) during the Empire. Action was necessary as, even in normal circumstances, the procedure tended to be somewhat slow.

lifetime...would hardly suffice: This was not the only time that the legal system had to deal with a back-log of cases. Previous emperors had had the same problem (*Aug.* 32.2; *Claud.* 23.1 and *Galba* 14.3), as, much later, did Justinian (*cod. Iust.* 3.1.13). Martial (7.65) refers to a trial that lasted for twenty years.

11 *[page 18]*

responsible for the Senate's resolving: Dio asserts that Vespasian 'regularly attended meetings of the Senate, whose members he consulted on all matters' (66.10.5).

that if a woman...regarded as a slave: i.e 'a free woman cohabiting with another's slave would be deemed to be a slave' (Bauman, 1982: 114). Vespasian was, in effect, re-enacting the *Senatus Consultum Claudianum* ('Claudian Decree of the Senate') that had been carried by the Senate in 52 on the proposal of Claudius (*Ann.* 12.53).

people who lent...death of the father: i.e. loans made to minors would not be repayable even on the father's death. Suetonius' summary resembles closely the wording of the *SC Macedonianum* (*Digest* 14.6) named after Macedo, the usurer involved. Tacitus also refers to a similar Claudian law (*Ann.* 11.13). Some believe that the two senatorial decrees mentioned here were really the work of Claudius wrongly attributed to Vespasian; but it is hard to accept that Suetonius could have confused the authors of two such different decrees and then list them as Vespasian's achievements when other material was available. Bauman (1982: 114-15) argues convincingly that they were restated by Vespasian at the same time as he revived Claudius' deification after its cancellation by Nero.

12 *[page 18]*

behaved like a citizen: Citizens should treat each other with respect, insult no one and accept insults from no one. Suetonius used this quality, or the lack of it, in his assessment of most emperors. According to Dio, Vespasian behaved:

> not as an emperor, but as a private citizen... He was looked upon as emperor only by reason of his oversight of public business, whereas in all other respects he was democratic and lived on a footing of equality with his subjects. (66.10.1-11.1)

The Elder Pliny said that 'he was equally accessible to all' (*NH* 33.41). On this quality (called *civilitas* by the Romans), see further Wallace-Hadrill, 1995: 32-48.

mercy: But see *Vesp.* 15 for the fate of Julius Sabinus and his family. That Vespasian was highly regarded by Suetonius is very evident and especially so from the fact that only Julius Caesar, Augustus and Vespasian are assigned this quality (*Iul.* 75.1, *Aug.* 51.1) and others are criticised for their lack of it (*Tib.* 53.2, *Nero* 10.1, *Vit.* 14.2 and *Dom.* 10, 11).

former modest background: For most of the Julio-Claudian period, the Flavians were wealthy and well-connected, so the term 'modest' could be applied to them only in comparison with the wealth and status of certain senatorial families.

trace back the origin: This sort of flattery was not without parallels – the Julians claimed descent from Venus (*Iul.* 6.1) and Galba from Jupiter and Pasiphae, wife of Minos (*Galb.* 2). There is a difference, however: they claimed it themselves whereas Vespasian had it claimed for him.

companion of Hercules: Hercules passed through Italy on his way back from Spain with the oxen of Geryon, but there is no reference anywhere to a companion or to any monument on the Salarian Way.

Salarian Way: The 'salt road' ran northeast from the Colline Gate (formerly called the 'Salt Gate – *Porta Salaria*) to Reate and, later, as far as the Adriatic.

day of his triumph: The joint triumph with Titus in June 71 for the victory over the Jews (*Titus* 6).

in his old age: He was over 60 (born 9).

did not even accept the tribunician power...until late: Some (e.g. Buttrey, 1980: 13) have criticised Suetonius' statement as 'mysterious', others (e.g. Hammond, 1959: 72) imply that he is referring to an unusually lengthy interval between the Senate's decree of 22 December 69 that assigned 'all the customary powers to Vespasian' (*Hist.* 4.3) and the assembly which passed the law. But such an explanation is unsatisfactory; for instance, an interval of fifty-three days is attested for Nero and one of forty-five for Otho (Bradley, 1978a: 65). To complicate matters further, many coins and inscriptions date his tribunician power from 1 July 69. Now the confusion is only apparent. Inscriptions that can definitely be assigned to 69 never list the so-called 'Republican' titles ('tribunician power, consul, chief priest, father of his country') but refer to Vespasian simply as 'Emperor Caesar Vespasian Augustus'. However, 'tribunician power' does appear on the earliest Vespasianic military diploma (26 Feb. 70: Roxan, 1996: 248-56). So Suetonius' point is that Vespasian did not immediately lay claim to the 'Republican' titles at a time when he was formally an usurper (Isaac, 1984: 144) and it was only later (but before 26 Feb. 70) that he 'back-dated' (Brunt, 1977: 107) it to 1 July 69. It could also be argued that Suetonius is being a little disingenuous as Vespasian could not receive tribunician power until the Senate and People conferred them and they could not do this whilst Vitellius was in power.

Father of his Country until late: The purpose of this (Republican) title (*pater patriae*) is stated by Dio:

> The term 'father' perhaps gives them a certain authority over us all, the authority which fathers once had over their children; yet it did not signify this at first, but betokened honour, and served as an admonition both to them that they should love their subjects as they would their children, and to their subjects, that they should revere them as they would their fathers. (53.18.3)

Cicero was so named by Catulus for 'saving the state' (63 BC) as was Augustus in 2 BC on his sixtieth birthday. Apart from Tiberius who refused to accept the title, most emperors accepted it some time after their accession – if they lived long enough (so not Galba, Otho or Vitellius). Vespasian did not assume the title of *PP* until after his return to Rome late in 70: it does not appear in the new diploma, Vespasian's earliest, of 26 Feb. 70 (see above).

For he had dropped the practice of searching...civil war still going on: All callers were searched during the reigns of Gaius (Dio 60.3.3) and Claudius (*Claud.* 35.1). Vespasian's practice (mentioned by Dio 60.3.3 and by Pliny, *NH* 33.41) is consistent with his reputation for 'behaving like a citizen'. Domitian, however, had the last word: see *Dom.* 21. Suetonius assigns this last item to the period of the civil war and introduces it with the word 'for' (*nam*), thereby linking it to Vespasian's 'late' assumption of two official titles. Once again, the reader is reminded of the emperor's *civilitas.*

13 *[page 18]*

lenient manner...free speech of his friends: Tacitus, *Dial.* 8.3; *Epit. de Caes.* 9.3 and Eutropius 7.20 agree. Dio states that he even 'enjoyed jokes at his own expense' (66.11.1). Suetonius now proceeds to give an example from each of his three categories – friends (Mucianus), barristers (Liberalis) and philosophers (Demetrius).

innuendos: See the discussion in *Dom.* 10.

obstinacy of the philosophers: Vespasian was ultimately forced to exile a number of them.

Licinius Mucianus: On his early career and his role in the events of 69, see *Vesp.* 6 and 7. Until Vespasian reached Rome, he was in control, and not the least of his services to the new emperor was his elimination of various opponents (*Hist.* 4.11; 48-50), including Vitellius' brother and son (Dio 65.22.1). In essence, Mucianus was an efficient organiser who silenced the ambitious Antonius Primus and began to reduce the excessively large praetorian guard, who dealt with the confusion prevalent in the senate (including moves against alleged Neronian informers) and with the behaviour of Domitian. Mucianus' reward was a suffect consulship in 70 and another in 72 – but nothing more. That was not what he had expected. In the seventies, he was pushed aside and seems to have devoted himself to writing, no doubt out of bitterness and frustration. His literary output was considerable – the Elder Pliny cited him by name on thirty-two occasions. As for the alleged rivalry between him and Titus (Crook, 1951: 162-75), there is little (if any) ancient evidence (Jones, 1984: 87-100). He may well have become resentful, yet would not have been so foolish as to intrigue against Titus. Had he done so, he would not have been the butt of one of Vespasian's jokes – he would have shared the fate of Helvidius Priscus.

notorious lewdness: Hinted at by Tacitus (*Hist.* 1.10). The accusation is that he was a passive homosexual. No doubt this is what Vespasian meant by the comment that follows.

'I, however, am a man': So, too, *Epit. de Caes.* 9.3.

Salvius Liberalis: An equestrian from Urbisaglia in Picenum, Salvius Liberalis Nonius Bassus (A.R. Birley, 1981: 211-2, 404-7) was adlected to the Senate at tribunician rank by Vespasian and Titus in 73/4 and immediately promoted (*Vesp.* 9); appointed legate of the V Macedonica in Moesia, he then became a judicial officer in Britain. On Domitian's accession, he was in Rome, serving as an Arval Brother, was subsequently appointed to the proconsulship of Macedonia and, c. 84, to a suffect consulship. Banished c. 87 (so it seems), he returned on Domitian's death, was appointed proconsul of Asia, but 'excused himself (from the post)' (*MW* 311). He was known for his outspokenness and as a powerful (*Ep.* 3.9.36) advocate for senators accused of extortion.

'What does it matter...sestertii?': Liberalis was implying that Vespasian, noted for his greed, might have had Hipparchus condemned so that his 100 million sestertii would revert to the emperor.

Hipparchus: He was presumably the Ti. Claudius Hipparchus whose property was confiscated after he had been condemned for treason (Philostratus, *V. Soph.* 2.1.2).

Demetrius the Cynic: This famous Cynic managed to earn Seneca's praise (*Ben.* 7.8.2-3), to attack Nero (Epictetus, *Dissert.* 1.25, 22), to discuss the nature of the soul with Thrasea Paetus during his last hours (*Ann.* 16.34) and, in 70, to defend the informer Egnatius Celer when attacked by Musonius Rufus (*Hist.* 4.40). According to Dio, it was Mucianus who had him and other philosophers expelled from Rome 'for teaching publicly many doctrines inappropriate to the times' (66.13.1). Philostratus also mentions Demetrius, claiming that he was exiled by Tigellinus, taught Titus (at Antioch) how to rule and lived at Puteoli during Domitian's reign (VA 4.42, 6.31 and 7.10).

barked out: In Dio's version, Vespasian said 'You are doing everything to force me to kill you, but I do not slay a barking dog' (66.13.2-3).

sufficient...as 'Dog': Martial 4.53.7-8 (and many others) used 'dog' (*canis*) in referring to Cynic philosophers. As ever, Vespasian's retort was very apt. In Greek, the word *kuon* means 'dog' and then it came to be used regularly of a Cynic philosopher.

14 *[page 18]*

little inclined to remember...insults: So, too, Eutropius 7.20 and the *Epit. de Caes.* 9.2. Presumably, Suetonius prefers to omit the fact that Vespasian authorised the execution of Julius Sabinus and his family for actions some nine years previously (see *Vesp.* 15).

daughter of his foe Vitellius...in marriage with great magnificence: The only daughter of Vitellius mentioned in our sources is that by his second wife Galeria Fundana (*Vitell.* 6). She had been betrothed to Valerius Asiaticus, governor of Gallia Belgica in 69 and partisan of Vitellius (*Hist.* 1.59); having made peace with the new régime, he was designated consul for 70 but died before taking up office. Vespasian then arranged for her to marry another senator. Although Mucianus executed Vitellius' young son (Dio 65.22.1), Vespasian treated other Vitellian relatives very generously, perhaps in view of that family's assistance some decades previously (*Vesp.* 4); so relatives such as Tampius Flavianus (*Hist.* 3.4) and Valerius Festus (*Hist.* 4.49) were awarded consulships and Silius Italicus' 'friendship with Vitellius' (Pliny, *Ep.* 3.7.3) did not prevent him from holding the proconsulship of Asia in 77/78 (Eck, 1982: 299).

banishment from court: For Vespasian's lapse, see *Vesp.* 4; Gascou, 1984: 323-6 and Wallace-Hadrill, 1996: 283-4.

someone: Dio's account is similar and he gives the official's name as Phoebus (66.11.2); but he assigns the anecdote to Nero's tour of Greece, whereas, in Suetonius' account of Vespasian's lapse during that tour (*Vesp.* 4), there is not a hint of Phoebus' role.

chamberlain: Entry to an audience with the emperor was controlled by an imperial freedman who admitted callers according to their rank (Seneca, *Ben.* 6.33.4). In the *HA*, Severus Alexander is said to have been gracious to visitors of first and second rank and even to those below them (*Alex. Sev.* 20.1) despite the fact that Trajan is supposed to have abolished such divisions (*Pan.* 47.5).

so far...driven to destroy anybody: Suetonius has (again) conveniently not cited the execution of Julius Sabinus and his family (*Vesp.* 15).

Mettius Pompusianus: Apart from a consulship during the seventies, little is known of Mettius' career (*PIR*2 M 570); but, despite Mooney (1930: 435) and Braithwaite (1927: 57), he is not to be identified with L. Pompusius Mettius (*PIR*2 P 783). Dio notes that 'Domitian first exiled him to Corsica and then put him to death' (67.12.2-4). Suetonius provides further details (*Dom.* 10). It would seem that he was one of the Mettii from Arles who fell out of favour during the nineties: Mettius Modestus (suffect consul in 82) was exiled (*Ep.* 1.5.5) and, in a number of papyri, the name of prefect of Egypt (in 91/92), M. Mettius Rufus, was erased. Perhaps they had come to grief through involvement in the fall of Mettius Pompusianus.

horoscope of the emperor: At this time, astrological predictions were often accepted as scientific (*Dom.* 10) and so eminent senators consulting an astrologer for an emperor's horoscope could be accused of planning to murder him – conspirators would always wish to know precisely when their would-be victim was destined to die. By Ulpian's time, consulting an astrologer even about an emperor's health was punishable by death.

guaranteeing: So, too, in the *Epit. de Caes.* 9.14 where the irony of Vespasian's reply (for he 'knew' that Mettius' horoscope had not been cast correctly [*Vesp.* 25]) is stressed. Dio also reports Vespasian's reply: 'He will surely remember me and will surely honour me in return' (67.12.3).

15 *[page 19]*

innocent person...punished: Vespasian's leniency is also mentioned by Aurelius Victor 9.2 and Eutropius 7.19.2.

not present: For the executions carried out by Mucianus before Vespasian's arrival in 70, see *Vesp.* 13.

misled: The reference may well be to Titus' activities as praetorian prefect (*Titus* 6) that earned him the reputation of being another Nero (*Titus* 6 and 7), whilst Vespasian was portrayed as publicly weeping even over those who were not 'innocent' (see below).

Helvidius Priscus: This son of a senior centurion had gained senatorial rank, married Thrasea Paetus' daughter but was banished (*Ann.* 16.33) after Thrasea's suicide. Recalled by Galba (*Hist.* 4.6), he became praetor in 70. In his assessment of Helvidius (*Hist.* 4.5-6), Tacitus sees him as inflexible and persistent in the pursuit of what he saw to be 'right'. He sorely tried Vespasian's patience (Epictetus, *Dissert.* 1.19-21, cited below), treating him with disdain, addressing him as 'Vespasian' and even reducing him to tears (Dio 66.12.1). What brought about his downfall was, in all probability, his persistence in asserting the Senate's traditional rights (but see *Vesp.* 25). He was again exiled and subsequently executed. His career is discussed by *RP* 7.574-7; Pigon, 1992: 235-4 and Levick, 1999: 87-9.

private name: i.e. as 'Vespasian', not as 'Caesar'. Pigon argues that the picture of Helvidius presented by Suetonius is impaired by his 'highly favourable' attitude towards Vespasian (1992: 243).

as praetor: As praetor in 70, Helvidius had officiated at the ceremony held at the Capitoline temple on 21 June 70 (*Vesp.* 8). During his praetorship, Helvidius opposed all measures that in any way involved the emperor (*Hist.* 4.6-9).

edicts: The emperor's name and titles would appear in the edict's preamble.

almost brought down...level of an ordinary citizen: This official expression was applied widely, e.g. to a magistrate who had been treated as though he were a private citizen (Livy 3.35.6, Pliny, *Ep* 1.23.1) and to Claudius (*Claud.* 38.1: by himself, complaining that the people of Ostia had treated him with insufficient respect).

extremely insolent: Epictetus provides an example:

> When Vespasian sent a message to him (Helvidius) not to come into the Senate, he replied, 'It is in your power not to let me be a senator, but, as long as I am one, I must come to the meetings'. 'All right' replied Vespasian, 'but when you come, keep quiet'. 'Don't ask me my opinion and I'll keep quiet.' 'But I must ask your opinion.' 'And I must say what appears just.' 'But, if you speak, I'll put you to death.' 'Did I ever say to you that I was immortal? You do yours, I'll do mine. It's yours to kill, mine to die without trembling. It's yours to send into exile, mine to leave without grieving.' (*Dissert.* 1.19-21)

banished: This was his second banishment, described by Suetonius as *relegatio*. There were different grades of exile (*Digest* 48.19.28) from deportation to an island (*deportatio*) to temporary relegation (*relegatio*). Relegation was a far milder penalty, involving (according to *Digest* 48.19.4) residence for a specified time (or indefinitely) outside (or within) a specified place or region, but did not include the loss of all civil and personal rights.

wept and groaned: A public display of emotion, never convincing, seems to have been a family trait (*Titus* 9 and 10). Suetonius' readiness to present the 'lenient' Vespasian in the best posible light has led him to avoid reference to any damaging evidence such as the fate of Julius Sabinus who:

> had once styled himself Caesar.... With him perished also his wife Peponila.... She threw her children at Vespasian's feet and delivered a most pitiful plea in their behalf. Yet, though she caused both him and the rest to weep, no mercy was shown to the family. (Dio 66.16.1)

See also *Vesp.* 25.

16 *[page 19-20]*

only thing...reproved...greed for money: Tacitus agrees (*Hist.* 2.5) but later sources are less disapproving: Dio reports that he refused to confiscate his opponents' property (66.10.2a) and Aurelius Victor assesses him as wise rather than greedy (9.9); similarly, Eutropius 7.19.2 and Ausonius, *De XII Caes.* 41-2.

reimposing taxes...dropped under Galba: Referring to Alexandria, Dio claims that 'Vespasian renewed many taxes that had fallen into disuse, increased many that were customary and introduced still other new ones' and adds that he also 'adopted this same course later in the rest of the subject territory, in Italy, and in Rome itself' (66.8.3-4). As for Galba's generosity, we have two statements by Tacitus to the effect that he granted some reduction in tribute to Spain and Gaul, provinces that had supported his bid for the throne (*Hist.* 1.8 and 1.51). Numismatic evidence in the form of an As of 68-9 from Spain (*MW* 29) advertises the 'removal of the two and a half per cent' customs duty levied on the frontier between Gaul and Spain.

adding new and burdensome ones: Thus the Alexandrians called him 'Herring-Stuffer': see *Vesp.* 19. Dio adds that the Alexandrians soon came to detest Vespasian:

> He collected large sums from them in various ways, overlooking no source, however trivial or however reprehensible it might be, but drawing upon every source, sacred and profane alike, from which money could be secured. (66.8.3)

Only Aurelius Victor reports that these new taxes 'were not imposed for very long' (9.6). Little detail about them survives. Apart from the tax on urine (*Vesp.* 23), the 'Jewish tax' was an annual tax (two denarii) imposed on all Jews from the age of three (*CPJ* 2.421). Other 'new taxes' possibly include the Alexandrian tax and the Asian tax, imposed on former crown properties in Egypt and Asia. In more general terms, the careful census of the early seventies must have resulted in a more thorough exaction of tribute – the epigraphic evidence (Dilke, 1971: 40-1 and Le Glay, 1981: 175-84) indicates how he attempted to define and widen the taxation base in Orange, Thrace, Cyrenaica and elsewhere.

increased the tribute for the provinces...doubling it: Tribute could be paid as a tithe remitted in kind, as a fixed amount (land tax, poll tax) or as a combination of both. Whilst we have no data on which provinces were required to pay twice as much in tribute, it is clear that massive changes came without delay following the appointment of a proconsul to Achaea and Vespasian's reorganisation in the east (*Vesp.* 8).

shameful: According to the Claudian Law (*Lex Claudia*), a senator could not engage in trade. Moreover, Roman aristocrats in general regarded such activity with contempt.

sell public offices: Caenis (*Vesp.* 3) acted as intermediary (Dio 66.14.3).

it is also believed: An unpromising prelude to a story of doubtful veracity. Compare, in *Vesp.* 1, 'despite my careful investigation...'.

procurators: The term was applied to a variety of imperial agents, but particularly to financial officers in imperial provinces and those in charge of various taxes. The more senior were members of the equestrian order. *OCD* 1251-2.

squeeze...wet: See *Vesp.* 4.

naturally very greedy: An assessment rejected by Aurelius Victor 9.6 – 'some wrongly believe that he had a weakness for money'.

fox...not its ways: According to rumour, he had long ago been found guilty of obtaining preferment for a young man and demanding payment for his services (*Vesp.* 4).

refused...for nothing: A slave could purchase his freedom from the money he had saved or the assets he has acquired; see further *OCD* 1130.

Treasury and the Privy Purse: In theory, the Privy Purse (*fiscus*) referred to the emperor's personal funds as opposed to the Treasury (*aerarium*). The precise nature of the *fiscus* has inspired extensive scholarly debate (*OCD* 598-9), a difficulty that (according to Dio) did not worry Augustus: 'In reality, Caesar...was master of the funds – nominally, to be sure, he had separated the public funds from his own, but he always spent the former as he saw fit' (53.16.1).

forty billion sestertii: Watkins (1988/89: 119) has questioned the figure, the largest sum of money mentioned in antiquity; four billion is a more likely figure. The causes of the deficit were clear enough – the economic disaster of Nero's reign, the widespread destruction caused by the civil war together with the need to pension off unsatisfactory and surplus soldiers from the Praetorian guard and the legions.

17 *[page 20]*

generous: So, too, Eutropius 7.19.2.

topped up: According to Dio, Augustus 'permitted all to stand for office who possessed property worth...1,000,000 sestertii' (54.17.3), supported by *Ann.* 1.75, 2.37. Less likely (Talbert, 1984: 10-11, 52-3) is Suetonius' 1,200,000 (*Aug.* 41.1). For an example of Vespasian's giving the census to a young man, see Frontinus, *Strat.* 4.6.4.

needy men...500,000 sestertii: According to Suetonius (*Nero* 10.1) and Tacitus (*Ann.* 13.34), Nero made the same annual grants.

restored to a better condition: So, too, Aurelius Victor who adds a detail not recorded elsewhere: 'Vespasian levelled hills on the Flaminian way to provide passage by a gentle gradient' (9.8). For examples of his work in restoring bridges and buildings, see *Vesp.* 9.

earthquake or fire: At Herculaneum in 76, he restored the temple of Rhea, Mother of the Gods (*MW* 433) that had been destroyed by an earthquake (*Ann.* 15.22). Natural disasters, including fires, were not infrequent during the first century AD (e.g. *RG* 6.4, *Ann.* 2.47 and *Tib.* 48.2) nor were imperial grants to the devastated areas (*Ann.* 12.58, 16.13).

supported...men of talent and the arts: Once again, Vespasian was following Augustus' example (Aug. 89.3). On the basis of the evidence provided by Suetonius, especially the grant to professors of rhetoric (*Vesp.* 18), Vespasian's patronage of the arts seems to have been genuine. There are other indications. In the seventies, the two leading orators of the day, Vibius Crispus and Eprius Marcellus, were amongst his most powerful friends (*Dial.* 8.3), as were the Elder Pliny (*Ep.* 3.5.9) and, before 69, the philosophers Barea Soranus and Thrasea Paetus (*Hist.* 4.7). He also seems to have been determined that his sons' education should not be neglected (*Titus* 3; *Dom.* 20 and Coleman, 1986: 3088-111). It is less clear, though, whether he had any genuine interest in the arts.

18 *[page 20]*

first to establish an annual salary...rhetoric: This grant (also noted by Dio 66.12.1a and Philostratus, *VS* 2.8.580, 10.589, 33.627) represents an important milestone in the history of Roman education. One hundred and fifty years previously, teachers of Latin rhetoric were expelled from Rome but, by the time of Augustus, it was possible for such teachers to gain great wealth and status (according to Suetonius, *Rhet.* 1.1). Quintilian was Vespasian's first appointee. The education of Domitian's heirs, the sons of Flavius Clemens (*Dom.* 15), had been entrusted to him, for which he received the rare award of consular decorations (Ausonius, *Grat. Act.* 10.7). From an edict found at Pergamum (*MW* 458), it appears that Vespasian also granted to teachers and doctors exemption from the payment of taxes and also from the obligation of providing lodgings for officials or troops; but this may not have been an innovation (Marrou, 1956: 301).

100,000 sestertii: That salary (equivalent to the second rank of equestrian procurators) remained unchanged at least until the beginning of the third century (*ILS* 9020).

outstanding poets: Saleius Bassus was one (*Dial.* 9.5; *Inst. Or.* 10.90).

Coan Venus: The Elder Pliny mentions a statue of Venus that Vespasian set up in his Temple of Peace (*NH* 36.27) and Suetonius may be referring to it (if, indeed, it came from Cos) – or perhaps he means a picture. If so, the likeliest candidate is the famous 'Aphrodite Anadyomene' of Apelles that was originally in the temple of Aesculapius at Cos (*NH* 35.91). Pliny also mentions another, even better, Aphrodite that Apelles started at Cos but which remained unfinished when he died (*NH* 35.92). Of the three possibilities, perhaps preference should be given to the statue rather than to one of the pictures: at least it would be consonant with the next item.

Colossus: The colossal bronze statue of Nero by Zenodorus was changed by Vespasian into a statue of the Sun (*NH* 34.45) with the addition of a radiate crown (Richardson, 1992: 92-3). It had first been set up in the entrance court of the Golden House (Martial, *Spect.* 1.2.1-3; denied by Howell, 1968: 292-9) and was moved by Vespasian to the Sacred Way (Dio 66.15.1). Later, Hadrian set it up in the Flavian Amphitheatre (*HA*, *Hadrian* 19.12-13) and Commodus, it seems, 'cut off (its) head and substituted for it a likeness of his own' (Dio 72.22.3; similarly *HA*, *Comm.* 17.9 and Herodian 1.15.9). On the Colossus, see Steinby, 1993: 295-8.

engineer: He was a technician, and possibly a freedman (Brunt, 1980: 82). So it is hard to accept Casson's theory (1978: 44-51) that he was, in essence, discussing labour problems with the emperor and proffering economic advice.

invention: Casson's argument (1978: 43) that the engineer proposed what could be described as a 'work for the dole scheme' has been persuasively rejected by Brunt (1980: 82). The 'invention' was not, despite Casson, an economic plan; rather it must have been some sort of labour-saving mechanical device, one that Vespasian rejected precisely because he had no intention of saving labour costs.

transport great columns: Compare the machine designed by a certain Paronius that was supposed to convey stone from a quarry (Vitruvius, *De Arch.* 10.2.13).

feed his poor plebs: Brunt has shown that the common people in Rome had to earn their living in casual employment and partly in the building trade (1980: 81-98). Despite Casson (1978: 43-51), there is not even a hint in Suetonius that Vespasian was forced to resort to a gang of slaves. On the contrary, Vespasian was not trying to save money but to maintain his people. The anecdote should be taken at face value, though Levick treats it with scepticism (1999: 129, 245).

19 *[page 20]*

In this chapter, Suetonius provides further examples of Vespasian's generosity, balancing it with two indications of his greed, neither particularly convincing, i.e. insults from the Alexandrians and, in effect, an anecdote on how to save the state ten million (less one hundred thousand) sestertii.

Theatre of Marcellus: Its foundations were laid by Julius Caesar and completed by Augustus who dedicated it in 11 BC (*NH* 8.65; Dio 43.49.2, 54.26.1), naming it for Marcus Marcellus (43-23 BC), who was both Augustus' nephew (by his sister Octavia) and son-in-law (married to his daughter Julia). There is a reference to it in the *Res Gestae* (21.1) and in *Aug.* 29.4 (*PA* 513-15).

Apelles: There was an Apelles in Gaius' reign, 'the most famous of the tragedians of the day' (Dio 59.5.2), and one was mentioned by Petronius (*Satyricon* 64), probably the same person. He could, just possibly, have still been on the stage some thirty-five years after Gaius' death.

400,000 sestertii: So he received the equestrian census. Vespasian gave the same amount to the woman in *Vesp.* 22.

Terpnus: He was the most prominent lyre-player of Nero's reign (*Nero* 20.1), took part in the tour of Greece (*Vesp.* 4), but, in the musical contest, failed to defeat the emperor (Dio 63.8.3).

Diodorus: Diodorus accompanied Nero on the musical tour of Greece and was defeated by him; but, on the latter's victorious return to Rome, 'by his side in the vehicle rode Diodorus the lyre-player' (Dio 63.20.3). These two received the equivalent of a year's salary for a third-level procurator.

gold crowns: Rewarding actors with golden crowns was hardly novel. Nero received them (*Nero* 53) and Plutarch tells of the younger Cato's cost-cutting efforts as aedile – 'he gave the actors crowns, not of gold, but of wild olive as was done at Olympia' (*Cat. min.* 46.3). The Elder Pliny refers to a variant of that practice, where thin leaves of Cyprus copper were used (*NH* 34.94).

dinner parties...in formal style: In this regard, Vespasian was once more following the example of Augustus (*Aug.* 74). So his dinner parties were frequent and formal. Despite his alleged greed, he apparently avoided the cheaper alternatives, a dinner in the Forum or a direct handout (*Dom.* 4) – and the formal dinner consisted of at least three courses (though Juvenal mentions seven in *Sat.* 1.94). However, they can hardly have endured for very long, given the financial problems facing Vespasian; and that suggestion is reinforced by Suetonius' next statement that 'Vespasian could not get rid of his former reputation for greed'. On all this, see Friedländer, 1968: 4.77-81.

food sellers: i.e. Stall-holders at the markets. For attempts to regulate what was sold there and the prices charged, see *Iul.* 43.2 and *Tib.* 34.

Saturnalia: The festival of the Saturnalia lasted from 17 to 23 December. It was a time of general enjoyment – law courts, schools and businesses were closed; there was a good deal of drinking, eating and gambling; slaves were allowed to behave as they liked and their masters wore leisure-wear instead of the toga. It was also the custom for men to exchange gifts: see next item.

take-home presents: The Latin term is *apophoreta* and is used of presents 'to be carried away' by guests, especially at the Saturnalia. It is also the title of the fourteenth book of Martial's Epigrams, consisting of couplets intended to accompany such presents.

Kalends of March: This day, the first day of the religious year, saw the ancient festival in honour of Juno Lucina (*matronalia*) that symbolised the sacredness of marriage and consisted of a procession of married women to her temple. As well, wives would receive gifts from their husbands – and from admirers (Martial 5.84.10-12; Juv. 9.53).

people of Alexandria: The Alexandrians displayed initial enthusiasm for Vespasian according to a papyrus fragment which purports to be an account of the moment when, early in 70, he came to Egypt (accompanied by Josephus: *Vita* 415) and was greeted by the Alexandrians as he entered the Hippodrome – 'In good health, Lord Caesar, [may you come!] Vespasian, the one saviour... Son of Ammon...' (*MW* 41: see Montevecchi, 1981: 484-96). But their enthusiasm did not last long, as Dio attests: 'The Alexandrians, far from delighting in Vespasian's presence, detested him so heartily that they were for ever mocking and reviling him' (66.8.2). It is possible that Vespasian reacted with vigour. In a speech addressed to the emperor Theodosius (Jones, 1997: 249-53), Libanius refers to the riots in Antioch in 387 when portraits and statues of the emperor Theodosius were destroyed and adds:

> Titus' father (had) undergone similar treatment with regard to his statues...and (had) meted out punishments.... So many Alexandrians were slaughtered by the soldiers stationed in the city that the swords grew heavy in the hands of those who used them.
>
> (20.30-2)

If Libanius' remarks are accurate, then Suetonius has avoided mention of an incident that would, to some extent, contradict the version of the emperor's character given in 12.

Herring-Stuffer...stinginess: The Alexandrians' enthusiastic greeting of the new emperor was soon replaced by unconcealed hostility at his imposition of new taxes. They called him *Cybiosactes*. Since *cybium* means 'chopped and salted pieces of young tunny-fish' (*OLD* 480), *cybiosactes* can refer to a 'dealer in salt-fish' (*ibid.*), an occupation that was traditionally despised; but there was more to the insult. It could also be taken to refer to the historical and extremely unpleasant Cybiosactes. He claimed to be descended from Syrian royalty, perhaps the son or illegitimate son of Antiochus X. When the Alexandrians declared Berenice IV Queen, they arranged a marriage for her with Cybiosactes (57 BC). The union was brief: she 'had him strangled to death within a few days (of the marriage), being unable to bear his coarseness and vulgarity' (Strabo 17 c. 796). No doubt the Alexandrians were also aware of the fact that, in Vespasian's retinue, was another Berenice, once married (or perhaps only betrothed) to Tiberius Julius Alexander's brother and now the mistress of Titus.

leading mime actor: The mime was a loosely-constructed presentation of everyday life and a leading mime such as Favor would train his own company of performers. OCD 982-3.

mask: This is the only reference to an actor wearing a mask of the deceased at the funeral (Mooney, 1930: 449).

funeral and procession: A detailed description of the funeral rites appears in Toynbee, 1971: 56-61.

exclaimed: We have a number of examples (but none from funerals) of double-meaning references by mime actors to an emperor's behaviour or activities, e.g., from Nero's reign, there is Datus' comment 'Farewell, Father! Farewell, Mother!' as he pretended to drink and swim (*Nero* 39.3).

hundred thousand sestertii: There is very little information on the cost of imperial funerals (Nero's cost two hundred thousand sestertii: *Nero* 50), but ten million sestertii is obviously excessive and intended to give more point to Vespasian's offer. The highest tomb cost recorded epigraphically in Italy was five hundred thousand sestertii (Popillius Theo...: *CIL* 10.5624) and the Elder Pliny mentions a freedman who died in 8 BC and requested that one million one hundred thousand sestertii from his substantial estate be spent on his burial (*NH* 33.135).

20 *[pages 20-1]*

Some idea of Vespasian's physical appearance can be gleaned from his coins and from those few busts which survive: see Daltrop, 1966: 9-17 and *MW* (facing p. 49). Suetonius' interest in his subject's physical appearance could have resulted from the Alexandrian biographical tradition of including every possible detail about his subject (Evans, 1935: 77-9, 1969: 51-2; but see Bradley, 1978a: 281). He was also interested in physiognomy – the 'science' of interpreting a man's character from his personal appearance. In this field, the contemporary expert was Polemo of Laodicaea (88-144/5) who, like Suetonius, was a member of Hadrian's court. Evans has argued that, at times, Suetonius listed those physical characteristics 'which from the point of view of the physiognomists indicate either the virtuous or vicious nature of an emperor's character' (1935: 63; similarly 1969: 53). Couissin goes much further. He suggests that Suetonius does not try to describe his subject's personal appearance but uses the 'rules' of physiognomy to provide a description consistent with his character (1953: 234). Baldwin's summary is accurate: Suetonius 'avoided the major nonsenses of physiognomy' (1983: 500).

emptying your bowels: The comment is remarkably apt as is attested by the bust of Vespasian in *MW* (p. 49), the Florence bust from the Uffizi in Daltrop, 1969: Tafel 8d, and the Copenhagen Vespasian in Southern, 1997: 120. There may also be a reference to Vespasian's last actions (*Vesp.* 24) and his own witticisms tended to be 'scurrilous and vulgar' (22).

excellent health: However, Dio mentions his 'accustomed gout' (66.17.1).

ball courts: They were part of the public baths and could be found in the more elaborate private homes and villas (Pliny, *Ep.* 2.17.12 and 5.6.27).

fasting: Celsus recommended it (2.16) – but in moderation (7.7.4), as was practised by Vespasian. Otherwise, it could become a means of suicide (*Aug.* 53.3).

21 *[page 21]*

ordering of his life: Vespasian's accessibility and the simplicity of his lifestyle is reported elsewhere. According to Dio:

> Vespasian's own style of living was very far from costly and he spent no more than was absolutely necessary... He received anybody who desired to see him, not only senators but also people in general. (66.10.3-4)

Similarly, Tacitus *Ann.* 3.55 and the *Epit. de Caes.* 9.15.

wake up quite early: So, too, Dio 66.10.4. That he was at work before dawn is attested by the Elder Pliny (*Ep.* 3.5.9) and Philostratus:

> When Apollonius came to the palace at daybreak and asked what the emperor was doing,...(he was told that) Vespasian had been up for a long time and was busy with his correspondence. (*V. Apoll.* 5.31)

correspondence: For the imperial correspondence, see Millar, 1977: 213-28.

admit his friends: Vespasian consulted trusted friends (*Titus* 7), be they senators or equestrians, on matters of importance. The astute Vespasian was not adverse to giving two of his, Vibius Crispus and Eprius Marcellus, a completely free rein (*Dial.* 8.3). For a list, see Devreker, 1977: 223-43.

put on his shoes himself: For those of high rank, this task was usually performed by servants known as *calciatores*.

sleep: i.e. the siesta.

deceased Caenis: See *Vesp.* 3. She died in the early seventies (Dio 66.14.1).

private retreat: i.e. from the private section of the palace.

bath and dining room: The usual time for bathing was the early afternoon, after the midday meal (Vitruvius 5.10.1). For Vitellius (*Vit.* 13.1) and Domitian (*Dom.* 21), it was a fairly substantial meal, whereas Augustus confined himself to bread and dates (*Aug.* 76.1). Suetonius is completely silent on Vespasian's eating habits: what he stressed was the emperor's availability at all times, meals included.

22 *[page 21]*

Vespasian's sense of humour is further exemplified in a carefully linked series of chapters (22-5) culminating in the death scene. We have eight instances of Vespasian's ready wit: (1) Mestrius Florus, (2) woman dying of love, (3) the man with large genitals, (4) Cerylus/Laches, (5) the pretended brother, (6) the muleteer, (7) the urine tax and (8) the base of the statue; with two of them (2 and 3) in the category of 'scurrilous and vulgar'. Reminding the reader that there will be more instances of imperial ready wit, he introduces the last four by harking back to the theme of Vespasian's greed (*Vesp.* 16) and concludes by linking his ready wit to the omens portending Vespasian's death ('Not even amidst the fear and extreme danger of death did he refrain from jokes': *Vesp.* 23). With the phrase 'fear and extreme danger of death', Suetonius is stressing the incongruity of Vespasian's sense of humour: death should be a source of 'fear and danger', but seemingly not for Vespasian, who reacts to the threat of it (the omens) and the reality with further jests: 'I'm becoming a god' (*Vesp.* 23). For more detail, see Gorringe, 1993: 436.

genial: The theory was that one was unassuming to one's fellow citizens and genial to one's friends. Dio states that Vespasian 'was looked upon as emperor only by reason of his oversight of public business whereas in all other respects...he lived on a footing of equality with his subjects' (Dio 66.11.1). See also *Vesp.* 12. According to Seneca, a ruler with these qualities 'was loved, defended and worshipped by the whole state' (*Clem.* 1.13.4).

dinner: The usual time for the last meal of the day was the ninth (Cicero, *Ad Fam.* 9.26.1) or tenth hour (Martial 1.108.9); and it lasted for some time (*Ep.* 3.1.9).

transact business...joke: His fondness for jokes is noted in Dio 66.11.1 and in *Epit. de Caes.* 9.3. Suetonius' point (repeated at the end of the chapter) is that Vespasian would try to take the sting out of some unpleasant piece of business by joking about it.

scurrilous and vulgar: Vespasian's occasional ribald sense of humour was part of what would now be dubbed 'a carefully cultivated image' and should not be interpreted as indicative of lowly birth or a 'peasant' upbringing. On the contrary, his father was extremely wealthy, he himself was a welcome member of the courts of Gaius, Claudius and Nero, his son was educated with the imperial prince Britannicus and he may have been granted patrician status as early as 47.

Mestrius Florus, a former consul: A friend of Plutarch, Mestrius Florus (*PIR2* M 531) appears frequently in his *Quaestiones Conviviales* and also in his *Otho* 14.2, where Mestrius is described as a 'Roman of consular rank and one of those who then (i.e. 69, at the first battle of Bedriacum: see *Vesp.* 5) accompanied Otho (but) not of his own free will'. However, despite Braithwaite (1927: 65), he was not then of consular rank. He held that post c. 75 and, some ten years later, became proconsul of Asia (Eck, 1970: 85-6).

'wains' not 'woins': Suetonius attests that Vespasian's fondness for the older pronunciation was quite deliberate. Priscian describes this precise usage as an archaism (1.52).

Flayrus: What Vespasian did was to avoid the Latin word *Florus* and use the form *Flaurus* which recalls the Greek equivalent meaning 'useless'.

400,000 sestertii: Vespasian gave the same amount to the actor of 19 above.

treasurer: Usually a slave or a freedman.

object of a passion: The phrase has been discussed in detail by Zinn, 1951: 10 and Hudson-Williams, 1952: 72-3.

23 *[pages 21-22]*

'Striding...spear': The quotation (*Iliad* 7.213) is from the description of Ajax about to fight Hector.

freedman Cerylus: Probably, he is the Cerylus of Martial 1.67.

evade the claim of the imperial purse: In Roman law, the patron was regarded as the heir of any of his childless freedmen or was entitled to a share in the estate if there were any legitimate children born after manumission. Cerylus must have been an imperial freedman and so, on his death, his estate (or part of it) would revert to his imperial patron. A change of name and a statement that he was freeborn would fool neither Vespasian nor the Treasury officials who, once Cerylus/Laches was dead, would soon claim whatever he had left.

Laches: Hardly an appropriate choice as 'Laches' was one of the standard names for slaves in Greek comedy.

'When..will you': This is from the *Theophoroumene* ('Girl Possessed') of Menanander (frag. 223,2: Kock), with the last line added by Vespasian himself.

witticisms: For a comment on Vespasian's sense of humour and the eight anecdotes in these sections, see *Vesp.* 22.

animosity...witty saying: Vespasian's greed is the theme of the last four anecdotes.

close servants: i.e. one of his favourite freedmen.

shoes on the mules: In antiquity, shoes were not usually put on horses or mules, and, when they were (e.g. on bad roads), they were never fastened by nails but by strings or straps. Shoes were generally of iron (Catull. 17.26), but sometimes of silver (*Nero* 30.3) or even gold (*NH* 33.140 and Dio 62.28.1: Poppaea's mules). See *Vesp.* 4.

tax even on urine: So, too, in Dio 66.14.5; but, despite this public pose, Titus was said to be as careful a financier as his father (Dio 66.19.3). On one level, the anecdote could be said to exemplify Vespasian's greed, but it also indicates that, for Suetonius, Titus was not co-ruler with Vespasian (compare Rogers, 1980: 90). This was a discussion not between two partners but between an apprentice (in money matters) and his master. It also illustrates an on-going debate – should the source of money prevent its being used for good works?

Urine was used by the fullers. The practice was for wool to be taken immediately from the loom to the fullers so that the grease and dirt could be removed, and this was done in a mixture of water, stale urine and fuller's earth. Now the fullers had to pay for the urine. The procedure adopted by Vespasian in collecting this particular tax remains obscure, but one explanation emerges from a sentence of Macrobius, i.e. 'wherever they go, there is no amphora that they don't fill' (*Sat.* 3.16.15). So receptacles must have been placed in each alley, but now the right to empty them was made subject to a tax. Vespasian's interest in such matters has been immortalised in French where the word for 'urinal' is (or, rather, used to be) 'une Vespasienne' and in Italian, where, with a change of gender, it is 'il Vespasiano'.

no small sum: 1,000,000 sestertii (Dio 66.14.5).

displaying his empty hand: The money was to be the statue with Vespasian's hand as the base. According to Dio, he said 'Give me the money; this is its pedestal' (66.14.5). This is the last of the four anecdotes illustrating Vespasian's alleged greed.

danger of death...refrain from jokes: Similarly in the *Epit. de Caes.* 9.17. For a comment on this brief transition to the death scene, see *Vesp.* 22.

prodigies: Dio (66.17.2) refers to the same two prodigies. Once again, Vespasian's reaction was 'to indulge in jests' (Dio 66.11.1). Note the connection between *Calvina* and the adjective 'bald' (*calvus* in Latin) that points unmistakably to Vespasian himself.

all the other prodigies: Suetonius gives no more detail on the nature of these 'other prodigies', an omission all the more noteworthy in view of the prominence ascribed to the omens that heralded Vespasian's accession. But further detail would be inappropriate here, given the inclusion immediately before the death-narrative of two omens (the Mausoleum and the comet) as yet further examples of Vespasianic wit.

Mausoleum: Built by Augustus in 28 BC, it contained the ashes of many Julio-Claudians and Nerva. No doubt Domitian had Vespasian's taken to the Temple of the Flavian clan (Blake, 1959: 114) together with those of Titus and Julia, whilst his nurse, Phyllis, later placed his own there as well (*Dom.*

17). The opening of its doors also heralded the death of Nero (*Nero* 46.2). See further Steinby, 1996: 234-9.

comet: The appearance of a comet (*stella crinata* in Latin – i.e. 'hairy star') heralded the death of a ruler, so it was thought (*Nero* 36.1; *Claud.* 46). Thus, 'when beggars die there are no comets seen; the heavens themselves blaze forth the death of princes' (Shakespeare, *Julius Caesar* 2.2).

Junia Calvina: She was one of the four children of Junius Silanus Torquatus (consul 19) and Aemilia Lepida. The fate of her three brothers (Marcus, Decimus and Lucius) was determined by the fact that they were great-great-grandchildren of Augustus. Calvina and her brother Lucius proved to be obstacles to Agrippina's dynastic plans for her son Nero (*Ann.* 12.4): in 49, Lucius was forced to commit suicide and Calvina was banished (*Ann.* 12.8); after Agrippina's death, she was recalled by Nero (*Ann.* 14.12).

clan of Augustus: Augustus' daughter Julia married Agrippa, their daughter Julia married Aemilius Paullus and their daughter Aemilia Lepida married Junius Silanus Torquatus.

Parthian King...thick head of hair: Since a comet was, literally, a 'hairy star' (see above), the prodigy could not be aimed at the bald Vespasian. On the other hand, as the Parthians were long-haired (Hdt. 6.19), a more likely candidate would be Vologaesus (*PIR*1 V 630, successor to the Vologaesus of *Vesp.* 6, V 629). Vespasian's interpretation of the omen is reported both by Dio 66.17.3 and in the *Epit. de Caes.* 9.18.

'I think I'm becoming a god': Dio 67.17.3 has the same report. This is the ultimate instance of Vespasian's ready wit. Suetonius' use of his comment is no doubt (Schmidt, 1988: 83-9) intended to recall the last words attributed to Claudius, i.e.'Oh, dear, I think I have messed myself' (*Apocol.* 4.3) and also, perhaps, to provide an ironical reminder of other links between Vespasian and Claudius (*Vesp.* 4). Gorringe aptly comments that

> not only does the joke...correspond with the rather earthy nature of Vespasian's preferences in humour, and also with his penchant for using literary quotations, but gains added impact from the fact that his own last illness was compounded by attacks of diarrhoea. (1993: 438)

But Vespasian was perfectly well aware of the political value of deification. In Rome and Italy, he 'behaved like a citizen' (*Vesp.* 12) and made no claim to superhuman powers – but not so in Alexandria in 69/70 where he was addressed as 'Serapis' (*Vesp.* 19). In the provinces, he never discouraged those who proclaimed his divinity. Quite the contrary; in fact, throughout the western provinces of the empire, it was under Vespasian that the extension of the ruler cult reached its climax and he was also responsible for installing the provincial cult in Lycia and Armenia (Fishwick, 1987: 299-300).

The honour of deification was decreed by the Senate on a motion of the reigning emperor and the ceremony (*consecratio*) normally held soon after his predecessor's death (Clarke, 1966: 318-21). However, it seems that Titus waited for more than six months (Buttrey, 1976: 457). Of Suetonius' twelve Caesars, only five (Julius Caesar, Augustus, Claudius, Vespasian and Titus) were deified and two of them were Flavians. For a detailed discussion of Vespasian's famous last words, see Fishwick, 1987: 295-300.

24 *[page 22]*

ninth consulship: He was in office until 13 January 79 (Gallivan, 1981: 215).

light attacks of fever: Celsus mentions the curative powers of the waters of Cutiliae in a discussion of why the stomach does not retain food (*Med.* 4.12). So, when Vespasian was in Campania, he may have been suffering, not so much from a fever, but rather from a stomach disorder that became even more serious with his visit to Cutiliae and resulted in a series of gastric attacks.

Cutiliae: That Vespasian died at Cutiliae (a Sabine village about 12 km. from Reate) is confirmed by Dio 66.17.1. The Elder Pliny refers to its lake (*NH* 3.10) and a number of ancient sources mention the curative powers of its springs (*NH* 31.10; Vitruvius, *De Arch.* 8.3.5; Celsus, *Med.* 4.12.7).

Reate: See *Vesp.* 1.

spend the summer: During the extremely hot summer months, most senators abandoned Rome. The Flavians must have regularly withdrawn to their Sabine retreat and it was here, and during much the same time of the year, that Titus died two years later (*Titus* 11).

embassies: For their significance, see Millar, 1977: 375-85. In the late republic and the Julio-Claudian period, multi-member embassies were the norm; but after Nero's death a limit of three representatives per embassy was imposed, as is stated in one of Vespasian's edicts (*Digest* 50. 7.5.6). No doubt financial considerations swayed him, for this was an expensive practice both for Rome and for the provinces (Sherwin-White, 1966: 625). Embassies to him from the Vanacini and Sabora are attested (Millar, 1977: 235-6 and 435; Souris, 1982: 242).

sudden relaxation of the bowels: Similar details appear in the *Epit. de Caes.* 9.18 and Eutropius 7.20.2. Dio, however, states that Hadrian and others 'in an endeavour falsely to incriminate Titus, spread the report that he was poisoned at a banquet' (66.17.1), recalling how Caecina was removed (*Titus* 6). But the administration of poison is often associated with gastric attacks – by Tacitus with diarrhoea (*Ann.* 12.67 and 13.15) and by Suetonius with vomiting (*Claud.* 44.3 and *Nero* 33.2); in each case the victims were Claudius and Britannicus. Suetonius, however, has no hint whatsoever here of foul play.

'emperor ought to die standing up': Similarly Dio 66.17.2 and the *Epit. de Caes.* 9.18.

straining: Perhaps Suetonius is deliberately harking back to the physical description of Vespasian in 20 above ('face like somebody straining to relieve himself').

ninth day before the Kalends of July: 23 June 79. Buttrey (1980: 7, 20), however, nominates 24 June, but only on the basis of Dio's inconsistent statement that 'he had lived for sixty-nine years and eight months, and reigned for ten years less six days' (66.17.3). See further Braithwaite, 1927: 68.

aged sixty-nine years seven months and seven days: The calculation is accurate, for Vespasian was born 17 November 9 and died 23 June 79. Dio, less precise, says that he lived sixty-nine years and eight months (66.17.3).

25 *[page 22]*

natal star: The reference is to Vespasian's horoscope. Astrology (*Vesp.* 15) was widely practised during the empire and its predictions had acquired intellectual respectability (see Liebeschuetz, 1979: 121-4). The Flavians and many others believed in this so-called science (*Dom.* 14). That Vespasian consulted astrologers on the subject of the succession is also mentioned by both Aurelius Victor 9.4 and Eutropius 7.20.3. Dio adds that 'Vespasian banished the astrologers from Rome, even though he was in the habit of consulting all the best of them himself' (Dio 66.9.2).

incessant conspiracies: Not many can be identified and the comments by Aurelius Victor 9.3 and Eutropius 7.20.3 add nothing to Suetonius' statement; but some details can be gleaned from Dio who refers to two incidents that occurred in 79 (*Hist.* 4.67 for the date). Julius Sabinus, his wife and family were executed (66.16.1). He had claimed to be descended from an illegitimate son of Julius Caesar and so, claiming the title *Caesar*, had taken part in Julius Classicus' unsuccessful uprising (see *Vesp.* 15 and Wellesley, 1975: 183). There was also the alleged conspiracy of Eprius Marcellus and Caecina Alienus. The former (Birley, 1981: 228-30), a consistently loyal and highly rewarded Flavian supporter, had received from Vespasian a three-year proconsulship of Asia and a second suffect consulship in 74. Caecina Alienus (*PIR2* C 95), on the other hand, commanded one of Galba's armies, then one of Vitellius and, ultimately, became a close associate of Vespasian. The so-called epitomator of Aurelius Victor even claims that Titus had Caecina executed 'on suspicion of having raped his (Titus') wife Berenice' (10.4). Dio believes that there was a conspiracy involving them both, that Titus had Alienus 'slain as he rose from a meal with (Vespasian); Marcellus...cut his own throat with a razor' (66.16.3). But Suetonius makes no mention of Marcellus and links the removal of Caecina with Titus' actions as the new régime's 'enforcer' (*Titus* 6). One wonders why there would be 'incessant conspiracies' against a well-loved emperor. Perhaps they were directed against Titus and led to Vespasian's outburst reported in the next item.

'either his sons would succeed him or no one would': Similarly, Aurelius Victor 9.4 and Eutropius 7.20.3. Dio, however, has Helvidius Priscus attacking Vespasian who replies that 'My successor shall be my son or no one at all' (66.12.1). Both versions, though incompatible, are internally consistent. The general context of the remark in Suetonius indicates that it was made late in the reign, but the nature of Vespasian's dynastic policy was obvious as early as 70 and Dio's use of the singular ('son') is appropriate if Vespasian's outburst occurred after Helvidius had denounced the role assigned to Titus and advocated that the 'best man' be the next emperor. However, Suetonius' 'sons' was accurate. Domitian was clearly designated by Vespasian as Titus' successor – his dynastic intentions could not have been stated more clearly.

house on the Palatine...Claudius et Nero: Vespasian liked to be portrayed as the legitimate successor of the Julio-Claudians and hence the scales are located, not in the Gardens of Sallust that he preferred, but in the imperial palace on the Palatine.

same number of years: twenty-seven, i.e. 41 to 68 for Claudius and Nero, 69 to 96 for the Flavians. See Mooney, 1930: 465 for the calculation in days, months and years.

THE DEIFIED TITUS

1 *[page 23]*

same surname: In fact, before 69, both father and son were called Titus Flavius Vespasianus. As was customary, the elder son was given his father's last name, whilst the younger son (Domitian) took his from his mother (Domitilla) – just as Vespasian, the younger of Titus Flavius Sabinus' two sons, took his *cognomen* from his mother (Vespasia).

beloved and darling of the human race: This assessment, so prominently placed and so highly favourable, sets the tone for what follows and is repeated by later writers, including the Elder Pliny (*NH Praef.* 1), Tacitus (*Hist.* 2.1), Eutropius (7.21), Aurelius Victor (10.6), Augustine (*Civ. Dei.* 5.21), Pacatus (*Pan. in Theod.* 11) and Ausonius (*Caes.* 11). In the opening scene of Mozart's *La Clemenza di Tito* of 1791, Titus' friend Sextus proclaims 'non togliamo in Tito la sua delizia al mondo' – 'Let us not in Titus take from the world its delight'.

talent, art, fortune: The same qualities are assigned to Titus in *Hist.* 2.1 and 5; and this entire passage recalls Suetonius' description of Germanicus in *Calig.* 3.1. Dio, however, reflecting a less favourable tradition, comments that, had the emperor lived longer, his good reputation might have been due 'more to good fortune than to merit' (66.18.5) and he compares him with Augustus who 'would never have been loved had he lived a shorter time'.

hatred: This negative criticism, the result of his activities as praetorian prefect (*Titus* 6), is another indication of the tradition hostile to Titus but rejected by Suetonius and later writers.

popular vituperation: In view of his lifestyle, people thought that he would be a second Nero (*Titus* 7).

third day before the Kalends of January: 30 December. The Kalends was the first day of the month and the Romans counted inclusively.

year made famous by the assassination of Gaius: The assassination occurred on 24 January 41. According to Dio's figures (66.18.4: Titus was 39 years, 5 months and 25 days old on his accession on 24 June 79), Titus was born on 30 December 39. Suetonius, however, claims here that the year was 41, but, later (*Titus* 11), gives the correct year.

Septizonium: The only Septizonium (or Septizodium) recorded is that of Septimius Severus built in 203 at the south-east corner of the Palatine. The location of Suetonius' building is unknown, but McGuire (1980: 25-7) argues ingeniously that Suetonius is referring to the Pantheon.

very small and dark: Suetonius repeats (see *Vesp*. 1, 4 and 5: *Dom*. 1) the Flavian propaganda that Vespasian did not prosper under Caligula and other 'bad' Julio-Claudians.

still there: Suetonius' claim underlines both his careful collection of historical evidence and also the fact that Titus' memory was still venerated more than forty years after he died.

2 *[page 23]*

brought up at court: In the early years of Claudius' reign, while Vespasian was in Britain, Titus had probably been sent to live with his grandfather Sabinus at Aventicum in Switzerland (van Berchem, 1978: 269-70), just as Sabinus, when in Ephesus, had arranged for Vespasian to be raised by his grandmother Tertulla, at Cosa (*Vesp*. 2). However, at the age of about seven (i.e. in 47), on Vespasian's return to Rome, Titus received the unusual honour of being educated at Claudius' court with (amongst others) Britannicus and the Herodian Agrippa II. The reason for Claudius' action is not hard to guess. Vespasian had been a member of the court of Claudius' mother Antonia, with the latter's freedwoman Caenis as his mistress (*Vesp*. 3); he and his brother Sabinus had, with considerable success, commanded two of Claudius' legions in the recent invasion of Britain; the year 47 was not only marked by Vespasian's triumphal return, but also by Sabinus' elevation to the consulship (A.R. Birley, 1981: 227) and (just possibly) by the family being awarded patrician status (McAlindon, 1957: 260).

Britannicus: Born 12 Feb. 41, this son of Claudius and his third wife Valeria Messalina was first called *Tiberius Claudius Caesar Germanicus*, the title *Britannicus* being decreed by the Senate following Claudius' British triumph

(*Claud.* 27.1). In 49, his father married Agrippina and adopted her son, Domitius (Nero) who was given precedence over Britannicus; a few months (*Ann.* 13.15) after Claudius' death (13 Oct. 54), Britannicus also perished (see below).

same subjects: Until the age of eleven, the boys would have been taught the basics (reading, writing and arithmetic); then (from twelve to about fifteen) they would have faced a broader curriculum (mathematics, philosophy music, literature and rhetoric – in both Latin and Greek) under a *grammaticus*. Titus would have advanced to the later stage at around the time of his father's consulship, but, whatever the extent of the family's loss of influence after Claudius married Agrippina, the quality of Titus' education did not suffer – as Suetonius attests (*Titus* 3).

same teachers: We know of one, the *grammaticus* Sosibius, appointed by Messalina who gave him 1,000,000 sestertii for 'giving Britannicus the benefit of his teaching' (*Ann.* 11.4); his opposition to Agrippina and Nero led to his death or exile (*Ann.* 11.1, 12.41 and Dio 60.32.5).

forehead-diviner: Such a person (*metoposcopus*) claimed to tell a person's future by examining his forehead, to 'prophesy people's future by their countenance (or) pronounce the year of one's death or the number of years (one) has lived' (Pliny, *NH* 35.88). This and other types of pseudo science were in vogue at Hadrian's court. Suetonius was particularly interested in the cognate area of physiognomy (see *Vesp.* 20, *Titus* 3) – the 'science' of deducing one's character from one's physical appearance. As early as the age of Pericles, a certain Zopyrus had claimed proficiency in this field (Evans, 1935: 47) and Latin authors before Suetonius were well aware of it (Couissin, 1953: 239-40), especially Seneca. By the second century AD, the practice had become well-established and fashionable; the contemporary expert was Polemo of Laodicaea (88-144/5) who enjoyed the patronage of Trajan and Hadrian (Philostratus, *V. Soph.* 1.532-3), being as well (like Suetonius) part of the latter's court. As the word *metoposcopus* is used in Latin only by Suetonius (here) and the Elder Pliny, one is tempted to speculate that Suetonius used Pliny as his source for this and, perhaps, other anecdotes.

Narcissus: *Vesp.* 4. Suetonius may also have found the anecdote in the writings of Balbillus (*PIR*2 C 813) who accompanied Claudius to Britain and took part in his triumph. Later, he became Vespasian's favourite astrologer (Dio 65.9.2) and would have recorded 'prophecies' such as this soon after Vespasian's accession.

tasted the potion...died: In another version of this incident (*Nero* 33.2-3), Suetonius states that Nero's poisoner Locusta first tried the mixture on a young goat which took five hours to die. Nero ordered her to strengthen the mixture and give it to a pig; the resultant poison was so virulent that the animal died at once – as did Britannicus. Titus' miraculous survival, indeed his very presence at the meal, is not mentioned in this version. Another possibility is suggested by Barrett: Britannicus may simply have suffered a severe and fatal epileptic fit (1996: 171-2).

reclining: Another error – imperial children sat at table. As Suetonius himself notes elsewhere, Augustus' grandsons 'sat on the lowest couch' (*Aug.* 64.3) and Claudius' children, 'together with the sons and daughters of distinguished men, sat at the ends of the couches' (*Claud.* 32).

troubled...serious illness: Titus' presence (but Suetonius does not vouch for it: 'it is believed') is not mentioned in any of the other versions (Dio 61.7.4, *Ann.* 13.16 and his own at *Nero* 33.1-3) of Britannicus' death. Perhaps it was an invention of the Flavian historians who, whenever possible, linked their heroes with the 'good' Julio-Claudians.

set up a golden statue...Palace: Golden statues set up in public (see *Dom.* 13) were regarded by the Romans as the equivalent to deification; but no such opprobrium was attached to statues in (as here, presumably) the private section of the imperial Palace on the Palatine.

equestrian statue made of ivory: Suetonius states clearly that this statue of Britannicus was displayed not within the Palace but openly for all to see. In his *Life* of Julius Caesar, he describes such a practice as 'an honour too great for a mortal man' (76.1), in reference to the fact that, during Caesar's lifetime, an ivory statue of him in triumphal garb was carried in a litter. Germanicus was similarly honoured, but only on his death (*Ann.* 2.83). Titus' public veneration of Britannicus' statue was intended to suggest another link between the Flavians and the 'good' Julio-Claudians.

still to this day: By continuing to honour Britannicus' statue, later emperors (Hadrian – or Nerva or Trajan) were trying to indicate their 'legitimacy', the link to the deified Claudius being provided by the deified Titus and Vespasian. The Flavians' (and, perhaps, Trajan's) seizure of power was disguised in this official propaganda by linking the 'good' dynasties to the 'young prince' who had been murdered by the 'tyrant' Nero.

carried in the processions at the Circus games: Games held in the Circus Maximus had always begun with an elaborate procession (see *Vesp.* 5) that started from the Capitol and passed through the Forum. Towards the end came images of the main deities carried in litters.

3 *[page 23]*

gifts of body and of mind: As in Titus 1, we have a passage closely resembling Suetonius' description of Germanicus in Calig 3.1.

not tall...a stomach that was a little too prominent: Some idea of Titus' physical appearance can be gleaned from his coins and from those busts which survive: for an example, see *MW* (facing p.96). The comment on his 'little too prominent stomach' might seem surprising, but results from Suetonius' interest in physiognomony (*Vesp.* 20 and *Titus* 2) and also, no doubt, from the fact that iconoclastic evidence of Titus' physique was available to his readers. Now the Pseudo Aristotle reveals that a paunch was a sign of strength (810b) – shared by Nero (*Nero* 51), Vitellius (*Vit.* 17.2) and Domitian (*Dom.* 18)! Here, but not with the other emperors, Suetonius qualifies the description ('a little too'). Again, according to Pseudo Aristotle 813b, lack of height was an advantage: he could not have been lazy since his blood did not have to travel so far! In general, though, Suetonius manages to 'avoid the major nonsenses of physiognomony' (Baldwin, 1983: 500).

virtually all the arts of war and peace: It was regarded as rare to excel in both. Other notable exceptions were Scipio Aemilianus (Vell. 1.12) and Trajan (*Pan.* 4.5). Titus' military ability appears throughout the *BJ* and is commented on in *Hist.* 5.1; Eutropius called him *bellicosissimus* ('very warlike': 7.21).

very skilful...riding: Suetonius uses the same words about Julius Caesar (*Iul.* 57).

pleading: The Elder Pliny praises his 'supreme eloquence', adding that 'in no other person does the dictatorial power of oratory and the tribunician authority of wit ever radiate more genuinely' (*NH Praef.* 5, 11). Versions (for what they are worth) of Titus' speeches in Judaea are provided by Josephus, both direct (*BJ* 3.494-6; 5. 121-5; 6.34-53; 6.328-50) and indirect (6.215-19; 7.6-12).

composing poetry: Titus' poem on the comet of 76 is praised by the Elder Pliny (*NH* 2.89) who also lauds his general ability as a poet ('How eloquently you thunder forth your father's praises! How great you are in the poet's art!': *Praef.* 5).

in Latin and Greek: The Elder Pliny refers to Titus' poem in Latin (*NH* 2.89), Eutropius to his tragedies and poems in Greek (7.21).

music: Though criticised by Nepos (died c. 24 BC) as 'unsuited for a person of importance' (*Epam.* 1.2), music was practised or at least appreciated in imperial circles (by Nero, Hadrian. Marcus Aurelius, Commodus, Alexander Severus, Elagabalus and Caracalla: Friedlaender, 1968: 2.337-65).

I have heard from many people: Here we have another indication of Suetonius' research methods.

shorthand: Shorthand, often called 'Tiro's shorthand' (*notae Tironianae*) from Cicero's Tiro, was first (Plutarch, *Cat. Min.* 23.3) used to record Cato's speech against Julius Caesar in 63 at the time of Catiline's conspiracy (5 December 63). Tiro's system was widely used during the empire; Seneca mentions 'signs for whole words enabling us to take down a speech' (*Ep.* 90.25) and Martial comments on a shorthand writer whose 'hand is swifter than (the speaker's) words' (14.208). Later, it was taken over by the Church. A Greek system also existed: *P.Oxy.* 4.724 is an apprenticeship contract with a shorthand teacher. More than a thousand years later, Thomas Becket, when Archbishop of Canterbury, encouraged research into Tiro's shorthand.

excellent forger: Titus possibly made use of this particular skill on any (or all) of three occasions during these years: the forgery of Otho's letter to Vespasian (*Vesp.* 6); of Caecina's signed speech (*Titus* 6); and of Vespasian's will (*Dom.* 2). Elsewhere, Suetonius mentions the punishment of forgers advocated by Claudius (*Claud.* 15.2: hands cut off) and lists the measures used to prevent the forging of wills and other documents under Nero (*Nero* 17). In the Republic, banishment and confiscation of property were the penalties provided by the Cornelian Law of 81 BC.

4 *[pages 23-4]*

in Germania: Probably, he served (from c. 57 to 59) in Lower Germany under Duvius Avitus (*RP* 2: 747), sharing the company of the Elder Pliny (*NH Praef.* 3). As laticlave tribune there, he was praised by Mucianus (*Hist.* 2.77), who provides no details of just what Titus did at a time when the province was 'abnormally peaceful' (Chilver, 1979: 236).

in Britannia: He may have arrived c. 60, bringing with him the reinforcements needed after Boudicca's rebellion; if so, he possibly served in the IX Hispana under his relative Q. Petillius Cerialis and even met Agricola who was tribune in Britain around this time (Birley, 1981: 75 and 296). However, Dio's account of his heroic rescue of his father in Britain (60.30.1) is to be rejected since Titus was a baby during Vespasian's service there.

military tribune: On the post, see *Vesp.* 1 and 2; but whatever Vespasian's status, Titus was definitely a laticlave tribune.

industry...unassuming behaviour: Suetonius' highly favourable assessment of Titus' qualities was expressed in *Titus* 1 and is enlarged on here. Tacitus called him 'fit for the most exalted station' (*Hist.* 2.1) and (in Mucianus' speech: 2.77) '*capax imperii*' ('capable of being emperor').

large number of statues...inscriptions of him: Suetonius provides further evidence of his careful research. However, no statue or honorific inscription survives of the type mentioned by Suetonius. The few that do (e.g. the Verulamium inscription: *AE* 1957, 169) are to be assigned to the period 79 to 81.

gave attention to the forum: Ambitious young men regularly advanced their careers through the law. Titus, then, after his military service, returned to Rome and served in the Centumviral court (*Vesp.* 10) probably during the years 63 and 64. At this time, apparently, admission to the Court was far from automatic. According to the younger Pliny, 'there was no place for a young man, however well-born, unless a consular senator introduced him' (*Ep.* 2.14.3): Titus' father and brother would no doubt have filled that role.

honourable rather than assiduous: Suetonius means that Titus' real purpose was to advance his political (rather than his professional) career.

Arrecina Tertulla: The marriage (from c. 63 to 65) with Arrecina Tertulla produced a daughter, named (Flavia) Julia (see *Dom.* 22) almost certainly after Arrecina's mother Julia [?Lupa]. There were a number of links between the Flavians and the Arrecini that dated at least from Gaius' reign. Arrecina's father M. Arrecinus Clemens had been praetorian prefect at the time of Gaetulicus' conspiracy (*Vesp.* 2) and had been involved in Caligula's assassination (*AJ* 19. 38-43). Although his son (also M. Arrecinus Clemens) was 'a member of the senatorial order' (*Hist.* 4.68), he too held the same post as his father: for his subsequent career, see *Dom.* 11. It is also possible that one of Arrecina's sisters (?Arrecina Clementina) married into the Flavian family; Townend (1961: 56) has suggested that she became the husband of Flavius Sabinus (i.e. Vespasian's nephew) and mother of Flavius Sabinus and Flavius Clemens (see *Dom.* 10 and 15). Other family members were appointed to strategically significant posts. Julia [Lupa]'s nephew Ti. Julius Lupus (*lupus* = 'wolf') was prefect of Egypt in 72/3 (*BJ* 7.420; Townend, 1961: 57) and his (?) brother L. Julius Ursus (*ursus* = 'bear') held the same post later in Vespasian's reign, then became praetorian prefect and was granted a consulship by Domitian in 84 (see Jones, 1992: 40-2).

prefect of the Praetorian cohorts: At this time, the praetorian guard consisted of nine cohorts (sixteen under Vitellius) of 1,000 men each under the supreme command of the emperor who delegated his authority to the praetorian prefect (or prefects: usually two but increased to three after Commodus). The post was the highest available to a member of the equestrian order from the Flavians onwards, but, before that, was regarded as inferior to the Prefecture of Egypt.

Marcia Furnilla: Arrecina must have died c. 65 and Titus married Marcia soon afterwards. Daughter (*PIR*2 M 265) of Q. Marcius Barea Sura (M 219: brother of Barea Soranus, consul 52) and Antonia Furnilla, she was closely related to the Annii Polliones and Annii Viniciani, a number of whom had been implicated in conspiracies since the time of Claudius (Jones, 1984: 19-20). Far worse was the fact that her family had fallen into official disfavour during the Pisonian conspiracy: her uncle Soranus and his daughter Servilia perished in 65, being 'offered free choice of death' (*Ann.* 16.33). So the marriage with Titus must have been severed early in 66, well before Nero selected Vespasian and Titus for the Jewish campaign.

illustrious family: Suetonius was correct: her grandfather (consul 34) had been proconsul of Africa in 41/42 and her uncle (consul 52) had the same post in Asia (c. 65-66: Birley, 1981: 75). So the marriage considerably increased the Flavians' social status.

daughter: Titus had more than one daughter (Philostratus, *V. Apoll.* 7.7) and, as there was a Julia in Arrecina's family but not in Marcia's, it seems (Castritius, 1969: 492-504) that (despite Mooney, 1930: 475 and others) this child was Julia's step-sister and must have died young.

quaestor: He probably held the post c. 65/66, at the minimum age, for (apart from being the father of at least one child) he had powerful patrons –

his uncle, the city prefect and his father, a former proconsul of Africa – and was also well known to Nero. Of course, if the family had been granted patrician status in 47 (*Titus* 2), then Titus would almost certainly (Birley, 1981: 13) have been *quaestor Augusti* (quaestor of the emperor). In any case, election to the quaestorship meant automatic admission to the Senate.

in charge of a legion: In the winter of 66/67, Vespasian was given command of the war in Judaea with three legions, one of which, the XV Apollinaris, was commanded by Titus – an unprecedented appointment (see *Vesp.* 6). Titus was sent to Alexandria to bring his legion (c. 5,000 men: he was twenty-seven) to Judaea (*BJ* 3.64-5), whilst Vespasian went from Achaea via the Hellespont towards Syria and, in February 67, reached Antioch (*BJ* 3.8, 29) where he met his other two legions (V Macedonica and X Fretensis) and proceeded to Ptolemais.

Tarichaeae: Situated in Galilee at the southern end of the Lake of Gennesaret, Tarichaeae was fortified by Josephus but fell to Titus with great loss of life late in September 67 (*BJ* 3.462-542).

Gamala: For seven months, Gamala (a city to the east of Tarichaeae) had been resisting the forces of Agrippa II. Vespasian then atttacked with his three legions in a siege that lasted from August to October (*BJ* 4.17-83). Titus, however, was absent, having left to visit Mucianus in Syria (see *Vesp* 6) after the fall of Tarichaeae. Returning to participate in the final siege of Gamala, he led a successful attack on the town. All the inhabitants apart from two women were either killed or else committed suicide.

losing his horse...legs: This incident is not included in Josephus' detailed (Jones, 1992: 408-20) account of Titus' heroics.

5 *[page 24]*

sent to congratulate: He was sent by Vespasian (*Hist.* 1.10) to 'pay his respects' to Galba or, as was subsequently claimed, to stand for the praetorship (*Hist.* 2.1). But, even though he was of the appropriate age, it was far too late for him to offer himself as a candidate, since the elections for 69 had already been conducted. A more likely motivation was a determination to discover the legal status and ensure the continuation of Vespasian's Judaean command, for it had expired on Nero's death (9 June 68). If Josephus' chronology is correct (*BJ* 4.502), the Judaean campaign of 69 did not begin until June of that year: presumably, Galba had not confirmed Vespasian's command by the end of 68. Other issues were more delicate: Galba's dismissal (c. November 68) of the city prefect, Vespasian's brother Flavius Sabinus and, according to Suetonius (*Galba* 22), Vespasian's belief that Galba had sent 'agents to Judaea with orders for his assassination'.

purpose of adoption: It is unlikely (so too *Hist.* 2.1) that Galba would have considered adopting a moneylender's grandson. Titus was no match for

L. Calpurnius Piso Licinius Frugi Licinianus, a descendant of Pompey the Great. However, there was much to be gained in not denying the rumour once the Flavians had secured power.

But when he perceived: Tacitus (*Hist.* 2.1) fills in the details. Towards the end of 68, Titus, Agrippa II and some prominent officials left for Rome but, on reaching Corinth (c. end January 69), they heard that 'Galba was dead and Vitellius was arming for war'. At a meeting of the delegation, Titus argued that it would be foolish for him to continue and become a hostage of either Vitellius or Otho; on the other hand, to return to Judaea might be interpreted as an insult, one that would probably be forgiven so long as his father joined the winner's side. However, if Vespasian claimed the principate, any insults would be forgotten. At Rome, Otho had been proclaimed emperor by the Praetorians (15 January) and remained in office until 16 April; Vitellius was proclaimed by the German legions early in January.

returned: Tacitus again (*Hist.* 2.2) explains. From Corinth, Titus sailed along the coast of Attica and Euboea, thence across the Aegean towards Asia, stopping at Rhodes and Cyprus. From there he crossed the open sea direct to Syria.

having approached the oracle of Paphian Venus: The famous temple and oracle at Paphos in Cyprus was situated on the spot where Aphrodite is said to have landed when she rose from the sea. Titus' visit is described in much the same way but in more detail by Tacitus (*Hist.* 2.1-4), whereas there is no reference whatsoever to Paphos in Josephus who merely states that Titus 'sailed back from Greece to rejoin his father at Caesarea' (*BJ* 4.501). If Titus did land there briefly, the details reported by Suetonius and Tacitus may have been added later in the seventies.

consulting...sea voyage: One of the supposed functions of this sea-born goddess was to grant sailors a safe voyage and Titus was planning to cross the open sea (in the middle of winter) to Syria. Tacitus (*Hist.* 2.4) provides more details. On being assured of 'a clear passage and an open sea', Titus then asked about his own future; the reply 'raised his spirits'.

confirmed in his hope: Vespasian was similarly encouraged when he consulted the oracle at Mt Carmel (*Vesp.* 5).

Having soon obtained this: On Vespasian's accession, Titus' hopes for imperial power were realised.

left to subdue Judaea: So, too, *Hist.* 5.1 and Orosius 7.9. Suetonius compresses the timetable for 69. Titus rejoined Vespasian at Maritime Caesarea (?late February), but, between then and June, whilst preparations were being made for civil war, little is heard of Titus. Presumably, his diplomatic talents were being put to use in dealings with Mucianus in Syria, Agrippa II and Berenice in Caesarea and Ti. Julius Alexander in Alexandria. After the proclamation of Vespasian on 1 July, both he and Titus spent the remaining months of 69 in Syria and Judaea, arranging matters to their satisfaction. With the departure of Mucianus for Italy, Titus was probably left in temporary control of both provinces, though Pompeius Collega may have been responsible for the civil administration of Syria (Jones, 1984: 46-7). Before the end of 69, Vespasian and Titus were in Alexandria, 'planning to invade Africa by land and sea and to shut off Italy's supplies of grain' (*Hist.* 3.48). Vespasian remained in Alexandria until the middle of 70, but Titus was left in charge of completing the Judaean campaign. Presumably, he officially assumed command in January 70, when (and as) he was consul *in absentia*. Occupying a very senior position on his staff was Ti. Julius Alexander, whose 'loyalty, wisdom and experience' was lauded by Josephus (*BJ* 5.45-6). Titus was assigned a substantial force by Vespasian. He retained the three Judaean legions to which were added the XII Fulminata from Syria and 2,000 men from the two Egyptian legions (III Cyrenaica and XXII Deiotariana) who were intended to replace the soldiers taken by Mucianus for the campaign against Vitellius. The auxiliary forces remained as before (see *Vesp.* 4) and the client kings actually increased theirs (Jones, 1984: 50).

slew twelve defenders: According to Josephus, 'he killed a dozen with his own hand' (*BJ* 5.288).

captured it: The campaign began c. 14 April 70. By the middle of June, the circumvallation of the city was complete and attention turned to the Antonia, which was taken c. 5 July. On 10 August, the Temple was captured and destroyed. Only the Upper City remained in Jewish hands and it fell on 8 September; for a discussion of the chronological problems involved, see Levick, 1999: 41-2.

birthday of his daughter: As Marcia Furnilla's daughter died young, the reference is presumably to Julia (*Titus* 4).

saluted him as victorious commander: So, too, Orosius 7.9.6. Josephus (*BJ* 6.316) assigns the salutation a little earlier, to the period immediately following the destruction of the Temple. During the Republic, it had been the soldiers' privilege to bestow the title *imperator* on their commander after a victory. The first so honoured was Scipio Africanus in 209 BC, the last (non-imperial recipient) being Junius Blaesus in AD 22 (Livy 27.19; *Ann.* 3.74). After that, an emperor claimed the title whenever he or one of his generals won a victory and the number of salutations appeared in his official titles – but it was the practice for each emperor to claim the title for the first time on his accession to power. The salutation, however, did not imply a grant of secondary proconsular *imperium*. In itself, the action by Titus' soldiers was comprehensible in the excitement of the moment after a long siege, but Titus' reaction to it (his addresses to his troops: see Jones, 1984: 58) as well as his subsequent behaviour (see below) was to give rise to adverse comment.

demanding...threats: Titus did not give in to their demands – XII Fulminata was sent to Melitene, V Macedonica and XV Apollinaris accompanied him on his tour of the east (then were sent back to their former bases, Moesia and

Pannonia) and X Fretensis remained in Judaea.

suspicion he had tried to rebel: Only Suetonius mentions this rumour. There is no hint of it in the relevant sections of Dio (66.8.6) nor of Josephus (*BJ* 5.1-2).

en route to Alexandria: Although Suetonius compresses Titus' activities after the fall of Jerusalem, details are provided by Josephus (*BJ* 7.23-105). As it was too late to sail to Italy, Titus decided to spend the winter at Agrippa's palace at Caesarea Philippi, but first he and his large retinue (including well over 10,000 soldiers: legions V and XV) proceeded to Maritime Caesarea to celebrate Domitian's birthday (24 October) with elaborate games (more than 2,500 prisoners perished), and from there to Berytus where Vespasian's birthday (17 November) was similarly honoured. After a brief visit to Antioch, Titus and his retinue went to Zeugma on the Euphrates where envoys of the Parthian king Vologaesus (*Vesp.* 6) presented him with a golden crown and congratulated him on his victory over the Jews (see Jones, 1984: 56). He then returned to Antioch, where he remained briefly before setting out for Alexandria, stopping at Jerusalem and Memphis (see below) on the way. He reached Alexandria (according to *P.Oxy.* 2725) on 25 April 71 at 7am (though the papyrus may be referring to his arrival at Memphis: Bowman, 1976: 157).

wore a diadem: In essence, a diadem was a band encircling the head; it was worn by priests – and, as a symbol of sovereignty, by the kings of Assyria and Persia. Romans were always suspicious of those wearing one. In 249 BC, Claudius Rursus had 'set up his own statue with a diadem on its head and tried to take possession of Italy' (*Tib.* 2.2); for Cicero, it was a sign of kingship (*Phil.* 3.5); Julius Caesar had refused to accept one from Antony at the Lupercalia (*Iul.* 79.2) and Gaius came close to wearing one and thereby 'changing the semblance of the principate into the form of monarchy' (*Calig.* 22.1). It was not until the reign of Constantine that a Roman emperor was represented on coins wearing one (*RE* 1.304; Alföldy, 1970: 263-8). So it had connotations that Titus should not have disregarded.

Apis bull: Open deference to eastern deities by Romans of Titus' rank was inappropriate – hence Augustus had refused to 'make a slight detour to visit Apis' (*Aug.* 93), the sacred bull worshipped in Memphis. The cult had reached its height under the Ptolemies and the Roman rulers gave it official status. Apis was regarded as the incarnation of Osiris and was connected with the river-god Nilus. When the bull died, he became Osiris-Apis (the likeliest origin of the name Serapis); he was mummified and entombed under the temple of Serapis at Memphis which was called the Serapeum. The ceremony of consecration is described by the Elder Pliny *NH* 8.71. Titus' behaviour, diplomatically useful though it may have been, would not have been viewed in the same way in Rome as it was in the east – as he should have known.

Memphis: The oldest capital of Egypt and about 25 km south of Cairo, it was rated by Strabo as second only to Alexandria.

interpret in a bad sense: The implication is that news of Titus' behaviour in general and of the Apis incident in particular had reached Italy, had fomented hostility in the capital which, when reported back to Titus, had caused him to return in haste to reassure Vespasian. But as he had reached Memphis only around the end of April and was back in Rome by the middle of June, it was chronologically impossible for an account of what happened at Memphis to have reached Rome and for the subsequent hostile reaction there to be reported back to Titus. At best, Suetonius' version is misleading.

Regium: Rhegium (modern Reggio di Calabria) is located in the extreme south-west Italy.

Puteoli: Situated near Naples, Puteoli (modern Pozzuoli) was an important trading port as early as the Second Punic War and remained so. Rome's eastern exports and imports, including grain, passed through it and it was linked to the *via Appia* by the *via Domitiana*.

rumours: Suetonius' comments and the persistent *CONCORDIA* legend on the coinage from 71 to 73 (e.g. *BMC* 2: 113 and 150) suggest that rumours concerning his behaviour had ultimately reached Rome, fuelled, no doubt, by his addresses to his soldiers following his salutation as *imperator* and his wearing of the diadem. Now, it is not impossible that Titus regarded himself as co-ruler; he may even have hinted at it in the heat of the moment in Jerusalem. However, the salutation did not imply a grant of *imperium* and there is no evidence to suggest that he ever rejected the statement (dated to his own reign) that his victory in Judaea was gained 'under the precepts, advice and auspices of his father' (*MW* 53). But the salutation and the Memphis incident (when news of it finally reached Rome) were open to misinterpretation, especially by the malicious. Opponents may also have made much of his seven-month tour, characterised by elaborate displays and games and by rapturous welcomes in the cities of the east. On the other hand, Vespasian had presumably instructed his son not to return to Italy before the middle of 71 – decades later, Trajan was equally reluctant to enter his capital – and must have intended that a tour of the east (especially the public despatch of so many prisoners) would demonstrate the futility of rebellion against Rome, and also keep his son out of public (and senatorial) gaze, limiting (perhaps) comment on the eastern origins of the family's seizure of power. If so, Titus' occasionally unwise behaviour must have caused him concern.

not expecting him: Josephus, on the contrary, claims that Vespasian was expecting Titus and went to welcome him (*BJ* 7.119).

6 *[pages 24-5]*

partner and protector of the imperial position: Suetonius' summary is not unreasonable. Titus' position was anomalous. He had received a far greater range of powers than any previous imperial heir. Tiberius had received proconsular *imperium* (equal to Augustus') in the last years of the reign; he as well as Agrippa and Drusus had been given tribunician power (*Ann.* 3.56) – but that was all. Now, Silius Italicus (*Pun.* 3.603) and Philostratus (*V. Apoll.* 6.30) both suggest that Titus' powers were equal to Vespasian's; but he was not co-emperor (despite Rogers, 1980: 90) and Suetonius does not make that claim (Jones 1984: 85-7). Vespasian alone appears as *Augustus*, *Chief Priest* and *Father of his Country* on coins and inscriptions; Titus' *imperium* (not discussed by Suetonius) was inferior to Vespasian's (Jones, 1984: 102) as was Titus' actual role in everyday affairs (*Vesp.* 23).

triumphed: On Titus' return to Rome in June 71, the Senate decreed triumphs for both Vespasian and Titus, the first time that a father and son had triumphed at the same time. But they preferred a common ceremony (*BJ* 7.121), described in detail by Josephus, i.e. *BJ* 7.123-31 (preliminaries), 132-47 (procession), 148-52 (spoils) and 153-7 (execution of Simon, the Jewish leader). Suetonius refers to it on two other occasions (*Dom.* 2 and *Vesp.* 8), as does Pliny (*NH Praef.* 3). The standard procedure was for the procession to pass, by a fixed route, from the Campus Martius to the temple of Jupiter on the Capitol. It consisted of the magistrates and Senate, the captives and spoils and finally the triumphant general (magnificently garbed) and his army. To be awarded a triumph, he had to have killed over 5,000 of the enemy in battle, have *imperium* and be fighting under his own auspices. It was also the custom for the soldiers accompanying the general to sing ribald songs directed at him: for two examples, see *Iul.* 49.4 and 51. In this instance, Titus was entitled to a triumph for the successful siege of Jerusalem; before that, he was fighting under his father's auspices (*Titus* 5).

census: See *Vesp.* 8.

colleague in the tribunician power: This was one of the most important of the imperial titles since the bearer was recognised by the Senate as emperor or heir; those failing to obtain senatorial recognition (Clodius Albinus and Pescennius Niger) also failed to assume tribunician power. Titus received it in 71, at some time between June 14 and 7 September (*CIL* 16.24, 26), but most probably on 1 July just after his triumph. So, between 71 and 79, there was a two-year difference between the tribunician numbers of Vespasian and Titus.

seven consulships: Titus' first consulship was held in 70 as his father's colleague (both *in absentia*), then in 72, 74, 75, 76, 77 and 79, all with Vespasian (Gallivan, 1981: 186-9). The Flavians' virtual monopoly of the ordinary consulship was bitterly criticised by the younger Pliny as an example of 'their wretched ambition to match their lifelong power with a perpetual consulship... (and) to appropriate every year and pass on the official purple only when its lustre was tarnished after use' (*Pan.* 58.4). But Vespasian's motives presumably included a desire to establish Titus even more firmly as his successor and to enhance the family's prestige after seizing power in a civil war.

management of almost all official duties: Suetonius exaggerates. Despite

Titus' unprecedented powers, the really important decisions were made by Vespasian alone. According to Suetonius himself, it was Vespasian who created new provinces and sent additional legions to Cappadocia (*Vesp.* 8); who had new buildings erected (8); who revised the senatorial and equestrian orders (9); and who instigated various legal, social and cultural reforms (9-10, 17). Suetonius' anecdotes are equally instructive. A number were directed at the one who formulated financial policy (16), whereas Titus' lack of expertise in these matters appears in the urinal anecdote (23). Moreover, it was Vespasian who poked fun at Demetrius and at Mucianus' sexual preferences (13) and who appointed Mettius Pompusianus consul after being warned of him (14).

dictated letters and drew up edicts: For a discussion of an emperor's role in such matters, see Millar, 1977: 213-28, 253-4, 258-9. In this instance, there seems no reason to doubt Suetonius' claim. Vespasian and Titus would have had a similar approach to administrative problems as was shown after June 79: as far as one can tell from such evidence as is available, Titus' policies as emperor were virtually identical to his father's. Surviving edicts of the period (*MW* 458, 460 and 461) are of no real help, being formulaic in structure and, in any case, may have been composed by the imperial *ab epistulis* along the lines dictated by either Vespasian or Titus.

read out his speeches...quaestor: This was not unusual. In fact, reading an emperor's speeches to the Senate was one of the tasks allocated to the quaestors nominated by the emperor (*Aug.* 56.2; *Ann.* 16.27). When Hadrian held the latter post, he performed that function for Trajan (*HA, Hadr.* 3.1), and, according to a senatorial decree on gladiatorial games, Marcus Aurelius' speech 'was read to us' (*ILS* 5163). Dio also notes that, whenever Vespasian was prevented either by old age or for other reasons from attending the Senate, he had his speeches read out by one of his sons (66.10.6).

prefecture of the Praetorian guard: Suetonius is wrong. The appointment was not unprecedented as Titus' predecessor (Arrecinus Clemens: *Dom.* 11) was a 'member of the senatorial order' (*Hist.* 4.68). Titus may well have had a colleague in the post, for a papyrus (*MW* 329) names Tiberius Julius Alexander as 'prefect of the praet(orians)'. So, perhaps, as Griffin (2000: 10) suggests, Clemens and Alexander were joint prefects for a short time until Clemens was designated to the consulship for 73. Alexander may then have continued in the post with Titus and acquired a reputation similar to his, if one judges from Juvenal's comment (1.131-4), neatly summarised by Turner:

> for Juvenal's unnamed 'Egyptian and arabarch', towards whose statue Juvenal recommends the action of dogs against lamp-posts, no candidate except Alexander has been put forward by commentators. (1954: 63)

On the other hand, Alexander may simply have been recorded as commanding those praetorians who were with Titus in Judaea during the siege of 70. The reasoning behind Titus' appointment is clear enough – witness the significant role of prefects such as Sejanus, Burrus, Tigellinus and Nymphidius Sabinus.

acted in a violent manner: Titus' activities as prefect went beyond what was accepted and regular. Bauman (1974: 182) has conjectured that, although Vespasian and Titus refused (Dio 66.9.1, 19.1) to accept charges of *maiestas* (treason), Titus found an effective substitute in the doctrine of the *manifestus*. The extrajudicial punishment of a 'manifest' criminal required no charge (so no trial) but resulted from popular pressure, which (according to Suetonius) Titus actually encouraged: 'he executed all...whom he most suspected, after suborning men to demand them for punishment'. Some sort of precedent for such a 'procedure' could be found in the Republic: in his speech to the Senate in 63, Cato urged that the Catilinarian conspirators be executed 'just as if they had been caught in the very act of committing capital offences' (Sallust, *Cat.* 52.36). In short, he wanted to sanction the infliction of summary justice.

somewhat uncivil manner: Suetonius frequently praises 'good' emperors for 'behaving like a citizen' (*civilis*), for treating other citizens with respect (*Vesp.* 12), whereas 'bad' emperors are accused of actions unbefitting a good citizen (*Calig.* 52; *Dom.* 12).

Aulus Caecina: Aulus (only Suetonius records his *praenomen* Aulus) Caecina Alienus (*PIR*2 C 95) had a varied career, outdoing even the Vicar of Bray: he had managed to be, in turn, a supporter of Galba (commanding a legion in Upper Germany); of Vitellius (leading one of his armies in the battle of Bedriacum); and finally of Vespasian (being numbered 'amongst his best friends': Dio 66.16.3). For his fate and that of Eprius Marcellus, see *Vesp.* 25. By 79, Vespasian was probably ailing and those senators who feared an unrestrained Titus or hoped to influence an inexperienced Domitian may have planned direct action but were forestalled.

copy of an address: No doubt this was the official version, but it should be regarded with some scepticism. Apart from Titus' expertise as a forger (*Titus* 3), can one imagine an experienced Roman orator (*Hist.* 3.13; Dio 65.10.3-4) reading out a prepared speech? As Levick (1999: 193) points out, had he done so, he would have received a frigid reception from the Guard. The so-called epitomator of Aurelius Victor's *De Caesaribus* provides another explanation for Caecina's execution: 'Caecina was invited to a meal, and hardly had he left the room when Titus ordered him to be slain on the suspicion of having raped his wife Berenice' (10.4); the story appears nowhere else and should be rejected.

security in the future: That Titus faced serious opposition to his accession is stated quite clearly by Suetonius.

great amount of ill will: Support for Suetonius' contention comes from

Dio (66.17.1) who reports the false rumour believed by Hadrian (and others) that Titus had poisoned his father. But, despite the hostility to Titus, the loyalty of the troops was unquestioned and Vespasian's arrangements so thorough that any opposition, whatever its strength, would soon have been crushed.

7 *[page 25]*

brutality: In this section dealing with more of Titus' faults, Suetonius does his utmost to avoid open criticism of his hero; so, whilst he regularly accuses 'evil' emperors of brutality (*Tib.* 61.2, 75.3; *Calig.* 27.1, 32.1, 34.1; *Nero* 26.1 and *Dom.* 3, 10 and 11) and even Vespasian of greed (*Vesp*, 16), he is most careful to stresses that Titus was only suspected of them both.

riotous lifestyle: Suetonius accuses Nero of this at some length (*Nero* 26.1, 30.1-32.1) – and Nero was only two years older than Titus who had been educated with the imperial children from the age of seven or so. In view of Tacitus' comment that Titus' youth was 'enlivened by pleasure' (*Hist.* 2.2), it does not surprise that many feared he would be 'another Nero'.

revels: See *Dom.* 21.

middle of the night: Nero's lasted 'from midday to midnight' (*Nero* 27.2). So we have yet another example of 'Neronian' behaviour on Titus' part.

libidinous nature...eunuchs: Suetonius usually discusses the sexual proclivities of his imperial subjects (Baldwin, 1983: 501-7), even the 'good' ones. None of the unsatisfactory associates of Titus mentioned by Suetonius can be idenfified, though Mucianus could perhaps included amongst the former (on the basis of *Hist.* 1.10 and *Vesp.* 14); for the latter, see Hopkins, 1978: 172-96. Suetonius praises Domitian's action in forbidding castration and regulating the price of eunuchs by including them amongst his commendable acts (*Dom.* 7).

famous passion for queen Berenice: Born in 28 and so eleven years older than Titus, Julia Berenice (daughter of M. Julius Agrippa I) was a descendant of the Hasmoneans and the Herods, both Jewish royal families. She married Marcus (brother of Ti. Julius Alexander: *Vesp.* 6) and then her uncle Herod of Chalcis. On his death in 48, she lived for a time (incestuously according to Juvenal 6.156-8) with her brother Agrippa II; she certainly was regarded as joint-ruler with him (Josephus, *Vita* 180). Then she married Polemo of Chalcis (*AJ* 20.146) but soon returned to live with Agrippa. Her wealth (palaces, *BJ* 2.426; granaries, *Vita* 119; gifts to Vespasian, *Hist.* 2.81), influence and involvement in affairs of state (Tacitus twice calls her 'Queen': *Hist.* 2.2 and 8; she sent cavalry against Gessius Florus: *BJ* 2.310) were well known when Titus first met her in 67 (Jones, 1984: 107). Whatever the nature of their affair, she apparently did not come to Rome until 75 (or perhaps as late as 79: Young, 1999: 162); but 'when Titus perceived that the Romans were displeased with the situation, he sent her away' (Dio 66.15.4); later, 'she returned to Rome again' (66.18.1). Some authorities (e.g. Mooney, 1930: 486) state that she was dismissed twice, once in Vespasian's reign and again in Titus'. Suetonius, however, has no hint of two separate dismissals, though, in *La Clemenza di Tito*, Mozart has Vitellia complain 'e poi, perfido! e poi di nuovo al Tebro richiamar Berenice!' – 'and then, and then, the traitor recalls Berenice once more to the Tiber'. Braund (1984: 120-3) has examined the apparently discrepant versions, pointing out that, if Dio's reference to her dismissal (66.15.4) is assigned to the opening months of Titus' reign (and not the last year of Vespasian's – as Mooney does), then the accounts are consistent. Berenice arrived in 75 and was dismissed 'immediately' (Suetonius) on Titus' accession (24 June 79) and returned before his death (13 September 81). After all, she was exiled 'from Rome' (Suetonius) but not from Italy.

Whatever her role during the last years of Vespasian's reign, she was far from unobtrusive. Quintilian has an interesting comment on her activities at the time:

> Again, some have been judges in cases where their own interests were involved. I note, for instance, in the book of observations published by Septimius that Cicero appeared in such a case, while I myself, when I appeared on behalf of Queen Berenice, actually pleaded before her. (*Inst.* 4.1.19)

The precise nature of her role is puzzling. However, it has been suggested that Vespasian faced a situation where he was obliged to deal with:

> allegations that were a disconcerting mixture of Jewish political and theological charges deliberately formulated in an ambiguous way.... (He could hardly) profess a full knowledge of the minutiae of Jewish religious practice. Berenice would have proved useful in providing a repository of essential experience and information on Jewish practices...(therefore) her appointment to an imperial *consilium* might be defended on the grounds of temporary necessity.
>
> (Young, 2001; for more detail, see Young, 1999: 162-3)

Indeed, she did not lack judicial experience: the apostle Paul appeared before her and Agrippa II (*Acts* 25-6) and see also Josephus, *Vita* 343, 355. Useful, however, as such an appointment may have been, it would, almost inevitably, have aroused considerable opposition, rendering impossible her continued presence in the city. For further speculation on the problem, see Crook, 1951: 162-75 and Rogers, 1980: 86-95.

promised marriage: Whatever the nature of the promise – and at least one ancient authority, Aurelius Victor's so-called epitomator, believed that Titus had married her (*Titus* 6) – there was never a chance that it would have been fulfilled. Marriage to a fifty-one year old foreign princess was simply not possible. The mere hint of it apparently caused considerable unrest in Rome, culminating in the beheading of Heras and the public flogging of Diogenes – for, 'entering the theatre when it was full, Diogenes had denounced the pair in a long, abusive speech' (Dio 66.15.5).

Once the Flavians seized power after the calamitous events of 69, they had to distance themselves in their propaganda from the movement's real origins. Josephus provided the authorised version: Vespasian's acclamation was the spontaneous movement of patriotic soldiers angry on hearing of Vitellius' attacks on Italy and Rome; the reluctant Vespasian had to be forced into accepting the purple (*BJ* 1.24, 4.585 ff., 601). So, the Flavian movement starting as it did in Egypt with the support of Serapis (*Vesp.* 7) could do without links to a 'small-scale Cleopatra' (Mommsen, 1885: 219), for it would have had the appearance of reversing the decision of Actium. In these circumstances, Titus' liaison was an embarrassment and marriage even worse.

rapacity: According to Suetonius, Vespasian and Domitian were guilty for it (*Vesp.* 16 and *Dom.* 3), Titus (as with the charge of brutality in *Titus* 7) only suspected of it. Even though he had a reputation for generosity (*Titus* 8), he, was, in fact, a careful financial administator, as were all the Flavians: 'in money matters Titus was frugal and made no unnecessary expenditures' (Dio 66.19.3). That quality was easily translated into one of meanness and greed.

habit of selling favours: Suetonius presents Titus' serious defects in diminishing order of importance.

judicial decisions: This form of trial (the Latin word is *cognitio*) was the personal judgement of an emperor (assisted by his advisers) or of any holder of *imperium* such as, for example, a provincial governor (Pliny refers to a *cognitio de Christianis* in his letter to Trajan: *Ep.* 10.96). It was distinct from the procedure in the regular courts (*quaestio*: see *Dom.* 10 and *OCD* 1286-7). Titus would have been present at any *cognitio* in his role as praetorian prefect.

another Nero: He was regarded as the standard example of a 'bad' emperor. So Domitian was a 'bald Nero', according to Juvenal (4.38).

changed into the greatest praises: In most of his *Lives*, Suetonius has a clear division (*divisio*) between an emperor's virtues (*virtutes*) and vices (*vitia*), the order in which they are listed depending on the impression he wants to make on the reader. When dealing with a 'bad' emperor such as Nero, virtues (briefly dealt with) precede the vices, and one is left with the memory of the latter – and conversely with Titus. From this point, Suetonius has no reference to Titus' *vitia*; we hear only of his extraordinary *virtutes* and the inordinate praise they elicited.

friends...emperors after also acquiesced: Suetonius' comment is flatly contradicted by Dio – 'Domitian quite outdid himself in visiting disgrace and ruin upon the friends of his father and brother' (67.1.2). Such evidence as we have, however, suggests that Suetonius was correct (see Devreker, 1977:

223-5). In fact, the only 'friend' of Titus attested epigraphically (*AE* 1972, 288) is C. Cornelius Gallicanus who was later (84) appointed consul by Domitian and, under Trajan, was in charge of the *alimenta*. These 'friends' (*amici*) were of some significance. Important decisions were taken by the emperor but, often, in consultation with a restricted circle of available *amici*; they were advisers he could trust. They did not form a recognised constitutional body, but the same people were probably called in regularly for consultation. Most were senators but prominent equestrians (for example, the Elder Pliny: *Ep.* 3.5.9) were frequently invited to attend. The praetorian prefect would, almost certainly, have been present on most occasions (see Juvenal, *Sat.* 4): for other possible *amici*, see Jones, 1984: 135-40. With respect to Dio's comment quoted above, it is worth noting that, whilst we have no evidence that Domitian ceased to consult Titus' *amici*, he did dismiss the latter's senior freedmen. Ti. Claudius Classicus, Titus' chamberlain and chief steward, held no posts under Domitian but was re-employed by Nerva (as *AE* 1972, 574 clearly shows) and the chief financial official since 70 (Tiberius Julius, the father of Claudius Etruscus) was removed from office soon after Domitian's accession, being 'caned with a feather' – exiled to Campania (Jones, 1992: 68-9).

immediately sent Berenice away: This was her first and only dimissal; see *Titus* 7.

such artists in dancing...dominated the stage: Dancers as well as actors were prone to accusations of obscenity. Consequently, Augustus had Stephanio flogged through three theatres (Pompey's, Balbus' and Marcellus') before exiling him (*Aug.* 45.4) and Tiberius also banished them (*Ann.* 4.14). Pliny, too, was far from supportive, condemning 'entertainment where dancing and wailing ran through every kind of buffoonery and effeminancy, expressed in rhythmic antics and shrieks' (*Pan.* 54.1). So Titus' action was intended as a public statement that his behaviour as emperor was to be beyond reproach.

took nothing away from any citizen: Once again, his practice differed from that of bad emperors, described by Suetonius in *Tib.* 49.1-2, *Calig.* 38.1-42, *Nero* 38.3 and *Dom.* 12. What is less clear is Titus' policy towards bequests or legacies made out in his favour. Perhaps he decided to reject them if, in any way, they were to the detriment of someone else such as the testator's children or relatives.

did not accept contributions...permitted and customary: Pliny praises Trajan for the same reason (*Pan.* 41). The 'contributions' mentioned by Suetonius have to be distinguished from regular taxes, for the former were often intended to help in times of natural (or other) disasters. Sometimes they were voluntary (*Aug.* 57.2), at others involuntary (*Calig.* 42; *Nero* 38.3, 44.2); but, in view of the damage caused during Titus' short reign by the eruption of Vesuvius and the three-day fire in Rome, a policy such as this, if it were actually put into practice, borders on the reckless.

hot baths close by: Located quite close to the western side of the Esquiline wing of Nero's Golden House, Titus' baths were still popular under Domitian (Martial 3.36.6). Unfortunately, no physical traces remain, and so it is impossible to substantiate archaeologically the statements of both the Chronographer of 354 and Eusebius ascribing them to Domitian; no doubt Domitian's builders finished what Titus' had begun. We do know that the latter worked hastily – presumably, so that the baths might be completed in time for the dedication of the Flavian Amphitheatre.

sumptuous gladiatorial show: This was held in the amphitheatre; on gladiators, see *Dom.* 4.

amphitheatre: For the Flavian Amphitheatre, see *Vesp.* 9. Titus continued his father's work on the building and it is probable that he added the upper tiers of wooden seats which perished in subsequent fires. Whatever the extent of his contribution, he judged it enough to justify a second dedication in 80 with games lasting 100 days (Dio 66.25.1-5).

old enclosure for naval battles: The idea of staging a mock sea-fight (*naumachia*) on land was not an innovation. Similar contests took place in earlier reigns and at different venues (*naumachia* was also used of the venue) in and near Rome – even in the middle ages, the region between St Peter's and the Castel Sant' Angelo was called the *regio naumachiae* ('sea-fight area': Friedlaender, 1968: 2.76). First attested is that by Julius Caesar in 46 BC in an area called the Codeta Minor on the left bank of the Tiber (*Caes.* 39.1,4). Later, in 2 BC (Vell. 2.100), Augustus held one (*RG* 23, Dio 55.10.7) on 'an artificial lake near the Tiber where the grove of the Caesars now stands' (*Aug.* 43.1). Sea-fights were also staged by Claudius in 52 on the Fucine Lake (*Ann.* 12.56; *Claud.* 21.6) and by Nero (in 57: *Nero* 12.1; and in 64: Dio 62.15.1). Two (Dio 66.25.3) at least occurred in Titus' reign, one in the lake developed by Augustus (as here) and another in a flooded section of the amphitheatre (for a detailed discussion of the logistics involved in staging such a display there, see Coleman, 1993: 48-74). Later, Domitian had a special lake dug near the Tiber, 'in a new place' (Dio 67.8.2-3), indicating he did not use either Augustus' venue or that of Julius Caesar; however, the precise location of Dio's 'new place' is uncertain. See *PA* 358 and Auguet, 1994: 68-71.

gladiators in the same place: On the first day of the games held in the 'old enclosure', the lake was covered with planks supported on piles which enabled both gladiatorial contests and wild-beast hunts to be held; on the second, the planks were removed, the lake drained and chariot races staged; on the third day, the lake was filled and a naval battle took place between 3,000 Athenians and Syracusans (Dio 66.25.3-4).

five thousand wild beasts: Dio gives a figure of 9,000 (66.25.1) but Eutropius agrees (as he usually does) with Suetonius' 5,000. During the Republic, wild-beast hunts were essentially contests with at least an element of competition. Not so during the Empire. What counted was the extent of the slaughter. In Augustus' 26 hunts, 3,500 animals were killed (*RG* 22.3) but 11,000 in the celebration of Trajan's Dacian victory (over 123 days: Dio 68.15.1). For more detail on beast hunts, see Balsdon, 1969: 302-8 and Auguet, 1994: 81-119.

8 *[pages 25-7]*

most generous: Kindness was one of the qualities assigned to 'good' emperors or those close to them (e.g. to Germanicus in *Calig.* 3.1). Proof of it was manifested by an emperor's generosity. Titus stated that he was acting 'with generosity' in a letter (from the third month of his reign) to the people of Munigua (*AE* 1962, 288) remitting a fine imposed on them; but it is clear that it cost him nothing, since someone else had to pay it (Griffin, 2000: 51). Usually associated with this quality was foresight (*providentia*), which appeared not infrequently on the coins of both Vespasian and Titus (e.g. *BMC* 2: 476).

all past benefits: The Latin word for this (*beneficia*) was a technical term for a special privilege such as immunity from taxation granted to a community or even to an individual by a specific emperor and, at first, it was open to review by his successor. In fact, emperors frequently rescinded *beneficia* granted by their predecessors – *Calig.* 38.1; *Claud.* 11.3; *Nero* 15.2; *Galba* 14.3 and *Vesp.* 8 (with *Nero* 24.2: Achaia lost the liberty granted by Nero when Vespasian declared it a 'senatorial' province). On the other hand, in a letter of 12 Oct. 77 (*MW* 460), Vespasian confirmed the *beneficia* made by Augustus to the Vanacini (in Corsica) but which had been revoked by Otho. Titus' proposal apparently established a precedent, for 'Domitian issued a proclamation confirming all the gifts made to any persons by them (Vespasian and Titus) and by other emperors' (Dio 67.2.1).

a single edict: So, too, Dio 66.19.3 and Aurelius Victor 10.2. On edicts, see *Dom.* 2.

servants warning him: In Eutropius' version, Titus was warned by his friends (7.21.3). Suetonius, however, is presumably referring to senior imperial freedmen such as Ti. Claudius Classicus (*AE* 1972, 574; Weaver, 1980: 150-6) who was both chamberlain and head of the emperor's entire domestic organisation (holding these posts simultaneously was unprecedented) and to Claudius Etruscus' father (Ti. Julius), head of the Treasury. They would clearly have been in a position to comment with authority (and dismay) on Titus' generosity.

promising more...fulfil: Image and reality (or, in modern political jargon, promise and performance) should not be confused: Titus was frugal in money matters (Dio 66.19.3a). Suetonius reflects the enduring success of Titus' propaganda, in that the image of generosity he created was still in vogue some forty years after his death.

I have lost a day: The anecdote's propaganda value was not lost to posterity, being cited in the *Epit. de Caes.* (10.9), by Eutropius (7.21.3), Themistius

(*Orat.* 6) and Ausonius (*Grat. Act.* 16.72: he contrasts the 'excessive, scarcely tolerable *parsimonia et austeritas*' of Vespasian). Over a millenium later, Racine has Titus lamenting 'Et de ce peu de jours, si longtemps attendus, / Ah! malheureux! combien j'en ai déjà perdus' (*Bérénice* 4.4), whilst Sextus, in Mozart's *La Clemenza di Tito*, says of his friend Titus 'inutil chiama, perduto il giorno ci dice, in cui fatto non ha qualcun felice' – 'He calls the day useless and wasted in which he has not made someone happy'.

geniality: This was another desirable imperial virtue, denoting successful interpersonal relations between emperor and people. It was displayed by Augustus (*Aug.* 53.2) and even, at first, by Nero (*Nero* 10.1). Vespasian set an example for his sons: '(He spent) most of his time in the Gardens of Sallust. There he received anybody who desired to see him, not only senators but also people in general' (Dio 66.10.4). See Bradley, 1978: 74.

gladiatorial show: Suetonius almost always discusses an emperor's behaviour at the Games; it was another of his assessment-criteria. For instance, unlike Titus, Caligula decided what the people would like (*Calig.* 26.5-27). Titus' behaviour is also contrasted with his brother's (*Dom.* 10).

neither refused anything when people asked: Requests were often made to the emperors at the games – with varying degrees of success. According to Josephus, 'the assembled throngs make requests of the emperors according to their pleasure. Emperors who rule that there can be no question about granting such petitions are by no means unpopular' (*AJ* 19.24). But when the people at the games 'desperately asked Caligula to grant some relief from the burden of taxes', he refused and had 'a very large number' executed (19.25-6).

Thracians: They were a class of gladiators deriving their name from the fact that they were armed 'in the Thracian manner', with a small, round shield and a short, curved sword. Often, they fought against the *murmillones*, so called because of the image of a fish (*mormyr*) on their helmets. See further Auguet, 1994: 46.

like a supporter: We have instances of partisan support for particular teams in the Circus (e.g. Vitellius and Caracalla favoured the Blues, Caligula and Nero the Greens), as well as for individual gladiators and particular kinds of fighters. Indeed, the tombstone of a slave oil-dealer named Crescens recorded that he had been a supporter of the Blues in the Circus and of the Thracians in the amphitheatre (*CIL* 6.9719). Both Titus and Caligula favoured the Thracians, Caligula even appearing as one and appointing one to command his German Guard (*Calig.* 54.1, 55.2). Domitian, however, a supporter of the *murmillones* (above), opposed the Thracians as one of their supporters found to his cost (*Dom.* 10).

keeping his dignity safe: A balance had to be maintained between levity and dignity. Of the other emperors, only Augustus is attested by Suetonius as possessing dignity (*Aug.* 25.1), whilst Claudius (*Claud.* 21.5) and Vespasian are said to have lacked it (*Vesp.* 7 and 22).

impartial behaviour: Titus is effectively being ranked by Suetonius with Augustus, the only other emperor to whom he assigns this quality (*Aug.* 53.1).

hot baths: Efforts such as this, designed to secure popular approval, implied no loss of dignity. On the contrary, similar behaviour is attested for Augustus (*Ann.* 1.54) – and Charlemagne (Einhard 22: cited by Mooney, 1930: 491).

Vesuvius: An earthquake on 5 February 63 was the prelude to Vesuvius' first recorded eruption on 24 August 79 that destroyed Pompeii, Stabiae and Herculaneum. According to Dio, volcanic ash spread as far as 'Africa, Syria and Egypt, and it also reached Rome, filling the air overhead and darkening the sun' (66.23.4). He provides a detailed description of the event (66.21.1-23.5) as does the younger Pliny (in two letters to Tacitus: *Ep.* 6.16 and 6.20) – it caused the death of his uncle, the Elder Pliny who, as prefect of the Misenum fleet, had sailed up to the scene of the disaster. Dio adds that 'these (volcanic) ashes...later brought a terrible pestilence upon the Romans' (66.23.5).

fire at Rome: The fire occurred in 80 when Titus was on his second visit to the disaster area of Campania; it raged over the city for three days and three nights. Buildings destroyed (according to Dio 66.24.1-2) included the Temples of Sarapis, Isis and Neptune, the Saepta, the baths of Agrippa, the Pantheon, the Diribitorium, the theatre of Balbus, the stage-building of Pompey's theatre, the Porticus of Octavia with its libraries and, most seriously, the Temple of Jupiter Optimus Maximus on the Capitol (*Vesp.* 8), the reconstruction of which was begun by Titus at once (certainly by 7 December 80: *MW* 11, line 12) and completed by Domitian (*Dom.* 5). Its effect was all the worse as it was concentrated in the ninth Region that had largely escaped the fire of 64 and so still contained all the faults that enabled fire to spread rapidly – narrow streets and poorly constructed buildings.

plague of unprecedented magnitude: Plagues (probably typhus or smallpox) are known to have occurred previously, in 23 and 22 BC (Dio 55.33.4, 54.1.1-2) and in AD 65 (*Ann.* 16.13) when 30,000 died in a single Autumn (*Nero* 39.1). Other writers (Dio 66.23.5, *Epit. de Caes.* 10.13) refer to the outbreak in 80, presumably the one assigned by Eusebius to 77 when (he claims) almost 10,000 perished. Hopkins (1983: 209-10), in a discussion of the mass burials necessitated by these outbreaks, cites the example of a huge pit examined by Lanciani in the late 19th century that must have contained something like 24,000 corpses.

unparalleled love of a parent: Titus' personal involvement underlines the nature of the Empire. It was – or was seen to be – a benevolent autocracy, with the emperor as *pater patriae* ('father of his country').

consolation by means of edicts: As Millar notes, 'emperors normally used in their edicts language which implies that these are essentially personal decisions and pronouncements' (1977: 258). Again, we have Titus the benevolent autocrat.

offering help...property sufficed: Titus, it seems, assumed personal responsibility for all the expenses. True or not, it illustrates further the centralisation of power in the emperor's hands.

Campania: Dio states that two ex-consuls were appointed (66.24.3); they would have been involved in various judicial duties such as investigating claims and in supervising reconstruction (*Digest* 50.4.18.10). We have epigraphic evidence (from a Naples inscription: *MW* 54) of Titus' work in the restoration of damaged buildings in Campania.

property...no surviving heirs: Under Augustus, such unclaimed property would have legally passed to the *aerarium* or public treasury (Ulpian *Reg.* 28.7), but, by the time of the Antonines, to the (imperial) *fiscus* (*Reg.* 17.2). Less clear, however, is the legal position in the interim: already under Tiberius it seems that the *fiscus* was trying to assert its claims (*Ann.* 2.48). So Titus' actions may have been technically illegal – but the distinction between the public and imperial treasuries (see *Vesp.* 16) was not really significant as the emperor exercised control over both. Quite possibly the *fiscus*' claims had been 'legalised' by (or in) 79.

only one to have lost property: Perhaps he was regretting his much publicised generosity and not merely lamenting the general financial situation exacerbated by the expenses involved in assisting those who had suffered by the eruption of Vesuvius.

the adornements...villas: The property at Titus' disposal was not inconsiderable, for he had inherited not only Vespasian's land, villas and their contents, but also everything owned by the Julio-Claudians. Particularly valuable would have been the innumerable statues, golden objects and paintings, not least of which was Nero's ruthlessly ('he stripped many temples of their gifts': *Nero* 32.4) gathered collection (*NH* 38.84).

equestrian class: Equestrian appointments were made by the emperor alone. Titus' decision was consistent with the ever-increasing tendency during the first century of the Empire for effective control of public building to pass into imperial control, just one more indication of the increasing centralisation of power and influence.

swifter: Suetonius, the bureaucrat, obviously equated centralisation and efficiency.

no divine or human aid: No doubt Titus resorted to traditional Roman ritual as well as to the non-traditional such as the cult of Serapis, for its alleged healing power was familiar to the Flavians (*Vesp.* 7).

sacrifice: Epidemics could be interpreted as punishment inflicted on the world by the gods whose wrath had to be propitiated by sacrifice.

informers: In the absence of an office of public prosecutions, accusations were brought forward by private individuals to the president of the appropriate court; and informers found it profitable to produce as many accusations as possible, for successful prosecutions brought them a share of the accused's property. Before long, informers became a recogised group (*Ann.* 4.30). The attitude of the early emperors towards them was inconsistent. Titus had them flogged or exiled or sold into slavery (*Titus* 8; Dio 66.19.3); even Caligula and Nero began by discouraging them (*Calig.* 15.4; *Nero* 10.1). Tiberius both encouraged and discouraged them (*Tib.* 61.2; *Ann.* 1.73, 4.30). So too Domitian: at first, he discouraged them, but later his policy changed (*Dom.* 9 and 12).

The accession of the new emperor was obviously an ideal time for charges to be laid against informers, particularly against those who had escaped punishment in 70. Quite a few had been accused during the vigorous debate at that time (reported by Tacitus: *Hist.* 4.42-3), but 'Mucianus spoke at length in favour of the informers (and) the senators relinquished the liberty they had begun to exercise' (4.44). Years later, Pliny saw the accession of Nerva as a chance to act as Titus' senators had done in 79: 'Once Domitian was killed I decided on reflection that this was a truly splendid opportunity for attacking the guilty, avenging the injured, and making oneself known' (*Ep.* 9.13.2). Titus, then, acted on the assumption that immediate action would win him much-needed senatorial support.

accusers: Under the Antonines, the law provided that those who supplied informers with material should receive the same punishment as informers (*Dig.* 49.14.1).

ordered: That the action was taken on Titus' direct orders is confirmed by Pliny's reference to punishment being inflicted as a result of 'an edict of Titus' (*Pan.* 35.4 – a laudatory account of the action taken by Titus and Trajan against informers). By dealing with them so stringently, Titus would have earned popular as well as senatorial approbation, for their property would have been confiscated to the imperial *fiscus* and the proceeds no doubt used to assist those in need following the disasters mentioned above.

soundly beaten: The same account appears in Dio 66.19.3.

whips and clubs: So not all the informers were senators or even free men. The *Digest* (48.19.10) provided that slaves would be beaten with whips but free men with clubs. Hence, on Commodus' death, the senators shouted 'Cast informers from the Senate; the club for informers!' (*HA, Comm.* 18.16).

arena: Martial also refers to the incident – 'the huge arena could not hold the guilty and the informer has the exile he once bestowed' (*Spect.* 4.4-5).

sold: Again, some of the informers must have been slaves or aliens as Roman citizens could not be sold into slavery. In Roman law, the penalties varied according to the criminal's social status.

taken away...islands: Dio believes that the penalty was far less severe, since he states that Titus simply 'banished the informers from Rome' (66.19.2).

harshest islands: For the five degrees of exile, see *Vesp.* 15. Banishment to an island was common in the Empire. Julia was sent to Pandateria, Agrippa Postumus to Planasia (*Aug.* 15, 65); Agrippina was exiled to Pandataria and Nero (Germanicus' son) to Pontia (*Tib.* 53, 54); for Domitilla's place(s) of exile, see *Vesp.* 3. Even more remote, it seems, were the islands mentioned by Seneca who describes his place of exile (Corsica) as 'barren and precipitous on every side' and names the 'rockiest islands [as] Sciathus and Seriphus, Gyarus and Cossura' (*Helv.* 6.4 – the latter near Malta, the rest in the Aegean).

forbade actions...several laws: Someone charged and acquitted under one law could not be prosecuted for the same offence under another law.

status of...dead: A person's legal status (free born, freedman or slave) was of interest to an informer who would try to prove that a deceased person had had no right to the status of free born and that therefore the will was invalid.

certain number of years: The actual number of years in Titus' enactment is not recorded by any of our sources, but later refinements of the law by Nerva (*Dig.* 40.15.4) and by Marcus Aurelius (*HA, M. Ant.* 10.2) specified a period of five years. However, the *Digest* (above) also assigns the reform itself not to Titus but to Nerva ('The deified Nerva was the first of all to forbid [this] by an edict'). However, Suetonius' version should be preferred; as Hadrian's Chief Secretary, he was in a position to know the facts and perhaps Titus' limit differed from Nerva's.

9 *[page 27]*

Pontifex Maximus: All emperors until Gratian (c. 375) held the position of Chief Priest. He was head of the state religion, and of the sixteen official priests (Dio 42.51.4). Augustus was elected in the traditional manner, by seventeen of the thirty-five tribes chosen by lot; later emperors received the post from the Senate (separately from their other powers), with (possibly) a formal announcement in the assembly. Augustus' election did not occur until 12 BC because he continued to allow Lepidus to hold the office (*Aug.* 31.1; *RG* 10.2). On official documents, it was usually the first of an emperor's 'Republican' titles and it was in this role that he could deal with offences against religion – hence Domitian punished the errant Vestal Virgins (*Dom.* 8). It was conferred on Augustus in March, that month being retained by the Julio-Claudian emperors. Tiberius, for instance, did not become chief priest until March 15 AD, more than six months after Augustus' death (17 August 14). Not so Titus: *p[ontifex] m[aximus]* appears on a coin of July 79 (Buttrey, 1980: 25) and he was already a *pontifex* in 72 (*MW* 84). Probably, he assumed the title of chief priest on 1 July, at the same time as his ninth tribunician power (*Titus* 6).

hands clean: He would therefore be free of any defilement that might exclude him from the sacred rites (McGuire, 1980: 149). We are also reminded that he was soon to be praised 'for not having put a single senator to death' (Dio 67.2.4). All this is illustrated by the next anecdotes.

neither instigator...death of anybody: Such statements were essential to counteract the odium attached to his activities as praetorian prefect, not least of which was the execution of Caecina (*Titus* 6). Dio asserts that 'during his reign, Titus put no senator to death, nor, indeed, was anyone else slain by him during his rule' (66.19.1).

not lacking a reason: Suetonius implies (and Dio states bluntly: 66.19.1) that there were conspiracies against Titus; later (*Titus* 9), he assigns responsibility to Domitian.

two men of patrician family: Dio has the same story – but about Nerva (68.3.2); Aurelius Victor repeats Suetonius' account, although he describes the two offenders as senators rather than as patricians (10.3). While Suetonius does not reveal their identity, he does indicate that they aspired to the throne and that they suffered under a later emperor. On that criteria, six candidates emerge. Five were executed by Domitian: Civica Cerialis (probably a patrician: Eck, 1970: 109), Salvidienus Orfitus, Salvius Cocceianus, Acilius Glabrio and Aelius Lamia (see Dom. 10 for their careers). Last and likeliest was Calpurnius Piso Crassus Frugi Licinianus. Apart from the fact that he was descended from Pompey and Crassus, his father was one of the four sons of M. Licinius Crassus Frugi (consul in 27) and of Scribonia, both of whom were put to death by Claudius c. 46 together with one of their sons, Cn. Pompeius Magnus. Of the surviving three, M. Licinius Crassus Frugi (ordinary consul in 64 and father of the patrician in question) was killed by Nero c. 67, L. Calpurnius Piso Frugi Licinianus, the Piso adopted by Galba, perished with him in 69 (*Hist.* 1.44) and M? (Licinius) Crassus Scribonianus was assassinated in 70. Furthermore, Calpurnius' maternal grandfather and uncle had also been executed under Nero (Dio 63.18.2). With that pedigree, it is not surprising that he was banished by Nerva to Tarentum (Dio 68.3.2: *Epit. de Caes.* 12.6), then by Trajan to an unknown island (Dio 68.16.2) only to be killed by one of Hadrian's procurators 'whilst trying to escape' (*HA, Hadr.* 5.5).

The theme of Titus the merciful endured. Sixteen hundred years later, Mozart was clearly impressed by it since it is the basis of *La Clemenza di Tito*; but that opera's libretto (by Metastasio) had first been used by Caldara (in 1734) and by at least thirteen other composers (including Gluck) before Mozart (Osborne, 1972: 302).

convicted: Since Titus 'would not entertain cases based on the charge of treason' (Dio 66.19.1), the two patricians must have been tried in the Senate, 'convicted' under the Julian Law of Treason and only then was the emperor involved – they appealed to him.

warn them to desist: The anecdote illustrates Titus' adherence to one of the traditional imperial virtues, clemency (*clementia*). But this quality is not stressed in the official propaganda (for instance, it does not appear on Flavian coinage), no doubt because of its autocratic connotations.

given by fate: Vespasian and Titus always stressed the 'official line': their rise to power was due, not so much to military supremacy, but rather to fate (as here), good fortune (*Titus* 1) or divine support (*Vesp.* 4, 5; *Hist.* 2.78, 5.13).

his own runners: A further instance of imperial *clementia*. The runners were slaves employed as messengers; for Domitian's, see *Agr*. 43.3.

invited to an intimate dinner party: In view of Caecina's fate, a dinner invitation from Titus would have been received with more than a little apprehension.

swords of the fighters: These contests usually began with a parade of the gladiators, followed by a display with wooden swords. At this point, the real weapons were produced and inspected by the giver of the games (*editor*) to ensure that they complied with the regulations. By assigning this privilege to the conspirators, Titus made a public display of his clemency.

birth star: See *Vesp*. 14, *Dom*. 10 and 14.

brother...plotting: Similar accusations appear in other (post-Domitianic) sources (*Dom*. 2; Dio 66.26.2; *Epit. de Caes*. 10.11). Whatever their accuracy, it seems from a remark of Pliny that Titus' attitude to Domitian was far from friendly; Julius Bassus, we are told, being a friend of Domitian, was therefore afraid of Titus (*Ep*. 4.9.2). But, apart from the fact that brotherly hatred was someting of a literary topos, the notion of 'plotting' may have arisen from other factors: the difference of twelve years in the brothers' ages, their education (Titus' at court) as well as Titus' absences (for more than ten years) in Germany, Britain and Judaea – in effect, for most of Domitian's teenage years. Their relationship was probably characterised by mutual indifference and ignorance: the assured, gregarious and successful Titus must have had little in common with his retiring, uncertain and suspicious younger brother.

support of the army: According to Tacitus, Mucianus tried to limit Domitian's contact with the army (*Hist*. 4.68, 85) whilst Suetonius reports his offer of a double donative to the troops (*Dom*. 2). He wanted to be given command of the proposed campaign against the Alani and even tried to bribe oriental kings to request his leadership in similar circumstances (*Dom*. 2). Lack of military experience must have been galling to an eighteen-year-old Roman aristocrat who had a number of close relatives (Vespasian, Titus, Flavius Sabinus, Petillius Cerialis, Caesennius Paetus and Traianus) who not only had been given command of a legion but had actually led one into battle (which was comparatively rare). Perhaps Domitian's desire to emulate them was, after 96, reinterpreted as treason.

contemplating flight: That Domitian planned to lead an army against Titus (as Suetonius implies) seems to have been an invention of post-Domitianic historians.

kill him: This would have run counter to his promise not to put a senator to death. But at least he had other heirs, the son and grandson (*Dom*. 10) of Vespasian's brother Sabinus.

remove him: Exiling Domitian would have been a public admission of family disunity.

colleague and successor: The word 'colleague' (*consors*) appears in *Ann*.

1.3 and *Pan.* 8.6 associated with tribunician power, in Valerius Maximus (6.4.2) with the censorship and, in later Latin, the word is used of the relationship between the two Augusti (*Amm. Marc.* 26.4.1). Domitian received none of these positions or titles, nor was he made praetorian prefect nor given some form of proconsular *imperium*. Another significant omission appears in the grant of imperial salutations. The first of these (*IMP. I*) was normally awarded on an emperor's accession, the only known exception being Titus who was already *IMP. XIV* before Vespasian's death (and remained so for some months after it), so facilitating the change from father to son. Titus made no such offer to Domitian, who became *IMP. I* only on his accession. So, after Vespasian's death, he remained 'Caesar' and 'Leader of the Youth'; all that he received from Titus – who was young enough to marry again and produce a son – was the ordinary consulship of 80 and 82. Titus' repeated assurances were but empty words.

tears: Resorting to tears was something of a family trait, faithfully reported, no doubt by the pro-Flavian sources. So Vespasian wept even when those who deserved it were punished (*Vesp.* 15).

begging him in private: We are entitled to wonder about the identity of those witnessing this alleged emotive scene between the brothers – it may well have been just another post-Domitianic invention.

10 *[pages 27-8]*

death: Numerous versions exist of the circumstances surrounding Titus' death. Suetonius' account is followed by the so-called epitomator of Aurelius Victor (11.1), but Victor himself states that Domitian poisoned him (10.11). Philostratus believes that Titus died after eating a poisonous fish known as the sea-hare that had been introduced into his food by Domitian (*V. Apoll.* 6.32). According to Dio, Domitian placed Titus in a chest packed with snow while he was still breathing in order to hasten his end (66.26.2-3), whereas Plutarch claims that he died through unwise use of the baths when ill (*De Tuenda San. Praecepta* 3). In a Jewish version, Titus is said to have been tormented for seven years by a gnat buzzing in his brain (his punishment for the destruction of Jerusalem), finally growing into a large bird with iron talons and a bronze beak (Jones, 1984: 155).

humanity...the greater loser: According to Suetonius, death cost Rome a wise and benevolent ruler, replacing him with the harsh tyranny of Domitian. Ausonius, however, states that Titus was 'fortunate in the brevity of his reign' (*Caes.* 11), recalling Dio's comment that, had Titus lived longer, his good reputation might have been due 'more to good fortune than to merit' (66.18.5).

games: This is a contentious passage, as commentators differ as to which 'games' are in question. Mooney (1930: 502) believes that Suetonius is referring to the games of 80 at the opening of the Flavian Aphitheatre and criticises

Suetonius' account as 'inaccurate'. His interpretation gains support from Dio who (it must be admitted) states clearly that the reference is to the events of 80:

> The spectacles that were offered lasted for a hundred days... After he had finished these exhibitions, and had wept so bitterly on the last day that all the people saw him, he performed no other deed of importance, but in the next year...he passed away at the same watering-place that had been the scene of his father's death.
>
> (66.25.4, 26.1)

Now, if Dio is correct, then Titus must have been suffering from a terminal illness that (so Dio implies) kept him out of Rome for more than a year. But the games of 80 were not the only ones held in his reign (see, for example, *Titus* 8 and 9) and he is also attested as being present at the meeting of the Arval Brethren held in Rome on 19 May 81 (*MW* 12). Suetonius does specifically name the games of 80; presumably he means those held towards the middle of 81, perhaps in honour of the deified Vespasian (end June). Dio's account has been pressed into service by those arguing that Titus suffered from a progressive fatal illness of some sort – even a brain tumour, a theory given (!)support by the Jewish version of his death (gnat in the brain: see above).

wept copiously: So, too, Dio 66.26.1. See *Titus* 9 – but, in this instance, the implication is that Titus' tears represented a genuine reaction. Perhaps this public weeping was intended to reflect his concern for the victims of the various natural catastrophes of the year rather than his fear of imminent death.

Sabines: Both Vespasian and Titus spent the summer season at the family property situated at Cutiliae near Reate (*Vesp.* 1 and 24; Dio 66.26.1).

victim had escaped: The escape of a sacrificial animal was clearly a bad omen (*NH* 8. 183); such an event 'foretold Galba's end exactly as it happened' (*Galba* 18.1).

weather was clear: Thunder from a clear sky was thought to be a sign from Jupiter, and of an ambiguous nature, whereas it was regarded as quite favourable if it came from the left. But Titus regarded the former as a dire omen, confirming the first (clearly dire) one.

lodging place: There were lodging places at regular intervals on the Salarian Way (the direct road between Rome and Reate), the first being at Eretum (modern Grotta Marozza) about 30 km. from Rome, the next at Vicus Novus (modern Osteria Nuova) some 25 km. away and about 12 km. from Reate; Cutiliae was about 12 km. further on. See McGuire, 1980: 167-8.

fever: Bastomsky has argued (1967: 22-3) that Titus could have died from a malignant strain of malaria, but the evidence put forward is not convincing. Whatever the truth, when Titus left for his summer residence, presumably at the usual time of late June, he must (in view of his tears and the reaction to the omens) have had the symptoms of the disease from which he died more than two months later. Apparently, his condition worsened by the time he reached Eretum since this was where he was transferred to a litter. In these circumstances, there seems no reason to doubt Suetonius' assessment that the death was natural and that Titus died as a result of a 'fever'.

one and only one exception: Dio offers two explanations:

> The prevailing view is that of those who say that he referred to his having intercourse with his brother's wife, Domitia. Others, and these I am inclined to follow, say that what he meant as his mistake was that he had not killed Domitian when he found him openly plotting against him. (66.26.3-4)

Other (far less likely) suggestions are that he may have regretted executing Caecina or altering Vespasian's will (McGuire, 1980: 172) or destroying Jerusalem (Henderson, 1927: 11) – or, even, 'his impious entry into the forbidden Holy of Holies in Jerusalem' (Graves, 1957: 293).

Domitia: See *Dom.*1.

would not have denied: There is remarkably little evidence to support Suetonius' generalisation. Apart from Dio's reference to her affair with Domitian whilst still married to Aelius Lamia (66.3.4), the only hint of her 'unchaste activities' appears in both Suetonius (*Dom.* 3) and Dio (67.3.1) who refer to her alleged adultery with the actor Paris, for which he even planned to have her executed. The supposed liaison is discussed by Vinson (1989: 438-40) who dismisses it as 'belonging to the realm of invective fantasy'. Years earlier, Scott (1936: 83) had argued that she was to be identified with the 'imperial harlot' of Juvenal 6.118; but, as Syme observed, 'she was not that noctivagous and indefatigable empress' (1937: 33). The tradition, hostile to Domitia and well-represented by Suetonius, was not the only one, however. Five centuries later, she is portrayed as devoted to her husband despite his manifold failings. In his *Secret History*, Procopius saw Domitian as similar in appearance and actions to his *bête noire*, Justinian, whereas Domitia was always highly respected, had wronged no one and had approved of none of her husband's actions (8.12-22).

11 *[page 28]*

died in the same country house: These details also appear in the *Epit. de Caes.* 10.15, Orosius 7.9.14 and Eutropius 7.22. He died in the villa at Aquae Cutiliae; see *Vesp.* 24.

Ides of September: 13 September 81. It is only in March, May, July and October that the Ides fall on the fifteenth (and not the thirteenth) day of the month.

two years, two months and twenty days: His reign began on 24 June

79. Dio (66.26.4) and the *Epit. de Caes.* (10.1) agree with Suetonius, whereas Eutropius (7.22.1) has two years and eight months as the length of the reign and Aurelius Victor (10.5) two years and 'almost nine months'.

forty-second year: Most ancient sources (Dio 66.26.4, *Epit. de Caes.* 10.1 and Eutropius 7.22.1) agree that Titus died in his 42nd year. Aurelius Victor (10.5), however, gives his 40th year, which is at least consistent with the incorrect year of Titus' birth quoted by Suetonius in *Titus* 1. But chronology was not Suetonius' strong point. For instance, he claims that Nero was in his eleventh year when adopted by Claudius (*Nero* 7) and Tacitus assigns that event to AD 50 (*Ann.* 12.25); but Suetonius had already stated that Nero was born on 15 December 37 (*Nero* 6.1). Note also the chronological differences between Aurelius Victor and his so-called Epitomator.

mourning publicly...private grief: Titus is again portrayed as the nation's father, the *pater patriae* (*Titus* 8), in a passage recalling the outpouring of grief at the death of Germanicus (*Calig.* 5-6: see *Titus* 1). Details of the public reaction form a regular part of Suetonius' death-narratives but rarely are Senate, people and army said to agree – they do also at *Tib.* 75.1 and *Vit.* 17 where uniform hostility was evident.

convened by edict: The Senate was usually convened in this way (*Jul.* 80.4).

opening the doors...closed: Eutropius (7.22) alone reveals why the doors were closed – it was night when the announcement was made.

such great praises: The most famous record of his reign still exists, the Arch of Titus on the Sacred Way. It was erected by Domitian and commemorates both his victory in Judaea and his deification. Spoils from the Temple in Jerusalem are shown being carried into Rome and Titus himself appears in triumphal garb riding a chariot, surrounded by attendants, crowned by a winged figure of victory and about to pass through a triumphal arch with Roma guiding his horses. The deification is symbolised on the ceiling of the vault, with Titus astride an eagle being carried upwards (Jones, 1984: 156). For a list of the other honours he received (during and after his reign) in both Italy and the provinces, see Garzetti, 1974: 262.

DOMITIAN

1 *[page 29]*

Ninth day before Kalends of November: 24 October.

father was consul designate: In 51 (*Vesp.* 4). Vespasian's consulship began approximately one week after his son's birth.

sixth region: Augustus divided Rome into fourteen regions (*NH* 3.66; *Aug.* 30.1).

Pomegranate: A street on the Quirinal, corresponding more or less with the Via delle Quatro Fontane (*PA* 326).

temple of the Flavian clan: On the site of the house where he was born, Domitian erected a magnificently decorated temple, intended both as a family mausoleum and as a public expression of his novel policy, the deification of the entire Flavian clan. After his assassination, his nurse, Phyllis, placed his ashes there (*Dom.* 17). No definite traces of the temple have survived.

youth and early manhood: Probably in the years around 64-66, after Vespasian's return from Africa.

poverty and disrepute: Suetonius' summary, whilst exaggerated, is consistent with the 'official' Flavian version of the family's status under the Julio-Claudians – Vespasian could not possibly have been favoured by the (bad) Julio-Claudian emperors.

Clodius Pollio: Not attested elsewhere.

poem of Nero entitled 'Luscio': Nero's literary efforts are mentioned by Tacitus (*Ann.* 14.16, 15.49), Martial (8.70.8; 9.26.9), Pliny (*Ep.* 5.3.6) and Suetonius (*Nero* 24) who also claims (*Nero* 52) to have seen the originals of his verses. The word *Luscio* occurs nowhere else but it may possibly be connected with the adjective *luscus* meaning 'one-eyed'. So a tentative meaning of Luscio would be 'The One-eyed Man'.

nor were there lacking...his successor: At first sight, this reference is puzzling, as Nerva is not only mentioned but identified precisely. Suetonius, writing almost certainly under Hadrian, appears to be accusing the emperor's (adoptive) grandfather of sodomy. Now, whilst there is some dispute about the precise legal penalties, the situation is that a Roman male who engaged in same-sex relations, so long as he did not violate a free-born boy under sixteen, incurred punishment only if he took a passive role. Hence Cicero's attack on Antony for prostituting himself (*Phil.* 2.44) and Vespasian's comment, 'I, however, am a man' (*Vesp.* 13), on Mucianus. See also *Dom.* 8.

fled...Sabinus: For attempts to reconcile the differences in Suetonius' and Tacitus' (Hist. 3.59 ff.) accounts of Domitian's activities, see Wellesley, 1956: 211-14; 1981: 166-90 and Wiseman, 1978: 163-78.

his uncle Sabinus: He was City Prefect (*Vesp.* 1).

forces...present: The forces included the four city cohorts and the watch under Sabinus' command (as City Prefect); so too Tacitus, *Hist.* 3.69.

temple was ablaze: The temple of Jupiter on the Capitol; see *Vit.* 15.3 and *Dom.* 5.

devotee of Isis: Domitian saved himself by mingling in an Isaic procession, appropriately disguised.

across the Tiber...fellow-student: According to Tacitus, Domitian was on the other side of the river, in the house of Cornelius Primus. None of the sources indicate his fellow student's name.

one companion: Flavius Sabinus, the City Prefect's son (Dio 65.17.4).

saluted as Caesar: So, too, *Hist.* 3.86, 4.2 and Dio 66.1.1. Originally, *Caesar* was a *cognomen* used by some members of the Julian family, e.g. by

Julius Caesar. On his death, his adopted son, the future emperor Augustus, added Caesar's name to his own; subsequently, *Caesar* was legally transmitted to those whom Augustus adopted. Claudius and Nero used it, though not legally entitled to do so; presumably they would claim that it was another imperial title. With Vespasian, though, it became the *nomen* of each imperial family member and was used to designate the heir to the throne.

urban praetor with consular power: So, too, *Hist.* 4.3. Such an award was unprecedented.

formal manner: Domitian performed none of the praetor's judicial functions.

handed over...closest colleague: The identity of Domitian's colleague is unknown. Galli (1991: 59) suggests Helvidius Priscus, the only other known praetor for that year (*Hist.* 2.91, 4.53).

showed...would be like: For Suetonius, Domitian was essentially bad and became worse as time passed.

sex with the wives of many men: Three versions of Domitian's alleged profligate behaviour have survived. Dio (66.3.4) has Domitian spending most of his time on his return from Gaul seducing various unnamed married women at his Alban retreat and finally marrying one. Suetonius reverses the order and depicts an even busier Domitian – seduction and distribution of official posts (*Dom.* 1) followed by war (2). Tacitus, however, has Domitian living not at Alba but on the Palatine, engaged in debauchery as well as adultery (*Hist.* 4.2). For a detailed discussion, see Waters, 1964: 54-5 and Vinson, 1989: 431-50.

forcibly took in mariage Domitia Longina...married to Aelius Lamia: Daughter of Corbulo and wife of the eminent patrician Aelius Lamia (*Dom.* 10), Domitia Longina (*PIR*2 D 181) was one of the married women whom Domitian is supposed to have seduced between December 69 and his father's return late in 70. Vespasian then tried but failed to arrange a dynastic marriage for him with Titus' daughter Julia (*Dom.* 22), and subsequently acquiesced in his son's choice, for it was politically advantageous. There were her ties with the opposition. Her father, brother-in-law (Annius Vinicianus) and his brother (Annius Pollio) were victims of the purge following the discovery of the Pisonian conspiracy. No less important was her father's name and reputation. The suicide of Nero's most popular and successful general was now seen to be avenged.

twenty...successor for him also: Dio 66.2.2-3 relates that Mucianus (not mentioned by Suetonius) and Domitian appointed so many officials that Vespasian wrote to Domitian thanking him for allowing Vespasian himself to continue as emperor. Suetonius appears to have forgotten Vespasian's well-attested sense of humour.

2 *[pages 29-30]*

campaign against Gaul and the Germanies: Mucianus and Domitian marched north (*Hist.* 4.68) to assist Cerialis in suppresing the revolt of Civilis and Classicus. On their way, they were informed that the uprising in Gaul had failed and so they stayed at Lyons. Subsequently, there were hints that Mucianus had refused Domitian a command against the Gauls and that Cerialis would not accept Domitian's request for Cerialis to hand over his army to him (*Hist.* 4.86). However, claims such as those of Josephus that he caused the Treveri to surrender (*BJ* 7.85) are, like the comments of Silius Italicus ('even when you were a boy, the yellow-haired Batavians feared you'; *Pun.* 3.607-8), literary excesses at best.

Germanies: Upper and Lower Germany were officially military districts until they were given provincial status some time between 83 and 90.

not necessary: The comment is inaccurate. Mucianus must have regarded it as necessary if he was prepared to leave Rome at such a time.

contrary to the advice: The reference is probably to prominent Flavian senators such as Nerva, Vibius Crispus (*Dom.* 3) and senior family members, including Flavius Sabinus (City Prefect's son) and Arrecinus Clemens (*Dom.* 11), all of whom had a stake in the survival of the new dynasty which had two of its three members out of Rome on active service.

equality with his brother: According to Tacitus (*Hist.* 4.86), Domitian (at Lyons) may have intended to make war on either Vespasian or Titus. But perhaps he had merely expressed desire to see some action.

rebuked: The Cancelleria reliefs convey the opposite impression – not unexpectedly. See the illustrations in Pailler/Sablayrolles, 1994: 48-9.

lived with his father: This would be an unwelcome experience as he had had the freedom of the Alban villa since the end of 69.

aware of his age: Domitian was eighteen.

follow in a litter: Whilst both Vespasian and Titus travelled in sedan chairs where one sat upright, Domitian was obliged to recline in a litter (*Dom.* 19).

Jewish triumph: See *Vesp.* 8.

accompanied...on a white horse: So, too, Dio 66.12.1a and *BJ* 7.152. His place in the triumphal procession paralleled that of Tiberius, who, aged thirteen, rode on the left trace-horse of Augustus' chariot in his triumph for Actium (*Tib.* 6.4).

six consulships: Domitian is attested as suffect consul in April 71 with Pedius Cascus and in June with Valerius Festus; as ordinary consul II in 73 with Catullus Messallinus; as suffect consul III in March and April 75 with Pasidienus Firmus (*MW* 5 wrongly assigns this third suffect consulship to 74); as suffect consul IV in 76 (colleague unknown); as suffect consul V in June or July 77 (colleague unknown) and as suffect consul VI early in 79, possibly replacing his father. In 75, 76, 77 and 79, he could well have replaced the ordinary consul as early as 13 January. For the evidence, see Buttrey, 1980: 32-4 and Gallivan, 1981: 187-8.

one...as 'ordinary': In 73. The ordinary consuls held office at the beginning of the year and gave their names to the year, whilst those who replaced them were referred to as suffect (i.e. replacement or substitute) consuls. Augustus regularised the practice of having suffect consuls in 5 BC and it soon became the norm for one or both ordinary consuls to be replaced. With time, further modifications occurred. One reason for the change was the growing administrative needs of an empire that required more senators of consular rank and so an ever-increasing number of suffect consuls.

brother gave way to him: Titus was not ordinary consul in 73 and there is no evidence that he was ever so designated. Suetonius' statement is not only wrong but 'malicious' (Buttrey, 1980: 33) as well.

pretence of moderation: Suetonius and Tacitus (*Hist.* 4.86) interpret Domitian's modesty as assumed.

enthusiasm for poetry: Domitian's epic poetry seems to have been based on the Jewish War (Valerius Flaccus, *Arg.* 1.12-13) and on the struggle for the Capitol in 69 (Martial 5.5.7). Quintilian claims that no epic poetry could come near Domitian's (10.1.91) and the elder Pliny praises Titus as a poet worthy of comparison with Domitian (*NH Praef.* 5). But Tacitus uses the pejorative 'pretence' to describe Domitian's cultural interests (*Hist.* 4.86), and Suetonius is even less kind (see *Dom.* 20).

despised and rejected: See *Dom.* 20.

public recitals: According to the elder Seneca (*Contr.* 4 *praef.* 2), such recitals developed out of Asinius Pollio's practice of inviting guests to readings of his own works. By the end of the first century AD, they were an inevitable feature of literary/social life, as both Pliny (*Ep.* 1.13.1) and, far more vividly, Martial (3.44.10-13) attest. Imperial precedents for Domitian's performance had been provided by Claudius (*Claud.* 41.1-2) and Nero (*Nero* 10.2).

Vologaesus: After a period of persistent conflict with Rome, he offered Vespasian help in 69 (*Hist.* 2.81, 4.51) and renewed an alliance with Rome (*Nero* 52.2). But it was an uneasy relationship, not improved by Rome's activities on the eastern frontier. See *Vesp.* 6 and 8.

Alani: A nomadic people from southern Russia, they expanded to the south and west during the first two centuries AD, with consequent pressure on other tribes. But their remoteness meant that they never posed a serious frontier problem for the Flavians (despite Mooney, 1930: 514). Vespasian's target was Parthia.

Vologaesus had asked for help: In the early seventies, the Alani attacked Parthia (*BJ* 7.244-51) and Armenia. Two brothers of Vologaesus (Pacorus of Media Atropatene and Tiridates of Armenia) were amongst the first to suffer

(7.247-9). Vologaesus requested help, but compliance would have run counter to Rome's general strategy. Vespasian's deceptive reply was that 'it would not be proper...to interfere in the affairs of others' (Dio 66.15.3).

other kings: Suetonius probably means Vologaesus' brothers (above).

death of his father: See *Vesp*. 24.

double bounty: This bounty (*donativum*) was a sum of money given to the troops by an incoming emperor with the intention of ensuring their support – the military equivalent of the *congiarium* (*Dom*. 4). Not all soldiers received it – the marines and most auxiliaries were ineligible. The amounts paid by each ruler varied considerably. Augustus gave the praetorians 1,000 sestertii each (but in his will), Claudius and Nero made them an annual grant of 15,000 per man, Galba refused to pay any and Vespasian offered them 100 sestertii each. On Domitian's accession, it seems that he paid the same amount as Titus had done (Dio 66.26.3).

partner in the imperial position: See *Titus* 9.

fraud had been applied to the will: Elaborate precautions had been established to prevent the forgery of wills. In this instance, Domitian's barbs were directed against Titus in view of his ability as a forger (*Titus* 3).

plots against his brother: See *Titus* 9.

left as though dead: Accounts of Titus' death and its cause are many and varied (*Titus* 10), but Dio's account is not inconsistent with Suetonius' in so far as he claims that, while Titus was still alive, Domitian placed him in a chest packed with ice to hasten his end and rode off to the praetorian camp in Rome to 'receive the title and authority of emperor' and to give the soldiers the same bounty as his brother had done (66.26.2-3).

no honour except deification: Suetonius is incorrect. Domitian honoured his brother's memory in various ways. He was commemorated on Domitian's coinage (*BMC* 2:313) and on dedicatory inscriptions (*CIL* 6.943-6). He was also honoured in a number of his brother's new buildings – apart from the Temple of the Flavian Family (*Dom*. 1), the Arch of Titus (built in Domitian's reign: see *Titus* 11) and the Temple of Vespasian and Titus (*PA* 556), a shrine dedicated to Titus was set up in the Temple of the Deified (Flavians) in the Campus Martius (*PA* 152-3).

deification: The ceremony of deification must have been held soon after Titus' death (implied in Dio 67.2.1), as was usual – but has to be after 1 October 81 (*MW* 12).

edicts: In theory, an edict was an imperial statement with the force of law but addressed to no particular person (Millar, 1977: 252-9). We know of Domitianic edicts on the subject of (a) vines (*Dom*. 7); (b) the *subsiciva* (*Dom*. 9); (c) seating arrangements in the theatre (Martial 5.8.1); (d) castration (Bauman, 1982: 117); (e) benefits available to former soldiers (Campbell, 1984: 443); (f) informers (Dio 67.1.4); (g) the expulsion of philosophers and astrologers (*Dom*. 10) and, perhaps, (h) the bannng of the sacrifice of oxen (*Dom*. 9).

3 *[page 30]*

solitary retreat: Most ancient sources mention Domitian's preference for his own company. Suetonius refers to it again (*Dom.* 21). Dio repeats the claim (66.9.4-5), as do others, though with more malicious overtones (*Agr.* 39.3; *Pan.* 48.5, 49.2, 49.6). Outdoing both Pliny and Tacitus, Aurelius Victor has him killing flies in seclusion when exhausted by his sexual activities (11.5).

capturing flies: Domitian's practice of killing flies is reported by Dio (66.9.5), Aurelius Victor (11.5) and his so-called epitomator (11.8). Dio turns the item to his disadvantage – Domitian speared flies at the Alban villa whilst pretending to be mad in an effort to avoid Vespasian's displeasure! Since a proverbial method of referring to a deserted place was to say that not even a fly was there, a connection between two quite innocuous habits could be established – Domitian's habit of killing flies linked to his preference for his own company indicated a secretive and therefore cruel nature.

piercing...sharp pen: Made of material such as bone or ivory, the pen was very sharp at one end (for marking the wax as well as for spearing flies) but circular and flat at the other (for erasing what had been written on the wax tablet).

Vibius Crispus: He was one of the four Domitianic friends mentioned by both Statius (*On the German War*) and Juvenal (4.81-93). Suffect consul and the curator of the water supply under Nero, he continued in the latter post under Vespasian, became proconsul of Africa, governor of Spain, returning to Rome in 74 for a second consulship. Under Domitian came the rare award of a third. His wealth, acquired through informing (*Hist.* 2.10), was legendary (Martial 4.54.7). But, above all, Crispus was a survivor – a Neronian consul, drinking companion of Vitellius (Dio 65.2.3), senior advisor to Vespasian and Domitian. Juvenal's summary is memorable: Crispus never swam against the stream, and, by limiting his conversation with the emperor to safe topics such as the weather, he was able to survive the hazards of Domitian's court (4.84 ff.). See *RP* 7.525-35 and Jones, 1992: 57-8.

not even a fly: Only Suetonius attributes the witticism to Vibius Crispus.

Augusta: She received the title on Domitian's accession (14 Sept 81) or else not long after (it appears in the minutes the Arval Brothers for 1 October: *MW* 12). Livia was the first to be named *Augusta* (*Ann.* 1.8); Claudius granted it to Antonia after her death (*Claud.* 11.2), whilst Nero's mother (Agrippina), wife (Poppaea) and daughter (Claudia) received it in their lifetimes (*Ann.* 12.26; 15.23) as did Vitellius' mother (*Hist.* 2.89) and Titus' daughter Julia (*BMC* 2:250).

Domitia: See *Dom.* 1 and 14.

son: The boy's name is unknown. After his death, he appeared on his mother's coins (*BMC* 2:2-3) with the title 'Deified Caesar, son of the emperor Domitian'. However, Desnier's argument (1979: 65) that his name was 'Titus Flavius Caesar' rests on insubstantial grounds. Presumably, he died before 83, since the coins on which he appears do not show Domitian as *Germanicus*. The boy's deification is referred to by Statius (1.1.97), Silius Italicus (*Pun.* 3.629) and Martial (4.3).

second consulship: Held in 73.

after he gained the imperial position: The Latin text is suspicious here and these words are a conjecture of Ihm.

Paris: Paris was an actor from Egypt (Martial 11.13.3-5). Domitian is said to have had him murdered in the street because of his adultery with Domitia (Dio 67.3.1). But Juvenal describes Paris as a powerful member of Domitian's court (7.88). Now this Paris is not easily identified with an actor of Egyptian origin, who is not unlike an earlier Paris, freedman of another Domitia (Dio 63.18.1; *Nero* 54; Vinson, 1989: 440). Moreover, neither resembles the Paris described by Malalas: 'Domitian was in love with Paris, a dancer of the Green faction' (10.49).

divorced: Early in the reign, Domitian 'divorced' Domitia because of her adultery with Paris but was dissuaded from having her executed by Julius Ursus.

alleging that the people demanded it: Dio 67.3.1 also refers to popular support for Domitia's recall.

brought her back: After a brief separation, Domitia returned to the palace – but appears rarely in the sources (Statius, 3.4.17-9; Josephus, *Vita* 429 and *Dom.* 13). What is surprising is his statement that Domitian remarried her. If true, it would have been all but unprecedented, for the only attested example of remarriage within the senatorial aristocracy occurs in the late Republic (Plutarch, *Cat. Min.* 25.2-5, 52.3: for an example of remarriage within the equestrian order, see *Dom* 8). Humbert (1972: 173) and others (but not *RP* 7.559) accept Suetonius' statement. However, it is more likely that Domitian exiled her c. 83, but later was obliged to recall her to counteract the rumours about his relationship with his niece Julia. Dio associates Domitia's recall (not remarriage) with stories about Julia (67.3.1).

turned his virtues into vices: This is the intervening section or division separating imperial vices (1-3) and virtues (4-9), a regular Suetonian technique explained at *Nero* 19.3.

in addition to his natural disposition: Some scholars (Rolfe and Mooney) have translated the phrase as 'it was contrary to his natural disposition'. For Suetonius, however, Domitian was essentially bad but, for some time, hardly gave any indication of it; as time passed, he became worse. See also Wallace-Hadrill, 1995: 151.

4 *[pages 30-1]*

magnificent and sumptuous shows: These were the Capitoline and Secular Games as well as those held each year in honour of Minerva.

amphitheatre: See *Vesp.* 9.

circus: The Circus Maximus, situated in the valley between the Palatine and Aventine was one of Rome's largest (c. 600m by 200m) structures. Estimates of its seating capacity range from 140,000 to 385,000. See Auguet, 1994: 124-6.

two- and four-horse chariots: There were also six, eight and ten-horse chariots (Carcopino, 1956: 217).

battle...cavalry and infantry: So, too, Dio 67.8.2.

naval battle: Titus also staged one in the amphitheatre (*Titus* 7; Dio 66.25.3).

he put on: These words have to be supplied.

beast hunts: Wild beast hunts were introduced in 186 BC by Fulvius Nobilior. There were three types of contest – animals against unarmed criminals or against armed men or against other wild animals. See further Balsdon, 1969: 302-8 and Auguet, 1994: 81-119.

gladiators: Domitian held gladiatorial combats at night, sometimes with female competitors and even dwarfs (Dio 67.8.4). See further Hopkins, 1983: 1-30; Coleman, 1990: 44-73 and Wiedemann, 1992.

night time: Events at night posed no problem for the Romans. Statius, for instance, in describing the effect of the illumination in the amphitheatre, states that 'the sky blazed with light' (1.6.89).

lamp-stands: Suetonius' word (*lychnuchus*) was used of either a lamp-holder or a lamp-stand (*OLD* 1055). Suetonius mentions that they were 'borne by forty elephants' in Julius Caesar's triumphal ascent of the Capitol (*Iul.* 37.2).

fights...women: They are also attested under Nero (*Ann.* 15.32) and Titus (Dio 66.25.1).

quaestorian games: Claudius had forced the quaestors to provide gladiatorial displays at their own expense (*Claud.* 24.2 and *Ann.* 11.22), a regulation abolished by Nero (*Ann.* 13.5) but restored by Domitian.

right...two pairs: It was the practice, according to Seneca (*Ep.* 7.4), to keep some pairs of gladiators in reserve so as to be able to provide an appreciative audience with an encore.

from his own school: There were four at this period, all probably established by Domitian. Situated near the Flavian Amphitheatre, they replaced private gladiatorial schools, at least in Rome itself, and were controlled by imperial procurators.

small boy...head: Dwarfs, jesters and the like formed part of the court in imperial Rome. We hear of Tiberius' dwarfs and jesters (*Tib.* 61.6) and also of Claudius' jesters (*Ann.* 12.49). A special market for dwarfs was located in Rome (Plutarch, *De Curios.* 10.520c), and, under Domitian, we have women and dwarfs fighting in the amphitheatre (Dio 67.8.4), an unarmed dwarf in the arena (Martial 1.43.10) and a fighting group of dwarfs at the Saturnalia (Statius 1.6.57).

Mettium Rufum: This is Marcus Mettius Rufus (*PIR*2 *M* 572 and *Vesp.* 14). Despite Mooney (1930: 523-4) and Galli (1991: 64), he is not to be confused with M. Junius Rufus (J 812) attested in Egypt some years after Mettius.

Egypt: Augustus ordained that Egypt was to be controlled by members of the equestrian order (*Hist.* 1.11). So the prefect of Egypt was appointed directly by the emperor, with not even any pretence of senatorial involvement.

naval battles...lake...next to the Tiber: Dio describes the lake as 'in a new place' (Dio 67.8.2-3), but its precise location is uncertain. However, his artificial sea-battles were no innovation. See the discussion in *Titus* 7.

torrential downpours of rain: During a violent storm when many spectators perished, Domitian would not allow anyone to leave, even though he had changed into more appropriate clothes (Dio 66.25.3).

Secular Games: The Secular Games (lasting for three days and three nights) were held to mark the end of one era (*saeculum*: see next item) and the start of the next. His games in 88 were commemorated on an impressive series of coins (*BMC* 2:29-38, 419-38) and by Statius (1.4.17; 4.1.37) and Martial (4.1.7; 10.63.3). See Hannestad, 1986: 141.

chronological calculations: In this context, an 'era' was a period of either one hundred or one hundred and ten years. Augustus had celebrated the Secular Games in 17 BC and Claudius in AD 47. The former had at first intended to hold them in 23 or 22 BC, but decided to postpone them until 17. Domitian, then, was technically correct, since it would have been 110 years (22 + 88) since Augustus had intended to hold them. Moreover, Claudius did admit that Augustus' calculations were correct (*Claud.* 21.2).

hundred races: Suetonius' figures are extremely suspect. The normal number was twenty-four per day (Dio 59.7.2-3; 60.27.2), but Domitian is supposed to have quadrupled that figure, whilst reducing the laps per race from seven to five. If so, the chariots would have travelled 90 kilometres on a normal day, but 270 during Domitian's secular games. See also Auguet, 1994: 120-48.

three-fold five-yearly contest to Capitoline Jupiter: In 86 (Censorinus, *De Die Natali* 18.15), Domitian instituted the Capitoline Games to commemorate his restoration of the temple of Jupiter on the Capitol. Their format was the same as the *Neronia* (*Nero* 12.3), a competition in three areas (music, horse racing and gymnastics) introduced by Nero in 60, but discontinued on his death. Held every four years early in the summer, Domitian's Capitoline Games attracted competitors from many nations (Martial 9.40); in the games of 94, there were fifty-two contestants for the Greek poetry prize alone (*ILS* 5177). In addition, the Odeum (for musical performances) and the Stadium (for athletics) were erected, magnificent buildings regarded 300 years later as two of Rome's finest (Amm. Marcell. 16.10.14).

music, horse racing and gymnastics: We know of contests in music (i.e. singing, oratory, poetry), chariot racing and athletics (with gymnastics). The prize, a wreath of oak-leaves, was presented by the emperor himself (Statius 5.3.233-4).

stadium: See *Dom*. 5.

young girls: This Domitianic innovation, referred to also by Dio (67.8.10), disappeared after 96.

clad...in the Greek fashion: Suetonius here uses (for the only time) the word *Graecanica* rather than his more usual *Graecus* – hence 'in the Greek fashion' rather than simply 'Greek'. Just what Domitian wore is open to dispute, but it may well have been something similar to the 'purple robe and Greek cloak' worn by Nero during his triumphal entry into Rome after his victory in the Olympic Games (*Nero* 25.1). Suetonius was the author of a work on clothes, but that does not explain fully his interest in the emperor's attire. The answer lies in Domitian's philhellenism (Jones, 1992: 112) – but here, it is all to his discredit.

golden crown: Similarly, the only statues of himself that he permitted on the Capitol were in gold or silver (*Dom*. 13), the equivalent of divine honours, so it was believed.

priest of Jupiter: Suetonius here uses the general term *sacerdos* (i.e. someone who ministers in holy matters) rather than the more accurate *flamen*. There were fifteen of the latter, each one assigned to the worship of a particular god; in this instance, his official title was *flamen Dialis* ('priest of Jupiter'). He held the post for life. However, although he had a seat in the Senate, he was not permitted to touch a horse, dog, goat, raw meat, a corpse, beans, ivy, wheat or leavened bread, nor to cut his hair and nails with an iron knife nor have a knot on his person (Scullard, 1981: 15-16). It is little wonder, then, that, during the period 87 – 11 BC, no candidate for the position could be found.

Flavian priests: These priests, fifteen in number (*sodales Titiales Flaviales*) presided over the worship of the deified Vespasian and Titus. See Levick, 1999: 205.

identical dress: Traditionally, the priest of Jupiter wore the *Albogalerus*, a cap terminating in a sharp point, surmounted by a small wooden knob. Suetonius' detailed description is designed to underline Domitian's travesty of normality.

Alban Mount: Even before Vespasian returned to Rome, Domitian was living in a villa at the foot of the Alban Hills, some twenty kilometres from the Capital (Dio 66.3.4). Later, his residence was developed into a masssive complex, with aqueducts, reservoirs, baths, theatre, circus, a 300-metre-long cryptoporticus and a camp for the praetorians. For Tacitus (*Agr.* 45), Juvenal (4.145) and Dio (67.1.1), it was the 'Alban citadel', the abode of a tyrant. He spent considerable time there, indulging in hunting and archery (*Dom.* 19). Sometimes, the imperial *consilium* met there (Juvenal 4.145-7 and *MW* 462). It was also the setting, as residence of the chief priest, for the the trial of the Vestal Virgin, Cornelia. Each year (Dio 67.1.2), a festival was celebrated there in honour of Minerva, called the *Quinquatria* from the Latin *quinque* meaning 'five': it began on 19 March, five days (counting inclusively) after the Ides. It consisted of contests of poets, orators, wild beast shows and gladiators (Dio 67.1.2; Juvenal 4.99; Martial 5.1.1; Statius 3.5.28, 5.3.227-9). These special games did not survive Domitian's death. For a detailed account of the Alban villa, see Darwall-Smith, 1994: 145-65.

Minerva: Domitian's devotion to Minerva was absolute (Dio 67.1.2). That his reverence was genuine appears from the fact that he kept a shrine to her in his bedroom (*Dom.* 17). He even claimed to be her son and is said to have imprisoned a magistrate at Tarentum because he had forgotten to include that 'fact' in a prayer (*V. Apoll.* 7.24). Early in the reign, he named his new legion *Minervia*; and just before the end, she came to him in a dream, so he said, with the news that she was no longer able to protect him, since Jupiter had disarmed her (*Dom.* 15). On his coins, four different types were assigned to her each year and they appeared with amazing regularity on both silver and gold coins (Carradice, 1978: 159-60). She was also portrayed prominently with Domitian on the Cancelleria reliefs. Martial often links them (5.2.6-8, 6.10.9-12, 7.1.1-2, 8.1.4 and 9.3.10). It was in her honour that he erected the temple of Minerva Chalcidicia, set up a shrine to her near the Temple of the Deified Augustus (Martial 5.53.1-2) and began work on the Forum of Nerva with its temple to Minerva. See further Sablayrolles, 1994: 131-3.

beast hunts: See *Dom.* 4.

contests of poets: Statius was more successful at these Alban games than at the Capitoline, winning the golden olive-crown on three occasions (3.5.28-31; 4.2.63-7).

three occasions: Approximate dates can be assigned to two of them, since one is recorded on the Fasti of Ostia for 84 (*MW* 56) and the third by Martial 8.15.1. It seems that the first was given in 83 (victory over the Chatti), the second in 89 (Dacian victory) and the third at the beginning of 93 (the Suebian-Sarmatian campaign).

gift to the people: The technical term is a *congiarium*. Originally, this was a gift of wine and oil from the magistrates to the people (Livy 25.2.2), later replaced by cash from the emperor's private funds. The *congiarium* came to be regarded as the civilian equivalent of the donative.

three hundred sestertii: The same amount was given by Augustus (twice),

Tiberius, Caligula (twice), Claudius, Titus and Nerva.

lavish feast: Banquets were given at the expense of an emperor in a public place such as the Forum to which all or a part of the city population was invited. This banquet, also referred to in *Dom.* 13, may possibly be identical with the feast mentioned by Martial 5.49.8-9 and Dio 67.4.4-5.

festival of the Seven Hills: This festival was celebrated on 11 December and consisted of a procession round the Palatine and Esquiline with a sacrifice on the former; no carts or vehicles drawn by beasts of burden were allowed in the city. The ceremony was still celebrated in the time of Tertullian (third century AD).

scattered...presents: At the Saturnalia, the emperor showered a great variety of presents on the audience, including figs, plums, dates, cakes and partridges from Numidia (Statius 1.6.75-78). Similar attempts to win popular approval are recorded by Agrippa (33 BC; Dio 49.43.4), Caligula (*Calig.* 18.2) and Nero (*Nero* 11.2).

tickets: Originally, they were tokens given to those citizens entitled to the corn dole and were inscribed with the name of the article (money at *Aug.* 41.2; wheat at *Nero* 11.2) for which they could be exchanged. Sometimes, they were small wooden balls (Dio 61.18.1-2, 66.25.5) or tablets and could, it seems, be bequeathed by will or transferred or sold.

block of seats: Suetonius is referring to the areas set apart for spectators according to their rank. For the details, see *Dom.* 8.

5 *[pages 31-2]*

restored...magnificent buildings: Suetonius' summary of Domitian's public works does little more than hint at the enormous building programme of 'one of the greatest builders of the Empire' (Blake, 1959: 99). Particularly significant is his failure to list the spectacular palace complex on the Palatine that is finally referred to, in passing, at *Dom.* 15. Most later writers add nothing to what little Suetonius reveals – apart from Eusebius who names fourteen of his works, whilst the Chronographer of 354 lists six more. The latter's accuracy has been doubted (neither Mooney nor Galli mention him), but archaeological excavation since 1945 has forced a re-evaluation of his claims (Anderson, 1983: 93-105). Even his list was incomplete since at least thirty structures should be added to it (Jones, 1992: 82-4 and Sablayrolles, 1994: 113-44).

fire: This was the fire of 80 that raged in Rome for three days and nights, consuming whatever was in its path (*Titus* 8; *Epit. de Caes.* 10.12). Previous conflagrations had also caused considerable damage, and not all of it had been repaired immediately – Nero's work of restoration was not completed on Domitian's accession (*ILS* 4914).

Capitol...burned down again: The temple of Jupiter was first burned down on 6 July 83 BC and again in December 69 (*Vit.* 15.3). Rebuilt by Vespasian (*Vesp.* 8), it was again destroyed in 80 (Dio 66.24.2); early in Domitian's reign, the building was completed and re-dedicated. The result was magnificent, lauded by all the court poets. Its features include doors plated with gold, a roof covered with gilt tiles, and a hexastyle Corinthian facade of white Pentelic marble, a material found in this building alone. It was one of his most famous architectural achievements, enduring until the end of the Empire. See Steinby, 1996: 144-53.

under his name alone...original builder: But Domitian was following the accepted practice – his restorations were indicated by the words 'Domitian...restored' (e.g. at Thyatira and Megalopolis: *MW* 422 and 436).

Jupiter the Guardian: Domitian had built a small chapel to Jupiter on the site of the house where he had hidden in December 69, later replacing it with a large temple (*Hist.* 3.74).

forum...'Nerva's': Fourth of the imperial forums, it was built by Domitian but dedicated by Nerva. An integral part of Domitian's planned renovation of the area, it was very narrow (120 metres by 40) and, for this reason, it was sometimes named the *Forum Transitorium* (the adjective *transitorius* means 'adapted for passing through'). Its most notable feature was an immense temple of Minerva. Within the Forum, he erected a shrine to 'Four-faced Janus' (it was square, with four doors) where the statue of Janus was supposed to look out on four Forums and was intended to 'bind together the disparate parts of the area' (Anderson, 1982: 138). See Sablayrolles, 1994: 127-30.

temple of the Flavian clan: See *Dom.* 1.

stadium: The arena itself, about 250 metres long, is today covered by the Piazza Navona which preserves quite strikingly the shape and size of Domitian's building. It must have been very impressive: even in the fourth century, it was regarded as one of the most conspicuous and famous monuments of Rome (Amm. Marcell. 16.10.14).

odeum: This roofed theatre could hold some 5,000 spectators (*PA* 371).

naval battles: See *Dom.* 4.

Circus Maximus: Severely damaged during the fire of 64 (*Ann.* 15.38), it suffered again in Domitian's reign. The restoration was not completed until Trajan's reign (Dio 68.7.2), but it seems highly likely that Domitian planned and commenced it. See *Dom.* 4.

6 *[page 32]*

campaigns partly...free will and partly of necessity: Suetonius' neatly constructed summary of Domitian's campaigns is far from complete. A brief outline of a few campaigns and triumphs is followed by a longer section describing a single incident (Saturninus' revolt of 89) in far greater detail.

Campaigns are included on the basis of whether they were justified or unjustified. So he mentions the unjustified one against the Chatti (82/3), and then three that were justified (the Sarmatian campaign of 92 and then two earlier ones of 85 and 86 in Dacia). Next we have the double triumph of 89 (and the partial one of 93), but not those of 83 and 86. So, whilst omitting the triumph over the Chatti (of 83), he includes the war that provided the excuse for it; again, he refers to the triumph over the Dacians, but not to the war (of Tettius Julianus) that gave rise to it. Logically, he excludes any conflicts not attended by Domitian (Britain, Africa). Yet the emperor was present in Pannonia when the Suebian Germans defeated the Romans (Dio 67.7.1-2), a defeat Suetonius does not mention, even though the war was apparently unjustified. Nevertheless, Suetonius' summary is a less hostile than Tacitus' in *Hist.* 1.2.

Chatti: The war against them began early in the reign (in 82, according to Jones, 1992: 128-30; but the traditional date is 83) and the Romans were quickly successful. Domitian was able to strengthen the Rhine defences in the Taunus and provide a quicker route between Mainz and the Danube. At some time between 9 June and 28 August 83 (Buttrey, 1980: 52-6), he assumed the title *Germanicus* and quickly claimed a triumph that was scorned by Tacitus (*Germ.* 37.6; *Agr.* 39.1) and Pliny (*Pan.* 16.3) – yet not by Aurelius Victor (11.4) and the epitomator (11.2). Domitian was also designated to the consulship for ten years in succession, was granted twenty-four lictors and allowed to wear the triumphal toga whenever he entered the Senate (Dio 67.4.3). See Jones, 1982: 329-35.

of necessity...Sarmatians...legion cut down together with its legate: Rome's most formidable opponents on the Danube were the Sarmatians against whom Domitian led campaigns in 92 and 95/6 (Jones, 1992: 150-55). Early in May 92, he left Rome for the Danube, and, on this occasion, the Sarmatians had the Suebic Germans (Marcomanni and Quadi) as allies (Dio 67.12.5), a complication not mentioned by Suetonius. The Romans lost a legion, either the XXI Rapax or the V Alaudae (see Wilkes, 1983: 279, 283). After eight months' absence, the emperor was back in Rome, celebrating an ovation (possibly) but not a triumph (see below).

Dacians: Domitian's Dacian wars are mentioned by Dio Cassius 67.6-7, 67.10-3, 68.9.3; Tacitus *Agr.* 41; Orosius 7.10.3-4; Jordanes *Getica* 76 and Eutropius 7.23.4. The war seems to have began in 85. The Dacians crossed the Danube, attacked the Romans and managed to kill their commander. Together with his praetorian prefect Cornelius Fuscus, Domitian immediately visited the Danubian front, rejected the Dacians' peace overtures, named Fuscus commander of the entire Roman forces (even though he was of equestrian rank) and sent him out against the enemy (Dio 67.6.3-5). His initial success enabled Domitian to return to Rome by September or October and claim his tenth and eleventh salutations for driving the invaders from

Moesia. For more details, see Strobel, 1989 and Jones. 1992: 138, 141.

Oppius Sabinus: Little is known of him (*PIR*2 O 122), even though he had been ordinary consul in 84 with Domitian.

Cornelius Fuscus: After his initial success, Fuscus had invaded Dacia, crossing the Danube on a bridge of boats (Jordanes, *Getica* 77); but his well-attested impetuosity (*Hist.* 2.86; *Agr.* 41.2) led to his death. So, in August 86, Domitian undertook his second campaign against the Dacians. He divided the province into two, appointed experiences governors (Cornelius Nigrinus and Funisulanus Vettonianus) and achieved some successes by the end of the year (Wilkes, 1983: 283). So the campaign was not as disastrous as Suetonius suggests, nor was Fuscus left unavenged. The next governor of Upper Moesia, Tettius Julianus (not mentioned by Suetonius) defeated the Dacians at Tapae (Dio 67.10.2-3), presumably late in 88.

entrusted the whole war: Fuscus had commanded the Ravenna fleet (*Hist.* 3.12; 3.42) in 69 and was voted praetorian insignia by the Senate (*Hist.* 4.4). Early in Domitian's reign, he became praetorian prefect and was one of the imperial friends summoned to the Alban villa for the meeting recorded by Juvenal. Subsequently, despite his equestrian status, he was given control of the Dacian campaign. His promotion was both unprecedented and brief; in 86, he fell in battle (Juvenal 4.111; Martial 6.76).

double triumph...Chatti and Dacians: This 'double triumph' over the Chatti and Dacians was his third and last. Held in 89, it is not to be confused with the 'two triumphs' of *Dom.* 13 celebrated earlier (83 and 86). The celebration in 89 included the erection in the Forum of the colossal equestrian statue of Domitian (*Dom.* 15) and the games organised by Arruntius Stella (Statius 1.2.181). But Dio dismisses it as a sham triumph (67.7.4).

battles of varying outcome: i.e. defeats (*Agr.* 41.2; *Hist.* 1.2; Eutropius 7.23.4; Orosius 7.10.3) and victories (Dio 67.10.2-3).

Sarmatians...laurel wreath: Why Domitian failed to celebrate a triumph for this victory in 93 is not clear. According to Suetonius and Silius Italicus (*Pun.* 15.120), he merely dedicated a laurel wreath to Jupiter Capitolinus, which was only part of a regular triumph (*NH* 15.30). Martial refers to 'secret triumphs' (8.15.5-6), Statius to the emperor's clemency (3.3.171). A more plausible explanation might be Domitian's determination to crush the Sarmatians in a later war, one undertaken very late in the reign (Jones, 1992: 153-5); thereby he would be able to advertise his prowess twice, the earlier ovation being the prelude to a full triumph.

civil war...L. Antonius: Suetonius obviously rated highly the political significance of this revolt, since, despite the brevity of his account of Domitian's reign, he refers to it again in 7 and 10. On 1 January 89, the governor of Upper Germany, L. Antonius Saturninus, seized the savings of the two legions (XIV Gemina and XXI Rapax) stationed at Mainz and revolted against Domitian. As well as the support from his own legions, he had apparently reached an understanding with the Chatti. But he received no support from the two other Upper German legions. His immediate opponent was the commander of Lower Germany, Lappius Maximus (*PIR2* L 84: omitted by Suetonius, but called 'Lucius Maximus' by Dio) who resided in Cologne. Lappius moved quickly and, with the aid of the equestrian procurator of Rhaetia, Norbanus (*PIR2* N 162) defeated Saturninus somewhere between Coblenz and Bonn. At the same time, Trajan was summoned from Spain with the VII Gemina, whilst Domitian came from Rome with his praetorians. Punishments and rewards followed. Lappius' four Lower German legions and their auxiliaries were honoured; Lappius and Norbanus were promoted. Once the mutinous leaders had been dealt with severely (*Dom.* 10), XXI Rapax and XIV Gemina were transferred to the Danube. There were other administrative changes (*Dom.* 7). A Lower German legion was also moved to Mainz; thus both Germanies were now three-legion provinces. See Jones, 1979: 30-6 and Murison, 1985: 31-49.

civil war: In the official propaganda, it was a 'German war' (*MW* 60).

Rhine...thawed: The sudden thaw must have been quite unusual, for horses could regularly cross the Rhine in winter (Herodian 6.7.7). But the result was that Saturninus' German allies, including the Chatti, were stranded on wrong side of the Rhine.

messages: News of the rebellion reached Rome promptly, since it probably began on 1 January 89 and his victory was already being celebrated in the capital 24 days later (*MW* 15).

spread abroad: Plutarch's account is similar (*Aemilius Paullus* 25.3).

seen his head: Dio reports it as a fact (67.11.3).

7 *[pages 32-3]*

formal dinners...food parcels: Originally, a small quantity of food (*sportula*) was provided by a patron in return for some service; later, he would instead invite his clients to a formal dinner. Nero preferred the *sportula* (*Nero* 16.2), but Domitian reversed the process. However, the change proved unpopular and Domitian later revived the *sportula* (Martial 9.100.1; 10.27.3).

factions: The faction was a professional body that supplied the organiser of the races with teams of horses, charioteers and a full complement of officials. There were four (white, red, green and blue) and Domitian added two more (gold and purple). Suetonius was particularly interested in public entertainment, as is apparent from the frequent references in his imperial biographies and his treatise on it. See further Cameron, 1976: 5-23 and Auguet, 1994: 135-48.

gold and purple: Although Domitian introduced two new factions (also noted by Dio 67.4.4), he supported neither, preferring the Greens (Martial 11.33.1-4), as did Caligula, Nero and other emperors. Both the Golds and the

Purples disappeared after his murder.

four original: White and Red were the earliest, with the Green first attested under Tiberius and the Blue under Nero.

banned actors: Accusations of obscenity were often directed at them (*Aug.* 45.4). In practice, emperors either banished actors (e.g. Tiberius: *Ann.* 4.14) or recalled them (Caligula: Dio 59.2.5). Atypically, Domitian attempted a compromise, allowing them to continue performing in private houses; and although Nerva restored their privileges (*Pan.* 46.1-2), Trajan was soon forced to revert to Domitian's practice.

forbade the castration of males: Domitian's legislation (presumably an edict) forbidding castration was frequently mentioned and usually praised, e.g. by Martial (2.60.4, 6.2.2-4, 9.6.4-7, 9.8.5), Statius (3.4.74-7; 4.3.13), Philostratus (*V. Apoll.* 6.42), Dio (67.2.3: but Domitian did it 'to insult Titus' memory'). The edict was apparently ineffective and was reinforced by subsequent emperors, e.g. by Nerva (Dio 68.2.4) and by Hadrian (*Digest* 48.8.4.2). See further Hopkins, 1978: 193-4.

regulated the prices of the eunuchs: Slave-dealers might well raise the price of their remaining stock and then be tempted to break the law to maintain supply.

nobody should plant new vines in Italy...half at most: The edict (that no more vines were to be planted in Italy and that at least half the vineyards in the provinces were to be cut down) was later dropped after a poem appeared comparing Domitian to a vine-eating goat (*Dom.* 14). Statius associates the measure with neglect of the 'chaste goddess' Ceres (4.3.11-12) and continues with a glorification of Domitian's achievement (as Censor) in forbidding castration (13-15). Suetonius similarly includes the vine edict amidst such items as the abolition of castration. So they regarded it as more of a moral reform than an economic one (Wallace-Hadrill, 1995: 134), as did Philostratus (*V. Soph.* 520). Undoubtedly, he wanted to encourage cereal-production both in Italy and in the provinces, for shortages were not unknown. In any case, the difficulties involved in implementing a policy of destroying vines in both Italy and the provinces would have been formidable. Who would do it and what would be the attitude of the Italian and provincial élite at the loss of part of their livelihood? For a fuller discussion, see Levick, 1982: 66-73; Patterson, 1987: 115-18 and Jones, 1992: 77-9.

did not persist: Despite Suetonius' statement (repeated at *Dom.* 14) that the proposal was soon abandoned, some scholars believe that it was put into effect in Africa and elsewhere, and that it was subsequently reversed by an edict of the emperor Probus.

shared...Roman knights: The meaning of 'shared' is in dispute. Weaver translates it as 'shared' in the sense of 'caused to be held or performed together in a collegiate sense' and argues that it means 'the appointing, where appropriate, of procuratorial pairs, one equestrian, one freedman, both carrying the same (or close variations of the same) title' (1994: 357) Suetonius, of course, as (a former) chief secretary, would have regarded the first appointment of an equestrian to that post as particularly momentous.

forbade the encamping of two legions together: The reform was long overdue. But the situation at Mainz had been particularly unsatisfactory for some time, as the former Othonian unit XIV Gemina was stationed with the Vitellian XXI Rapax.

forbade deposition of more than a thousand sestertii: A maximum balance of one thousand sestertii per soldier, as stated here, would have been difficult to enforce. Apart from the regularly mounting balance in the soldiers' accounts, half of each donative had to be deposited (Vegetius: 2.20). Perhaps the new measure was only temporary (Watson, 1969: 150).

L. Antonius: Born in Spain, L. Antonius Saturninus (*PIR*2 A 874) was granted senatorial rank by Vespasian and later (? 76/77) appointed proconsul of Macedonia (so it seems); after replacing L. Flavius Silva as governor of Judaea, he reached the consulship, almost certainly in 82 and was subsequently appointed to the command of Upper Germany (Eck, 1982: 297, 302 and 314). With the failure of the insurrection (*Dom.* 6), he was executed and his head exposed in the Forum (Dio 67.11.3).

winter quarters of two legions: The legions were the XIV Gemina and XXI Rapax, transferred after the revolt to the Danube.

added a fourth payment of three gold pieces: Suetonius asserts that Domitian added three gold pieces (*aurei*) to the soldiers' pay. So he increased it from nine *aurei* to twelve (i.e. to 1,200 sestertii). What Domitian did was to introduce an additional 'pay-day' per year, without changing the amount of each instalment. After 96, his fourth instalment was abolished, but the amount of each of the remaining three increased, so that the annual total remained the same as before 96. Alston (1994: 113) and others argue that Domitian retained the three instalments (despite Suetonius' 'fourth' and 'added') whilst increasing the amount of each to 400 sestertii; and this is certainly what happened after he was murdered, according to Dio 67.3.5). In any case, a substantial increase in costs must have resulted.

8 *[page 33]*

dispensed justice with diligence and industry: Chapters 8 and 9 provide details of Domitian's jurisdictional, legislative, censorial and pontifical activities, but in a very haphazard fashion, and they do not support Suetonius' laudatory assessment (repeated by the so-called epitomator of Aurelius Victor 11.2). For instance, even though 8 begins 'he dispensed justice...in the forum', not one of the items in 8 deals with Domitian's decisions as judge in the first instance. Again, despite the introductory reference to his censorial achievements later in 8, the most extensive item is an account of his punishment of the errant Vestal Virgins, i.e. Domitian acting as chief priest, whereas 7 has an example of Domitian the censor (castration forbidden). Perhaps Suetonius' point is that Domitian dealt with a variety of cases in any order whatsoever or it may simply be an indication of Suetonius' hasty composition evident elsewhere in this Life. For a fuller discussion, see Bauman, 1982: 118-23.

even in the forum: i.e. as well as in the Palace and at the Alban villa, where criminal cases were usually heard, with civil cases being reserved for the Forum.

outside normal procedure: Suetonius is referring to the court's sitting on special occasions, e.g. on days exempt from legal business, as in Cicero, *Pro Caelio* 1.1.

rescinded...self-interest: So he was acting upon appeal and not in the first instance.

Centemviral Court: Court of the Hundred: see *Vesp.* 10.

Recoverers: They were arbiters used instead of a single judge in certain cases, e.g. of disputed legal status, debt or extortion. Suetonius is referring to investigators of status who were repeatedly warned by Domitian to be on their guard against false claims for freedom.

council: In civil cases, the arbitrator or judge was assisted in coming to a decision by his council of advisors.

tribunes...accusing a despicable aedile: Domitian presumably did so because a private accuser could not lay a charge against a magistrate in office. But, during the Empire, this matter would normally come before the Senate, not the emperor (*Ann.* 2.18, 13.14). So, again, we do not have an example of him acting as judge in the first instance.

judges...from the Senate: If the accused were found guilty of extortion by the Senate, the amount to be refunded would be determined by three or five specially appointed judges. On the extortion court, see *OCD* 1308-9.

never...more modest or just: Brunt (1961: 226-7) and others have doubted the accuracy of the Suetonius' assessment. However, the opinion of Hadrian's Chief Secretary should not be so easily cast aside; and, apart from the not-unexpected support of Silius Italicus (*Pun.* 14.686-8) and Statius (5.1.79), there was also the Alexandrian Jew who, more than a century after Domitian's death, praised him as the benefactor of all the provincials, as him whom 'all men worship and gladly obey' (see Levick, 1982: 61-2). Even hostile sources admitted his firmness as an administrator. Nerva's consul Fronto is supposed to have said that 'it was bad to have an emperor under whom nobody was permitted to do anything, but worse to have one under whom everybody was permitted to do everything' (Dio 68.1.3). In short, his selection of comparatively sound administrators coupled with a readiness to punish the blatantly dishonest provides ample justification for Suetonius' assessment. Only one trial is attested under Domitian, that of Baebius Massa

(Sherwin-White, 1966: 444-7), but six under Trajan (see below). See further Levick, 1982: 50-73 and Jones, 1992: 109-14.

we saw: Suetonius must be referring to the six attested senatorial trials of Trajan's reign, viz. those of the proconsuls Marius Priscus (Africa: 97/8), Caecilius Classicus (Baetica: 97/8), Julius Bassus (Pontus-Bithynia: 100/1) and Varenus Rufus (Pontus-Bithynia: 105/6); for their tenures, see Eck, 1982: 328, 334 and 341. Proceedings were also instituted against an official from Baetica (who was possibly a proconsul (96/7: Eck, 1982: 326) and against Hostilius Firminus, a legate of Marius Priscus (*Ep*. 2.11.23-4). Four of the trials were held in 100, one (Bassus) in 102 and one in 106 (Varenus).

improvement of morality: Suetonius' reference is to Domitian's assumption of censorial power (April 85), followed soon after by his appointment as censor for life. The ancient office of censor was held by various emperors, including Vespasian and Titus in 73/74. For a discussion of the censor's regulation of conduct and morals, see Hammond, 1959: 133-5.

knights regardless of rank: The seating arrangements in the Roman theatre were very elaborate. The orchestra was reserved for senators and distinguished foreigners (*Aug*. 35.2; *Ann*. 13.54); the next fourteen rows were occupied by the knights, whilst special areas were set aside for women, soldiers, married plebeians and for boys not of age together with their tutors (*Aug*. 44). But these regulations had been ignored and Domitian's edict (Martial 5.8.1-3) was intended to prevent what Caligula had encouraged (*Calig*. 26.2), the indiscriminate occupation of the seats reserved for the knights.

libellous: Justification for firm action in such matters already existed. In the Twelve Tables, the penalty for defamatory verse was death (Cicero, *Rep*. 4.10.12) and Augustus was the first emperor to apply the laws of treason to publications of this sort (*Ann*. 1.72). At first, though, Domitian reacted in a comparatively mild fashion.

abolished: The works were probably burned, as were Senecio's (*Agr*. 2.1).

removed from the Senate: At last, Suetonius has included an example under the correct heading. As censor, the emperor could remove morally delinquent senators.

man of quaestorian rank: He is identified by Dio 67.13.1 as Caecilius Rufinus (*PIR*2 C 73) who was expelled from the Senate for miming.

making theatrical gestures and dancing: Pliny described such gestures as 'perverted' (*Pan*. 46.4); Nepos thought that dancing was a 'vice' (*Epam*. 1.2).

women of ill-fame: Dio supports Suetonius' contention, but adds 'some had been debauched by Domitian himself' (67.12.1).

litter: Various restrictions had been placed on the use of the litter. It was available only to those of free birth, but not (since Julius Caesar) to women under the age of forty-five with neither husband nor children (*Iul* 43.1; *Claud*. 28.1).

right of receiving legacies and inheritances: The legal basis of such action is disputed. Mooney (1930: 547) and Galli (1991: 78) claim that the penalty was copied from that imposed on celibates by Augustus' Julian Law on Marriage, whereas Bauman argues that the action was taken under the Voconian Law (it apparently restricted the right of women to inherit), since the censor had to be involved (1982: 121-2).

struck off the list of judges: The judges in any trial were selected by the praetor from a list of those qualified to serve.

taken back...divorced her: Domitian punished a member of the equestrian order for doing what Domitian himself was alleged to have done, i.e. taking his wife back after divorcing her and charging her with adultery (*Dom.* 3). The positioning of this item is very significant, for it has been sandwiched between the punishment he meted out to 'women of ill-fame' on the one hand and to sodomites on the other, thereby underlining the imperial hypocrisy all the more and also serving as a prelude to the following item, the 'cruel' penalty he imposed on the Vestals.

Scantinian law: By this Law, sodomy with free-born boys attracted a fine of 10,000 sestertii (Quintilian, 4.2.69 and 7.4.42; Juvenal 2.44). Later, the penalty for that offence was death (*Digest* 47.11.1.2). The item is certainly out of place amidst Domitian's censorial activities.

Vestal Virgins: Domitian's treatment of the Vestals is also mentioned by Statius (1.1.35-6), Plutarch (*Numa* 10.8), Pliny (*Ep.* 4.11), Philostratus (*V. Apoll.* 7.6) and Dio (67.3.3-4). Since they were technically daughters of the community, any moral transgressions involving them were regarded very seriously. See further Vinson, 1989: 433-8, 445-8 and Jones, 1992: 101-2.

early acts...later ones: Two separate incidents are recorded. On the first occasion (early in the reign), Domitian found three of the six Vestals (the Oculata sisters and Varronilla) guilty, but allowed them to choose the manner of their deaths, and merely exiled their lovers. It was probably on this occasion that the senior Vestal, Cornelia was acquitted. Later in the reign, probably in 89, she was dealt with according to the letter of the law.

ancient manner: The original form of punishment was for the condemned Vestal to be beaten to death with rods; then, under Tarquinius Priscus, she was buried alive, but sometimes scourged first.

relegated: Relegation was an extremely light penalty, since it was customary for the seducer to be hung from a cross and be beaten to death with rods. Expulsion took several forms in the Empire (*Vesp.* 15).

Cornelia: She was found guilty at a trial held at the Alban villa and condemned to be buried alive. However, in Pliny's highly rhetorical (*Ep.* 4.11) account aimed at vilifying Domitian, her death is directly associated with Domitian's supposed incestuous relationship with his niece Julia and the fatal abortion he forced on her. Suetonius' briefer version carries more conviction – at least he separates the deaths of Julia and Cornelia (*Dom.* 8

and 22), which occurred around the same time.

Chief Virgin: She was the oldest Vestal (*Ann.* 11.32). The vestals were six in number, chosen between the ages of six and ten. After serving for a period of thirty years, during which time they had to remain virgins, they could retire and marry, if they so wished or else remain as Vestals. Most preferred the latter alternative since the former was considered unlucky. See further Beard, 1980: 12-27.

debauchers...flogged to death: Cornelia's lovers, including the equestrian Celer, were beaten to death, the exception being Valerius Licinianus (see below). The entire affair exemplifies the attention he paid to the letter of religious law.

in the Comitium: This was an enclosed area to the north of the Forum adjoining the Senate-house and separated by the Rostra from the Forum.

man of praetorian rank: According to Pliny, he was Valerius Licinianus (*Ep.* 4.11). He was probably guilty, since he was not recalled after Domitian's murder. But Domitian treated him leniently, for he was allowed to rescue what he could before his property was confiscated (4.11.13).

temple of Jupiter Capitolinus: Similarly, when the temple was being restored under Vespasian, the haruspices forbade the use of stones which had been destined for some other purpose (*Hist.* 4.53). For the temple, see *Dom.* 5.

9 *[page 33]*

Vergil: i.e. *Georgics* 2.536. In primitive times, killing an ox was regarded as impious (Varro, *RR* 2.5).

father still absent: Vespasian returned c. 13 October 70 (Buttrey, 1980: 12).

greed and avarice: In Suetonius' view, Domitian was always greedy and avaricious, but gave very little evidence of it until he was emperor, and, even then, not at once.

great proofs...generosity: Once again (as in *Dom.* 3), Suetonius' 'chiaroscuro' technique is in evidence – he praises his subject so as to highlight the inevitable decline to vice.

generosity: The theme of imperial generosity is discussed in detail by Bradley, 1981: 129-37.

all around him: Identification of them is extremely hazardous. Apart from his 'official' associates (Jones, 1992: 50-61) and his senior freedmen (*Dom.* 14), his attested intimates were understandably few and included Earinus (his boy lover), the actor Latinus (*Dom.* 15), and perhaps the satirist Turnus.

urged...do nothing in a mean fashion: Domitian seems to have behaved in this way until, possibly, 85 with the devaluation of the coinage to the Neronian level of 64 (Carradice, 1 983: 9-56). So his generosity lasted three years or so; then, limits were imposed.

inheritances...those who had children: During the Empire, the custom of leaving one's friends something in one's will was ominously extended. Caligula insisted on being named in wills and then sent poisoned cakes to those who did not oblige him by promptly dying (*Calig*. 38.2). Domitian did not maintain his refusal for long, and was soon claiming the estates of total strangers (*Dom*. 12). See further Hopkins, 1983: 235-47.

Rustius Caepio: He is not elsewhere attested.

as they entered the Senate House: This provision in Caepio's will may mean that a sum of money was to be given to all senators on entering the Senate for the first time each year or else to each new senator at his first entry. Domitian probably annulled the provision on the grounds that it was inappropriate to the dignity of the Senate.

defendants...case: Augustus had established a similar five-year 'statute of limitations' for charges of adultery, both emperors presumably being influenced by the congestion prevailing in the courts. See further Bauman, 1968: 82-3.

quaestors' clerks...Claudian law: Since the time of Sulla, there were thirty-six quaestors' clerks, some being freedmen, while others later gained senatorial rank. They worked in the public treasury, with two being attached to the staff of each provincial governor. Suetonius is probably referring to a law of P. Clodius c. 58 BC. This seems to be a (misplaced) example of Domitian acting as judge in the first instance (Bauman, 1982: 119).

pieces of land...left over: When a colony was being founded, the surveyors divided the territory into rectangular tracts and any irregular sections left over were known as *subsiciva*. They were still technically public land, even though occupied by owners of the nearby plots. Domitian's policy was always to confirm such squatters in their occupancy, as was also recorded in an epistle of 22 July 82 (*MW* 462) and by Siculus Flaccus (*De Condicionibus Agrorum* 163). Vespasian and Titus, on the other hand, favoured reassigning these illegally occupied tracts of land to the state.

acquired by long use: Suetonius' language is precise. As Bauman (1982: 119) has pointed out, the real difficulty is to reconcile this statement with the fact that this was expressly prohibited by law (*Digest* 41.3.9).

saying of his: Dio refers to 'a proclamation (by Domitian) to the effect that when an emperor fails to punish informers, he himself makes them informers' (67.1.4).

informers: See *Titus* 8. Tacitus names Baebius Massa, Mettius Carus and Catullus Messallinus as Domitianic informers (*Agr*. 45), whilst Palfurius Sura, Publicius Certus, Pompeius (? Silvanus) and Arrecinus Clemens seem to have been active.

10 *[pages 34-5]*

clemency...self-restraint: See *Dom*. 9.

cruelty...cupidity: The theme occurs in Dom. 3, picked up from *Vesp*. 1.

Paris: See *Dom*. 3.

Hermogenes of Tarsus: He is not the famous Hermogenes (born after 137) but may be the Hermogenes of uncertain date who wrote a mythological account of Phrygia (Janssen, 1919: 7).

allusions: Quintilian provides an example (9.2.67) of what Suetonius means – *duxi uxorem, quae patri placuit* ('I married a wife who pleased my father' or 'I married a wife and this pleased my father'; and Bauman offers the attractive conjecture that *patri* ('father') is Quintilian's 'discreet emendation of a *fratri* ('brother') in Hermogenes' history' (1974: 162), the allusion being to Titus' alleged affair with Domitia (Dio 66.26.4) – Domitian was notoriously sensitive to attacks on his wife, as Helvidius discovered (see below).

scribes: They were slaves used as copyists.

Thracian: See *Titus* 8.

net-fighter: For this class of gladiator, sometimes referred to as '*murmillones*', see *Titus* 8.

giver of the gladiatorial show: This was Domitian himself, known to be hostile to the Thracians. It was 'unwise' of the spectator to accuse Domitian of bias.

thrown to the dogs: Caligula (*Calig*. 27.3) and Claudius (*Claud*. 14) condemned prisoners 'to the beasts'.

impiously: As 'father of his country' (*Vesp*. 12), an emperor could expect to be shown due respect (*pietas*), disregard of which was equated with *impietas* or *maiestas* (treason). See Bauman, 1974: 1-59. The incident is also mentioned in *Pan*. 33.3-4.

put to death very many senators...several of consular rank: The charge is repeated precisely by Tacitus (*Agr*. 45.1) and more generally by Pliny (*Pan* 48.3; 90.5), Aurelius Victor (11.5), Dio (67.11.2-13 and frequently), Eutropius (7.23.2) and Orosius (7.10.2). However, Suetonius does not list all Domitian's senatorial victims, only those of consular rank. Three of them were charged with planning revolution, the remainder arraigned on trivial charges. But two consular victims, also imperial relatives, are not listed until later, i.e. Arrecinus Clemens (*Dom*. 11) and Flavius Clemens (*Dom*. 15), even though the latter's brother, Sabinus, is included here. See Jones, 1992: 180-92.

Civica Cerealis: He was executed in 87/8 (Eck, 1970: 86) whilst proconsul of Asia and replaced by an equestrian, Minicius Italus (*MW* 336), an unprecedented appointment not mentioned by Suetonius. Tacitus also refers to him (*Agr*. 42.1). The charge of treason was not necessarily groundless. It may have been connected with the appearance of a 'false Nero' c. 88 in Asia. However, his close connections with the Flavians were not enough to save him. He probably came from Vespasian's home town, Reate; his brother commanded one of Vespasian's legions in Judaea (*Vesp.* 6) and both had governed Moesia at various times after 70 (Eck, 1982: 295 ff.).

Salvidienus Orfitus: He received a consulship from Domitian (before 87), even though his father, of the same name, had been executed by Nero in 66 (*Nero* 37.1; Dio 62.27.1). In addition, the younger Orfitus was described (by Philostratus) as a 'suitable candidate for (imperial) power' (*V. Apoll.* 7.8). It would not surprise if such an aristocrat aroused Domitian's suspicion, especially in the latter part of the reign. Orfitus was banished to an island and killed.

Acilius Glabrio: Appointed ordinary consul in 91 with Trajan, the patrician Acilius Glabrio was made to fight a huge lion at Domitian's Alban villa (Dio 67.14.3; Fronto 5.23). According to Juvenal, he had been a member of Domitian's *consilium* (4.95-6). Exiled for 'plotting revolution', he was put to death on the grounds of 'atheism, a charge on which many others who had drifted into Jewish ways were condemned' (Dio 67.14.2-3). On the other hand, since a second century Acilius Glabrio may have been a Christian, there are some scholars (Sordi, 1994: 50-1) who believe that he was one as well, though this is doubtful.

Aelius Lamia: After Flavius Sabinus, he was the most eminent of these Domitianic consular victims. Almost certainly the son of Plautius Silvanus Aelianus (*RP* 4.169), he had been adopted by an Aelius Lamia. All that is known of his career is his particularly long suffect consulship (under Titus) of six months instead of the normal two (Gallivan, 1981: 198), an award that probably did not endear him to Domitian. The 'harmless jokes' mentioned by Suetonius would not have been appreciated by an emperor who lacked a sense of humour and resented personal criticism of the mildest sort.

wife: Domitia. See *Dom.* 1.

I keep it under control: According to an ancient belief, abstaining from sex (Domitian had married Lamia's wife) improved one's singing ability.

You don't...as well: Lamia suggests that the unmarried Titus might emulate Domitian in his search for a wife.

Salvius Cocceianus: Son of Salvius Otho Titianus, Salvius Otho Cocceianus was executed for celebrating the birthday of Otho, his paternal uncle. Salvius Cocceianus was a consular patrician and nephew of both Otho and Nerva. He ought to have heeded both parts of the advice given him by his uncle Otho in 69, i.e. 'My boy, this is my last charge to you; do not altogether forget, and do not too well remember, that you had a Caesar for an uncle' (Plutarch, *Otho* 16.2, repeated precisely by Tacitus, *Hist.* 2.48).

birthday of Otho: i.e. 28 April. Normally, such celebrations were perfectly acceptable – but Domitian had forbidden memorial games on Titus' birthday (Dio 67.2.6).

Mettius Pompusianus: The details recorded by Suetonius may well have been part of the charges officially brought against him, in particular the horoscope indicating that he would one day be emperor. See next item, *Vesp.* 14 and Arnaud, 1983: 677-99.

horoscope of the emperor: See *Vesp.* 14 and 25. The 'logic' of this was that the leaders of a conspiracy would always be able to muster more support if they were able to obtain a 'suitable' imperial horoscope predicting the precise time of the emperor's death. For an emperor who believed in this so-called science as firmly as did Domitian (*Dom.* 14, 15 and 16), astrological predictions were accurate and scientific.

map of the world...speeches from Titus Livius...slaves the names of Mago and Hannibal: With a map outlining possible conquests or weak points most susceptible to attack, speeches (from Livy) at hand to urge on his warriors and their leaders, to say nothing of slaves with Punic names and a horoscope indicating that he would one day be emperor, he must (so it could be alleged) have been plotting to seize power. Hannibal (247-183/2 BC) was the most famous of Carthage's generals and one of the world's greatest military tacticians. His most remarkable victory was over the Romans at Cannae in 216. His youngest brother, Mago, served under him in Italy, fought in Spain from 215 to 206, then returned to Italy and was defeated in 203.

Sallustius Lucullus: An enigmatic figure, Sallustius Lucullus must have governed Britain after Agricola's departure and before 94/5 (Eck, 1982: 312-22). Neither his consular year nor his full name is known, unless he is to be identified with the suffect consul of 89, P. Sallustius Blaesus. His demise could well be connected with the hostility shown by the general staff (and shared by Lucullus) to Domitian's rejection of expansionist warfare in Germany and Britain. Possibly he was accused of treason and the detailed charges may have included naming a lance after himself. Suetonius, then, in an effort to 'prove' that Domitian executed some senators for the 'most insubstantial reasons', may have omitted all the charges against Lucullus except the last. See also Birley, 1981: 82-3 and Jones, 1992: 133-4, 186.

Junius Rusticus: As tribune of the people in 66, he tried (*PIR*2 J 730) to veto the Senate's condemnation of Thrasea Paetus (*Ann.* 16.26); and he no doubt retained his enthusiasm for the tenets of Stoicism. Nevertheless, he and others like him were granted suffect consulships by Domitian – Rusticus in 92, Helvidius Priscus' son in 93 or before 87 and Avidius Quietus in 93. But in that same year, seven of this group were brought to trial, three (Arulenus Rusticus, Senecio and Helvidius Priscus' son) executed and the rest exiled. In Suetonius' version, Rusticus was executed for 'publishing eulogies of Thrasea Paetus and Helvidius Priscus'; but Pliny, Tacitus (*Agr.* 2.1) and Dio (67.13.2) state that Herennius Senecio composed Helvidius' eulogy.

Paetus Thrasea: Disgusted with the excesses of Nero's reign, he withdrew from public life (though of consular rank), was prosecuted for treason and subsequently (in 66) driven to suicide. He is often cited as the embodiment of Stoic or philosophic opposition to the emperors, but this is misleading. He was an outspoken senator with Stoic views, rather than a Stoic who just happened to be a senator. See further Syme, 1958: 555-9 and Bauman, 1974: 153-7.

Helvidus Priscus: See *Vesp*. 15.

removed all philosophers: Tacitus (*Agr*. 2.2), Pliny (*Ep*. 3.11.1; *Pan*. 47.1), Aulus Gellius (*NA* 15.11.4), Philostratus (*V. Apoll*. 7.8) and Dio (67.13.3) attest to an expulsion of the philosophers by Domitian; Suetonius and Dio associate it with the executions of 93. Dio, however, states that, under Domitian, they were 'banished once more' – so either the 'first' banishment occurred earlier in the reign or else the reference is to a Vespasianic expulsion, as recorded in Dio 66.13.1. For what it is worth, the late chronographers support the first interpretation, with both philosophers and astrologers being expelled in 88/9 and again in 93/4 or 95/6 (Sherwin-White, 1966: 764-5). It seems preferable to accept the contemporary evidence that there was only one Domitianic expulsion. Amongst those exiled were Artemidorus, Epictetus, Junius Mauricus, Gratilla, Arria and Fannia.

Helvidius, the son: There is no evidence that he ever bore the names 'Gaius' or 'Priscus'. Despite his father's fate (executed by Vespasian) and the family connections of his step-mother (*Vesp*. 15), he was awarded a consulship either in 93 or else before 87. But this was not all. In 85, his son-in-law Annius Herennius Pollio also became consul. In 93, however, he was executed.

divorce: See *Dom*. 3.

comic piece on the stage: This was a comic performance staged after more serious plays.

Paris and Oenone: Helvidius chose cleverly. Oenone (= Domitia?) was Paris'(= Domitian?) first wife whom he had deserted for Helen (= Julia?); learning that he had been wounded by an arrow, she refused to return and cure him. In addition, Paris was also the name of Domitia's alleged lover and Domitian himself was known to be particularly fond of archery (*Dom*. 3 and 19).

Flavius Sabinus: He was the grandson and not the son (as Mooney, 1930: 561 and Galli, 1991: 83) of Vespasian's brother. Only a few years younger than Domitian himself, he was always an ominously senior Flavian, a fact that he did little to conceal, parading his attendants in imperial white (*Dom*. 12). But, despite this, Domitian regarded the firm establishment of a dynasty as paramount and so chose Sabinus to be his colleague as ordinary consul for 82, the first year of the reign. It used to be thought that this appointment was made by Titus, an assumption refuted by Eck (1970: 48-54). Sabinus, however, did not retain imperial favour for long (see below).

another of his cousins: The other was Clemens (Sabinus' brother).

day of the consular elections: On elections for the consulship, see *Vesp.* 5. Under Tiberius, they were transferred from the people to the Senate (*Ann.* 1.15), but the people later did still meet formally to hear the result. So there were two quite distinct acts. Here, they occurred on the same day and the herald made his unfortunate error.

not as consul elect but as emperor: The error must have occurred either during the second month of the reign, October 81, when the ordinary consuls for 82 were announced, or (less likely) during a second consular designation later in the eighties. Suetonius and Dio together imply that he was executed very early in the reign, not long after he was consul in 82. The former has Julia living openly with Domitian after her father and husband were dead (*Dom.* 22) and Dio places the couple's unconcealed living together in Domitian's reign (67.3.2) but before the executions of the Vestals (67.3.3) and the outbreak of the war against the Chatti (67.4.1). So the mistaken announcement would have occurred at the second consular elections for 82 (held in October 81).

civil war: See *Dom.* 6.

tortured: A trial often involved torture (*Calig.* 32.1; *Claud.* 34.1).

many of the opposing side: Not one of these supporters has ever been identified. The likeliest candidates would be the legates and centurions of the two legions stationed at Mainz (XIV Gemina and XXI Rapax).

broad stripe: See *Vesp.* 2.

tribune: Julius Calvaster (Dio 67.11.4).

homosexuals: Dio states that, on offering this defence, Calvaster was acquitted (67.11.4) – as Suillius Caesoninus had been after using this argument in the trial following the execution of Messalina in 48 (*Ann.* 11.36). No doubt the tribune and centurion claimed that their association with the Antonius Saturninus was sexual, not political and so hoped to incur nothing more than the social disapproval (see *Vesp.* 13: Mucianus) that would result from the admission that they were passive homosexuals.

11 *[pages 35-6]*

cruelty...unexpected: So, too, *Pan.* 66.3, *Agr.* 39.1 and Dio 67.1.1-3; and the theme reappears below. Both Tacitus and Philostratus compare the cruelty of Nero and Domitian (*Agr.* 45.2; *V. Apoll.* 7.14).

portions from his dinner: Persian kings (Xen. *Anab.* 1.9) and Roman emperors (*HA Pertinax* 12.6) sent helpings of food from their tables to absent friends as an honour.

Arrecinus Clemens: M. Arrecinus Clemens (*PIR*2 A 1072) was related to the imperial family (*Hist.* 4.68) – his sister Arrecina Tertulla married Titus. Replaced by the latter as praetorian prefect c. 72, he was appointed consul in 73 and later governed Spain. Returning to hold a second consulship in 85, he became City Prefect not long afterwards. His period of eminence was brief, however, for he fell from favour, possibly c. 87. Suetonius' list of Domitian's consular victims in *Dom.* 10 is apparently meant to be complete and does include one imperial relative (Flavius Sabinus). Arrecinus, however, is omitted from chapter 10 but does appear here, where he is the second of three examples of Domitian's unexpected cruelty. The implication of the passage is that the death sentences were carried out in each case, but Suetonius is not explicit. The passage is reminiscent of *Nero* 37, where he lists three senators 'executed' by Nero; but one of them, Cassius Longinus, was merely exiled (*Ann.* 16.9) and was later recalled by Vespasian (*Digest* 12.2.52). Perhaps Arrecinus, too, was exiled.

one of his close friends and spies: Their friendship is mentioned by Tacitus (*Hist.* 4.68). He must have been an unofficial imperial agent, obtaining information that resulted in charges of treason. Suetonius uses the same word to describe Tigellinus (*Galba* 15.2).

driving with him: i.e. they were riding together in a litter (*Dom.* 2).

charge of treason: So, too, Dio 67.4.5. The incident is presumably to be assigned to Domitian's later years, for, at first, he had probably relied on the deterrent effects of censorial powers.

ancestral manner: Not even Nero knew what 'in the ancestral manner' meant when told that the Senate had recommended it for him; and, on being informed that the victim was stripped, fastened by the neck to a wooden fork and flogged to death, he thought that suicide was preferable (*Nero* 49.2).

interceded: In the Republic, the tribune of the people possessed the right of veto and any magistrate had the right to veto the motion of any magistrate not superior to him. Subsequently, it referred to the emperor's power of veto over a decree of the Senate, used by Tiberius (*Ann.* 4.30), Nero (*Ann.* 16.11) and Domitian.

difficulty: Note Suetonius' earlier reference (*Dom.* 10) to 'artful cruelty'.

free choice of death: So, too, Dio 67.3.4. Domitian also boasted of his 'clemency' in allowing the Vestals the same choice (*Dom.* 8).

understand that I was present in the Senate: Perhaps this also indicates that Domitian's attendance was not as regular as might be expected: he spent an enormous amount of time ouside of Rome and Italy (Jones, 1992: 26-7).

12 *[page 36]*

financially drained...shows:'Drained' is an exaggeration, and far more so than Pliny's opposing statement that Domitian had enough money but always wanted more (*Pan.* 50.5). The expenses of his building programme (the restoration of numerous buildings and the erection of new ones) were substantial, but construction continued throughout the reign (Jones, 1992: 79). Income, then, must have been matching expenditure. Apart from the enormous increase in army pay (see below) and the usual donatives (*Dom.* 2), considerable sums were spent on his three *congiaria* (*Dom.* 4), on his various wars (6), on the annual subsidy to Decebalus (Dio 67.7.4), the entertainment in the circus and amphitheatre (4), the games (Secular, Capitoline and Minervan: 4) and the public banquets (4). In brief, Domitian spent consistently throughout the reign. Not only that: he left Nerva sufficient funds for the normal *congiarium* and special distribution of corn, for the mitigation and remission of certain taxes, for the agrarian law, new colonies, various public works, and, not least, for the *alimenta*. So Suetonius' 'drained' is a myth. Scholars' views on Domitian's financial management differ substantially. See further Sutherland, 1935: 150-62; *RP* 1.1-17 and Jones, 1992: 72-7.

pay which he had added: See *Dom.* 7.

reduced the number of soldiers: Suetonius' simplistic explanation of how Domitian budgeted for the pay rise is repeated by Dio 67.3.5. There is little evidence to back up these claims (unless he deliberately discouraged recruitment, refusing to replace veterans as they retired). One legion, presumably the XXI Rapax, was apparently destroyed by the Sarmatians in 92 (Wilkes, 1983: 283-4). As for the V Alaudae, there is no evidence that it survived 69 (Jones, 1992: 138). Tacitus had already expressed similar sentiments to Suetonius' (*Agr.* 41.2). On the other hand, an additional legion, the I Minervia, was created early in the reign. A more general consideration, though, is the impossibility of estimating the actual as distinct from the theoretical strength of a legion at any particular time.

plundering in every way: Emperors deemed 'bad' are subject to such charges.

property...seized: So, too, *Pan.* 50.1, 5; but Pliny 'never suggests that (Domitian) acted as he did in order to raise ready cash' (*RP* 1.14). Suetonius' logic is faulty. An emperor in financial difficulties would be able to raise comparatively little by selling his victims' property (Jones, 1992: 74), since the market would soon be saturated and proceeds from sales slump accordingly. Syme's argument (*RP* 1.13-14) is more persuasive. Loss of property was an additional penalty for those guilty of treason, an added 'bonus' for the emperor rather than the cause of the accusation.

majesty of the emperor: Domitian's early reluctance to institute charges of treason soon changed (*Dom.* 8 and 11).

inheritances of totally unrelated people: i.e. Domitian lay claim to the estates of total strangers who were not related to him in any way, quite contrary to his previous policy of rejecting legacies from those with children (*Dom.* 9).

Jewish privy purse: See *Vesp.* 16.

most rigorously: The harshness of Domitian's procurators is illustrated below. Later, so it is claimed, Nerva abolished these abuses, an act commemorated on the coinage (*BMC* 3:15, 17, 19).

all...living a Jewish life...concealing their origin: The interpretation of this passage has long been in dispute. Griffin argues, probably correctly, that the contrast is 'between (1) those Jewish in lifestyle but not by origin; (2) those Jewish by origin but not in lifestyle' (2000: 75) – but see further Thompson (1982: 329-42), Goodman (1989: 41-4), Williams (1990: 196-211) and Griffin (2000: 74-5).

as a young man: His exact date of birth has long been a matter of some dispute (Wallace-Hadrill, 1995: 3); but he was probably about eighteen in 88.

procurator: See *Vesp*. 16.

circumcised: Circumcision was practised amongst Arabs, Samaritans and Egyptians as well as by the Jews.

not...civil: On this quality, see *Vesp*. 12.

impudent and immoderate...deed: These comments are of considerable value. Titus and Domitian differed remarkably in their ability to deal with people. Titus was an capable diplomat, Domitian could never be described as affable or courteous. Preferring his own company (*Dom*. 21), he lacked both the will and the ability to mix with others. In short, he was anti-social.

held out his hand: This was the mode of greeting appropriate to someone of inferior status, unworthy of a kiss.

Caenis: See *Vesp*. 3.

Istria: A peninsula in the Adriatic between Trieste and the Gulf of Quarnero.

offering him a kiss: The custom of the imperial kiss was well established before Domitian's reign (*Tib*. 10.2) and Domitian so greeted Agricola on his return from Britain (*Agr*. 40.3). The practices of the court aside, it was the custom for women to kiss their own relatives and those of their husband as far as the degree of second cousin. However, Vespasian was not her husband and Domitian's public stance was understandable. His reaction to her in private would be another matter and perhaps 'as was her practice' refers to behaviour within the Palace itself.

son-in-law of his brother: The reference is to Flavius Sabinus, married to Titus' daughter Julia (*Dom*. 10 and 22).

servants dressed in white: With the death of Flavius Sabinus (son of Vespasian's brother), his son became the most senior Flavian after Titus and Domitian. His position was strengthened when he married Titus' daughter (Julia), but he seemed to Domitian to be flaunting it when his attendants appeared in imperial white – hence the Homeric warning from an emperor ever suspicious over his personal safety (*Dom*. 14).

'A multiplicity...good thing': Odysseus' words (Homer, *Iliad* 2.204) also appear in *Calig*. 22.1.

13 *[pages 36-7]*

had given the imperial position to his father and brother: Although Domitian had no real power before Vespasian reached Rome in 70 (*Hist.* 4.39), the court poets and others later found it politic to gild the lily (Martial 9.101.15-16; Quintilian, 10.1.91).

bringing back his wife: See *Dom.* 3.

divine bed: The Latin equivalent (*pulvinar*) is the technical term for the sacred couch used for the images of the gods. In the *Vesp.*, such a comment would have been included amongst his commendable deeds (and not amongst his vices) as an example of his sense of humour.

heard with pleasure: Statius notes the emperor's refusal to be so addressed (1.6.84: dated to c. December 89). Suetonius, then, is referring to a later date, when persistent flattery had softened imperial inhibitions.

Lord: Augustus rejected this form of address (*Aug.* 53.1), as did Tiberius (*Tib.* 27; Dio 58.8.4) – in Latin, the word suggests a master of slaves or a political tyrant.

amphitheatre: See *Dom.* 4.

competition on the Capitol: See *Dom.* 4.

Palfurius Sura: See *Vesp.* 9.

worthy of no answer: At the games, favours were often requested but not always successfully: see Caligula's response in *AJ* 19.24-6. Refusal by an emperor to make any response was taken as a sign of arrogance.

ordered them...to shut up: Hadrian followed the Domitianic precedent (Dio 69.6.1).

arrogance: So, too, Aurelius Victor 11.2 and Eutropius 7.23.4. Pliny goes further, linking Domitianic arrogance and fear (*Pan.* 49.1), whereas Suetonius discusses the latter in *Dom.* 14.

dictating: i.e. to his Chief Secretary, probably the freedman Abascantus (*PIR2* F 194), unless the anecdote is to be assigned to the last years of the reign when the incumbent was the equestrian Titinius Capito (*PIR2* O 62).

Lord and God: Most scholars have accepted that Domitian insisted on being so addressed, even though the title is nowhere attested epigraphically; see Jones, 1992: 108-9.

statues to him on the Capitol...golden or silver: So, too, Dio 67.8.1 and Eutropius 7.23.2. Statues in silver or gold, when set up in public, held special significance for the Romans, who regarded the practice as equivalent to deification.

certain weight: The usually accepted weight is one hundred (Roman) pounds, since that is the weight of the golden statue of Domitian that the dying Priscilla is supposed to have asked her husband Abascantus to set up on the Capitol (Statius 5.1.191).

arcades: Even under Augustus, there were many in Rome and sometimes they were surmounted with statues (*Aug.* 31.5). Note Suetonius' hostility towards Domitian, since he includes part of his building programme amidst his non-commendable deeds.

arches: Platner describes an arch as a 'large monument...usually standing free from other structures and pierced by from two to three passage-ways', whereas the arcade 'is an arch or gate intended as a passage way' (*PA* 33, 275). As early as 196 BC (Livy 33.27.4), the Romans erected arches to mark victories in war and other achievements. Domitian maintained the tradition (Dio 68.1.1).

insignia: The insignia surmounting the arch consisted of the victor on horseback or (as here) in a chariot.

regions: See *Dom.* 1.

seventeen consulships: He was criticised for this by Pliny (*Pan.* 58.1) and Ausonius (*Grat. Act.* 6) but praised by Statius (4.1.1-2). Six consulships (five suffect) were held under Vespasian (*Dom.* 2), one under Titus and three between 89 and 96. See Eck, 1970: 55-76.

in successive years: i.e. from 82 to 88.

purely for the title: Suetonius means that he discharged none of the duties pertaining to the office.

majority only up to the Ides of January: i.e. 13 January. Epigraphic evidence (Gallivan, 1981: 190-1) supports Suetonius' statement. In 86 and 87, he was replaced by 22 January; in 92 and 95 by 13 January (*MW* 13, 14, 17). But Augustus once held the consulship for a few hours only (*Aug.* 26.3), Tiberius for a few days (*Tib.* 26.2) and Caligula until 7 January (*Calig.* 17.1). Moreover, Vespasian and Titus were the ordinary consuls of 70 without ever being in Rome, or even in Italy, as was Trajan in 98 when he remained in Germany.

assumed the name Germanicus: This title, claimed after his victory over the Chatti and first attested between 9 June and 28 August 83, remained part of his official titulature throughout the reign (Buttrey, 1980: 52-6).

two triumphs: Domitian celebrated triumphs on three occasions, i.e. in 83, 86 and 89 (see *Dom.* 6). Suetonius assigns Domitian's renaming of September and October to the period after 86 (and before 89) which agrees with the papyrological evidence.

changed...months: Assigning new names to the months of the year would have interested Suetonius, for he was an authority on the Roman year (Censorinus, *De Die Natali* 20.2). Various emperors refused or accepted similar changes (*Julius* 76.1, *Aug.* 31.2, *Tib.* 26.2, *Calig.* 15.2 and *Nero* 55), whilst Dio 72.15.3 has Commodus renaming all twelve. In general, though, since *Quintilis* and *Sextilis* retained their new names, later emperors tended to concentrate on September and October, so as to continue the sequence. Domitian's changes were recorded by Martial (9.1.1-4), Statius (4.1.42),

Pliny (*Pan.* 54.4) and Aurelius Victor 11.4 – but the original names still occur in the minutes of the Arval Brothers for 87 (*MW* 14). After Domitian's death, neither was used (Macrobius, *Sat.* 1.12.36-7).

names of months: He named September *Germanicus* because he became emperor on 14 September 81, and October became *Domitianus* as he was born on 24 October 51.

14 *[page37]*

object of hatred...to all: Suetonius' 'all' is hardly consistent with his statement that 'the soldiers took (his death) very badly' (*Dom.* 23).

friends and close freedmen: Apart from Malalas (who states that Domitian 'was murdered in the temple of Zeus by the senators'; 10.52), the sources agree that the assassination was the result of a palace conspiracy, planned and carried out by those closest to him (Dio 67.15.1-6; Eutropius 7.23; Aurelius Victor 11.7; Orosius 7.10.7). Dio names the assassins as Parthenius (see *Dom.* 16), Sigerius, Entellus and Stephanus (17); he adds that, according to tradition, Domitia as well as the praetorian prefects Norbanus and Petronius Secundus were not unaware of the plot; and mentions that the conspirators had discussed their plans with Nerva. Whatever the truth of that allegation, no hint of his involvement occurs in Suetonius, nor could any be expected.

wife: Suetonius' version is repeated by Aurelius Victor 11.7 and his epitomator 11.11, who suggest a reason for her involvement ('her love for the actor Paris': *Dom.* 3). Neither Eutropius nor Orosius refer to her. Dio, however, mentions the tradition that she was not unaware of the plot (67.15.2) but then adds (67.15.4) that she had obtained a list of people whom Domitian suspected (her own name being included) and had given it to the conspirators who accordingly moved their plans forward.

year and last day...manner of his death: Domitian's obsession with astrology is also attested by Dio 67.15.60 and is apparent from *Dom.* 10.

Chaldeans: i.e. the astrologers. See *Dom.* 10 and MacMullen, 1966: 132-4, 325-7.

mushrooms: The anecdote is perhaps to be assigned to the period after Vespasian's accession, when Claudius' fate would have had an even greater impact on Domitian. The association of mushrooms with Claudius' demise began, in one sense, with Nero who called them the 'food of the Gods' (*Nero* 33.1) and was maintained by Tacitus (*Ann.* 12.67), Suetonius (*Claud.* 44.2), Martial (1.20.4) and Juvenal (5.147).

timid and nervous: Suetonius' theme is that Domitian's natural apprehensiveness was increased by the simultaneous elevation of his father to the principate, the murder of his uncle Sabinus and his own escape from death. Now, he believed, he was a target and would remain so; hence he became 'cruel because of fear' (*Dom.* 3).

decree...vines: See *Dom.* 7.

pamphlets: It was not unusual for people to show their disapproval of an emperor in this way (*Aug.* 55; *Tib.* 66; *Otho* 3.2; *Vit.* 14.4 and *Dom.* 8).

this verse: An epigram by Evenus of Ascalon, imitated by Ovid (*Fasti* 1.355-9). Sacrificing a vine-gnawing goat to Bacchus is referred to by Varro (*RR* 1.2) and Vergil (*G.* 2.380).

same fear: Pliny provides other examples of his timidity (*Pan.* 49.1; 82.1).

especially eager for all such things: So, too, Dio 67.4.2.

lictors: In the Republic, magistrates, priests and others were assigned a number of attendants (lictors) who went before them carrying a bundle of *fasces* (rods bound together by red thongs) and clearing a path for them; however, there is no evidence that they performed these functions during the Empire. Augustus appears to have had twenty-four lictors until 29 BC (*StR* 1.387), as did Domitian (according to Dio 67.4.3; but Statius 4.1.8-10 refers to his twelve lictors). See further Purcell, 1983: 148-52.

attendants: Roman magistrates were attended by scribes, messengers, lictors, personal servants and heralds.

official robe: It was a special toga with purple bands or stripes woven into it. Suetonius apparently commented on it in his work on clothing, according to Servius (on *Aen.* 7.612). Apart from the equestrians, those who could wear it were the kings, consuls (when opening the temple of Janus), augurs, the Salii, the Priests of Jupiter and Mars. The knights wore it on various public occasions, e.g. when they marched in procession before the censor (Martial 5.41.5) or acted as honorary bodyguards (as here) or served as funeral escorts (*Ann.* 3.2) or were part of public banquets (Statius 4.2.32).

time...danger: See *Dom.* 14.

decorated...the walls...with phengite: Phengite is a variety of Muscovite, either a crystallised gypsum (Bates and Jackson, 1987: 498) or else a high-silica Muscovite (Clark, 1993: 539). That Domitian was (rightly) concerned for his security also emerges from the design of his palace (Jones, 1992: 97-8), hinted at by Pliny (*Pan.* 49.1).

majority of prisoners...into his hand: Dio's version (67.12.5) is close to Suetonius'.

in order to persuade...good precedent: Dio (67.14.4) attributes a similar motive to Domitian.

household slaves: Suetonius is referring to the senior freedmen who had the greatest access to the emperor (*Titus* 8; *Vesp.* 21) and also represented a potential source of danger to him.

condemned...to death: Dio claims that he was first exiled then killed (67.14.4).

Epaphroditus: Nero's petitions officer, the freedman Epaphroditus (*PIR2* E 69), took part in revealing the Pisonian conspiracy (*Ann.* 15.55) and later helped Nero to commit suicide (*Nero* 49.3). Under Domitian, he was exiled, perhaps c. 93 (Dio 67.14.4) and subsequently executed. That he was the former master of the Stoic philosopher Epictetus is unlikely (Weaver, 1994: 475), and it even less likely that he retained his Neronian post after 68 or that he was the Epaphroditus to whom Josephus dedicated the *AJ* (1.8-9), *Vita* (430) and *Contra Apionem* (1.1, 2.1, 2.926). On him, see Weaver, 1994: 468-79.

petitions' officer: For a discussion of his role, see Millar, 1977: 77-9, 102-5, 240-52.

Nero...aided by his hand: For his role in Nero's suicide, see *Nero* 49.3. That this was the reason for his execution by Domitian is also mentioned by Pliny (*Pan.* 53.4).

15 *[page 38]*

his cousin, Flavius Clemens: Clemens was the grandson (not the son, as Mooney,1930: 580) of Vespasian's brother; his wife was Domitian's niece Domitilla (*Vesp.* 3). So both husband and wife were perilously close to the throne. In 95, Clemens was appointed ordinary consul with the emperor, no doubt to groom his sons for the succession. He was in office until 30 April and executed soon after (Jones, 1992: 47-8, 115-18).

suddenly: Sordi, believing that there is some connection between this word and similar phrases from *1 Clement* (e.g. 'sudden and repeated misfortunes and calamities'), argues unconvincingly that this is further proof that Clemens was a Christian who perished in the Domitianic persecution (1994: 50-1). It should also be noted that Christians are never mentioned by Suetonius. For a detailed discussion of Domitian and the Christians, see Keresztes, 1979: 257-72; Jones, 1992: 114-17 and Sordi, 1994: 43-53.

most contemptible inactivity: Clemens' 'inactivity' may have been inherited from his father (Wallace, 1987: 343-58). On the other hand, the word could have the sense of 'indifference to public affairs', a charge directed at Christians (and vigorously denied by Tertullian, *Apol.* 42).

slenderest of suspicions: Dio, on the other hand, states that 'the charge was atheism, on which many others who drifted into Jewish ways were condemned' (67.14.1). The precise reason for Clemens' execution is disputed as is the nature of his 'atheism'. Some argue that he was a Christian or a Christian sympathizer (Pergola, 1978: 407-23), others that he favoured Judaism (Kerestzes, 1979: 261-8). More recently, Sordi has restated her view that he 'died as a martyr in the year of his consulate' (1994: 188).

In Talmudic and Midrashic sources, reference is made to a Jewish proselyte named Onkelos (son of Kalonymos and a nephew of Titus) whom the emperor tried to arrest (Smallwood, 1956: 8). The vague similarity between Clemens and Kalonymos together with the reference to the imperial family may add some weight to Dio's version (67.14.2). Again, the Midrash and the

Babylonian Talmud refer to a senator and his wife who were converted to Judaism and executed by an emperor (Smallwood, 1956: 8, 10). However, none of this proves the existence of Clemens' sympathy with Judaism. The only 'evidence' that he was a Christian (apart from his 'inactivity' and his 'atheism') is archaeological (Pergola, 1978: 413-15), but the relevant Christian cemetery bearing the name *Domitilla* could be dated as late as to the end of the second century AD (Smallwood, 1956: 8). In fact, there is no direct link between his death and Christianity, though some modern Christian apologists have even argued that Flavius Clemens and bishop Clement (author of *1 Clement*) should be identified (Keresztes, 1973: 8). It was only in the eighth century that Clemens was hailed (by Syncellus) as a Christian (Prigent, 1974: 471), hundreds of years after his wife had been so acclaimed. Then, in the sixteenth century, Cardinal Caesar Baronius (*Vesp.* 3) was the first to link Clemens' execution with a general persecution of the church.

almost in his very consulship: In 95, Domitian held his seventeenth consulship, with Clemens as his colleague, an appointment connected with the public announcement of the adoption of two of Clemens' sons. On Suetonius' evidence, he must have been executed fairly soon after 30 April 95 (the suffects came into office on 1 May). Dio (67.14.1) and Philostratus (*V. Apoll.* 8.25), however, contradict Suetonius and claim that Clemens was consul when he died. In matters such as this, the unambiguous statement of the senior Hadrianic official is preferable – Dio and Philostratus presumably confused the terms 'consul' and 'consular'.

designated...sons as his successors: Clemens and Domitilla had at least seven children (*ILS* 1839), two of whom were designated by Domitian to succeed him. Presumably, 'publicly' indicates a public announcement of the adoption of Clemens' sons. The boys' education was entrusted to Quintilian (*Vesp.* 18).

hastened on his death: Philostratus also links the two events (*V. Apoll.* 8.25).

eight months in a row: Suetonius is referring to the first eight months of 96.

Let him strike: The 'him' is Jupiter.

Capitol and the temple of the Flavian clan: The lightning's targets were all intimately connected with Domitian.

hit from the sky: Similar portents preceded the deaths of Gaius (*Calig.* 57.2), Claudius (*Claud.* 46) and Nero (*Galba* 1). On omens and portents in Suetonius, see Wallace-Hadrill, 1995: 191-7.

Palatine house: The next targets (the imperial palace and bedroom) were even more intimately connected with him. The palace complex on the Palatine, designed by Rabirius (Martial 7.56.1), was virtually completed by the end of 92. Its style was unique. A spectator in the Circus Maximus would have looked up at a huge curved terrace in front of the palace and at buildings that towered over the terrace (Statius 4.2.1-67). It was some forty thousand square metres in area; the vestibule measured 23.5 m. by 32.5 m. with a height of over 27.5 m. One hall had walls of highly-coloured polished stone mentioned by Suetonius as enabling the emperor to see a reflection of what was happening behind him (*Dom.* 14). For Plutarch, the palace represented 'a disease of building, and a desire, like Midas', of turning everything to gold or stone' (*Publicola* 15.5); for more detail, see Blake, 1959: 115-22; MacDonald, 1982: 47-74, 127-9 and Sablayrolles, 1994: 118-21 (plan and illustrations).

inscription: The inscription must have been on a bronze tablet attached to the statue's base and not carved on to it.

base: There was now no doubt whatsoever about the identity of the target, since Jupiter had concentrated more and more obviously on Domitian – his temples, his palace, then his bedroom and finally the inscription bearing his name.

triumphal statue: The reference is probably to the massive equestrian statue of Domitian that was the subject of Statius 1.1.1-107. In 89, the Senate had voted that it be erected in the Forum to commemorate his victories over Germany and Dacia (1.1.7). Its concrete base was some 11.80 m. by 5.90 m.; however, like the rest of his statues, it was destroyed on his death (*Dom.* 23). See further Hardie, 1983: 131-2.

tree: On the tree's history, see *Vesp.* 5.

Fortuna of Praeneste: Situated twenty-three miles to the south-east of Rome, Praeneste (modern Palestrina) was the seat of the famous Praenestine oracle consulted by emperors (*Tib.* 63.1; *HA Sev. Alex.* 4.6) and others.

entrusted...to her care: Only Suetonius mentions Domitian's habit of offering sacrifice at the temple on the first of January each year.

Minerva whom he worshipped: See *Dom.* 4.

was departing from her chapel: Two unfavourable omens not noted by Suetonius are described by Dio – Domitian dreamed that Rusticus (*Dom.* 10) 'approached him with a sword and that Minerva, whose statue he kept in his bed-chamber, had thrown away her weapons and, mounted upon a chariot drawn by black horses, was plunging into an abyss' (67.16.1).

chapel: His reverence for her was such that there was a chapel to her in his bedroom.

disarmed by Jupiter: Athena (Minerva) sprang fully armed from Zeus' head, according to legend.

Ascletarion: Dio (67.16.3) has a similar account but does not name the astrologer.

Latinus: He was frequently mentioned by Martial. Juvenal (1.36) names him as an informer, as does Marius Maximus (scholiast on Juvenal 4.53). Suetonius indicates that he was an intimate friend of Domitian, an emperor who, despite his fondness for solitude, sought congenial company in unexpected quarters (*Dom.* 4).

16 *[pages 38-9]*

apples: These were African apples that came in two varieties, one white and the other red (*NH* 15.47).

Aquarius: Astrological predictions are supposed to be contingent on the relative positions of the stars and seven other heavenly bodies (Sun, Moon, Jupiter, Venus, Saturn, Mercury and Mars); and the zone of the heavens within which their paths lie is the Zodiac, itself divided into twelve constellations, the eleventh of which is Aquarius. Around 20 January, the sun enters the zone of Aquarius, the name being derived from the rains that are prevalent at that time of the year. In 96, the Moon would enter Aquarius on September 15/16 and leave on September 18/19 (Domitian was assassinated on 18 September). See further Brind'Amour, 1981: 338-44.

diviner: Dio names him: 'Larginus Proculus was condemned to death, but his execution was postponed in order that he might die after the emperor had escaped the danger; but in the meantime Domitian was slain, and so Proculus' life was saved and he received 400,000 sestertii from Nerva' (67.16.2).

sent from Germany: Dio (67.16.2) states that 'he was sent by the governor (of Germany)' – either Trajan in Upper Germany or Licinius Sura in Lower (Eck, 1982: 326).

lightning flash: See *Dom.* 15.

change: Suetonius has him predicting a change of government, Dio the date of Domitian's death (67.16.2).

sixth hour was reported to him: At this period, sundials and water-clocks were in use and, in the homes of the wealthy, a slave was employed to announce the hour (*NH* 7.182; Martial 8.67.1).

fifth: According to the astrological calculations of Brind'Amour, the fifth hour on 18 September 96 was around ten and eleven in the morning (1981: 339), which coheres well enough with what Suetonius says here and with Philostratus' statement that the assassination occurred around noon (*V. Apoll.* 8.26-7).

hurrying to his bodily care: The reference is presumably to such activities as a massage, bath and exercise. At this stage of his account, however, Dio states that 'he was ready to take his afternoon rest, as was his custom' (67.17.1); and the Suda similarly records that he was stabbed during his siesta.

chamberlain Parthenius: Parthenius was imperial chamberlain at the end of the reign, a post of considerable influence (*Dom.* 14). Martial often mentions him, asking him to ensure that Domitian saw his poems (5.6.2) and sending him a poem for the fifth birthday of his son Burrus (4.45). His was a major role in Domitian's murder, but, whereas Dio (67.15.1) and the later historians name him as the instigator of the plot and as one of the actual murderers (Eutropius 8.1; Orosius 7.11), Suetonius is more reticent, portraying him as the organiser who leaves the actual murder to someone else. When Domitian went to retrieve a dagger he kept under his pillow, he found that the blade had been removed; Dio (57.17.1) assigns responsibility to Parthenius; in Suetonius, no culprit is named (*Dom.* 17). Presumably, he was also one of the freedmen who, according to Suetonius (*Dom.* 14), formed part of the conspiracy. Dio is far more helpful, naming three of them (Parthenius, Sigerius and Entellus). Parthenius survived his master for about a year. Nerva, however, was unable to restrain the praetorians who 'cut off his genitals, stuffed them into his mouth and then cut his throat' (*Epit. de Caes.* 12.7-8).

someone bringing something of importance: The reference is to Stephanus. Philostratus (*V. Apoll.* 8. 25) says that Stephanus approached Domitian as he was returning from the law-court and asked him for a private audience; Domitian then took him aside privately into the men's apartment of the palace, where Stephanus stabbed him. In Dio's version, Parthenius removed the blade from the dagger under the emperor's pillow when Domitian left the court for his afternoon rest, and then admitted Stephanus (67.17.1). The only substantial difference is that Domitian's visit to the law-court is not mentioned by Suetonius.

17 *[page 39]*

conspirators: See *Dom.* 14.

Stephanus: One of the prime movers in Domitian's murder was Domitilla's freedman, Stephanus. His action, according to Philostratus, was foretold by a portent, a halo (*stephanos* in Greek) which surrounded the sun and dimmed its brilliance (*V. Apoll.* 8.23): he 'was also led by consideration for the murdered man (i.e. Flavius Clemens), or for all Domitian's victims' (*V. Apoll.* 8.25). Suetonius' explanation is less imaginative – he had been charged with theft. According to Dio (supported by Philostratus, *V. Apoll.* 8. 26), at exactly the same time as Domitian was being murdered, Apollonius of Tyana 'mounted a lofty rock at Ephesus...(saying) "Good, Stephanus! Bravo, Stephanus! You have struck, you have wounded, you have slain"' (67.18.1-2). But he was killed by those not involved in the conspiracy.

Domitilla: Domitian's niece (*Vesp.* 3).

wool and bandages: Only Suetonius records the important fact that – for some time – Stephanus was fully prepared to murder Domitian. So there was ample opportunity for the conspirators to consult the praetorian prefects and Nerva (or some other suitable candidate) had they wanted to do so.

claiming to have information: According to Philostratus, Stephanus claimed that Flavius Clemens was still alive and plotting against Domitian (*V. Apoll.* 8.25).

stabbed...groin: Philostratus claims that Domitian was first stabbed in the thigh (*V. Apoll.* 8.25).

adjutant: He would be attached to an officer of varying rank, and would be on pay and a half or double pay accordingly (Maxwell, 1981: 239). Clodianus was probably attached to one of Domitian's praetorian prefects.

Maximus, a freedman of Parthenius: In Dio, Stephanus had 'knocked Domitian to the ground...Then Parthenius rushed in, or, as some believe, he sent in Maximus, a freedman' (67.17.2).

Satur: He is possibly the same person as Siger(i)us, described by Dio as a chamberlain (67.15.2) and is coupled with Parthenius by Martial 4.78.8.

certain men from the gladiatorial school: Mentioned only by Suetonius. Perhaps they were from one of Domitian's four gladiatorial schools (*Dom.* 4). One wonders how they managed to enter the Palace.

boy...this piece of information: Mentioned by Suetonius alone (unless he is one of Dio's 'whispering boys' of 67.15.3).

Lares of the bedchamber: Other emperors are attested as having a shrine for the worship of the *Lares* in or near the bedroom – *Aug.* 7.1, *Calig.* 7 and *Nero* 25.2.

struggled...long time: Philostratus provides more details: 'Domitian, who had always been of strong pysique, grappled with Stephanus after the blow (to his thigh), knocked him down, and pinned him, and then gouged his eyes and beat his face with the stem of a golden cup which had been lying there for use in ritual. The bodyguards...burst in and killed the tyrant when he was already sinking' (*V. Apoll.* 8.250).

dagger hidden under the pillow: See *Dom.* 16.

fourteenth...Kalends of October: 18 September 96. Pliny regarded it as 'day of triple joy' (*Pan.* 92.4), referring to the murder of Domitian, the accession of Nerva and the birth of Trajan (? in 53).

forty-fifth year: So, too, Eutropius (7.23.6), Aurelius Victor (11.7) and the epitomator (11.12). Domitian was born on 24 October 51 and so Dio 67.18.2 is more precise than Suetonius (and the others), giving his age at death as 44 years, 10 months and 26 days.

fifteenth (year) of his rule: Suetonius is wrong and so is Eutropius 7.23.6; Domitian died in his sixteenth year as emperor. Dio states that he reigned for 15 years and five days (67.18.2). Less accurate are the epitomator of Aurelius Victor 11.1 and Orosius 7.10.1 (15 years) and Malalas (15 years and 2 months: 10.48).

corpse-bearers: According to Martial, a funeral bier was carried by four (8.75.9) or six (6.77.10) slaves.

common bier: Whereas the stock rhetorical tyrant received no burial, Domitian was at least allocated that of a pauper – hence Suetonius' vocabulary. A pauper's body was carried to burial on a bier (Martial 2.81.2), being placed in a cheap wooden coffin that was re-used and not burned with the body.

Latin Way: It branched off to the east from the Appian Way.

Phyllis...brought the remains: Procopius, however, states that Domitia collected the pieces of her husband's flesh (the people had 'carved up his body'), sewed them together and had a sculptor use the result as a model for a statue (*Secret History* 8.12-22).

Temple of the Flavian clan: See *Dom.* 1, 5 and 15.

Julia, the daughter of Titus: Her mother was, almost certainly, Arrecina Tertulla and not Marcia Furnilla (as Martinet, 1981: 29-33). See *Dom.* 22.

18 *[pages 39-40]*

Some idea of Domitian's physical appearance can be gleaned from his coins and from those few busts which survive – see Daltrop, 1966: Plates 23-35 and the Toledo Domitian (cover of Jones, 1992). More detail could be expected from the literary sources. Malalas portrays him as 'tall, slender, fair-skinned, with short fair hair, grey eyes and a slightly hunched back' (10.48), while Philostratus says that his 'his voice is harsh even when he is talking kindly, and his cheek is flushed with anger' (7.28). Suetonius' description, fortunately, is more substantial. Every Suetonian *Life* has some reference to his subject's physical appearance; see *Vesp.* 20.

tall in stature: This was supposed to be a sign of laziness since one's blood had further to travel (Pseudo Aristotle 813b)! and, as well as Suetonius (*Dom.* 19), both Dio (67.6.3) and Pliny (*Pan.* 14.5) do refer to his idleness.

countenance...modest: Statius (4.2.41-4) interprets his expression as one of serenity, as does Martial 5.6.10.

redness of blushing: The ancient sources used Domitian's readiness to blush to bolster their pre-determined interpretation of his character. For Tacitus, it hid his shame (*Agr.* 45.2); for Philostratus, his anger (*V. Apoll.* 7.28) and, for Pliny, his impudence (*Pan.* 48.4).

large eyes...vision dull: Weak eyes were a sign of cowardice (Pseud. Arist. 807b and 808a). Poor vision seems to be inconsistent with Domitian's attested ability as an archer (*Dom.* 19).

toes rather short: This was a sign of greed (Pseud. Arist. 810a) and so Domitian's appearance was hiding a nature that was vicious.

unsightly...baldness: His baldness is mentioned by Juvenal (4.38) and Ausonius (2.12).

obesity: Nero (*Nero.* 51), Vitellius (*Vit.* 17.2) and Titus (*Titus* 3) had a similar problem – but this was a sign of strength (Pseud. Arist. 810b)!

thinness of his legs: Polemo (*De Physiog* 2.5) states that it was a sign of timidity. Gaius (*Calig.* 50.1) and Nero (*Nero* 51) had this defect too, but Domitian's thin legs were the result of an illness.

so vexed by his baldness: Perhaps Domitian was not as sensitive about his baldness as Suetonius states. On four occasions, Martial mocks this condition and those who try to conceal it, e.g. at 2.41.10; 3.93.2; 6.57.1-4 and 6.74.2. At other times, he is even less tactful. His description of Marinus' bald patch is blunt enough (10.83.1-3) as are his lines on Labienus' (5.49.6-7) and this was intended for the emperor's eyes (Garthwaite, 1978: 93-4). Needless to say, the recently discovered Toledo marble bust of Domitian has no suggestion of baldness.

inserted even the following: The dedication Domitian appended to his work 'On the Care of Hair' (an unusual topic for someone so worried about his baldness) consisted of a line from Homer (*Il.* 21.108, where Achilles is speaking and refusing to spare Lycaon).

19 *[page 40]*

intolerant of toil: The physiognomists explained this by his height. See *Dom.* 18.

on campaign rarely on horseback: Suetonius' statement is contradicted by both Aurelius Victor (11.3) and his so-called epitomator (11.2).

carried on a litter: The prime example is Verres (*Verr.* 2.5.27).

no enthusiasm for arms: The Romans did not classify arrows as weapons (Festus, p. 3; Lindsay).

archery: Both of Vespasian's sons were skilled with the bow (*Titus* 5). In the Roman army, archers were part of the auxiliary forces.

Alban retreat: See *Dom.* 4.

passed through gaps between his fingers: But this is inconsistent with his poor sight (*Dom.* 18).

20 *[page 40]*

neglected the humane studies: The term includes literature, rhetoric, music, mathematics and legal studies. Both Tacitus (*Hist.* 4.86) and Suetonius (*Dom.* 2) portray Domitian as a philistine, hypocritically pretending in his youth to be interested in literature. More diplomatic is Quintilian's comment that 'government of the world has diverted (Domitian) from the studies he had commenced (10.1.91); and, writing in Vespasian's reign, the Elder Pliny (*NH Praef.* 5) had rated Domitian's poetry more highly than Titus'. However, his interest in music was minimal (Philostratus, *V. Apoll.* 7.4). See further Coleman, 1986: 3088-111.

libraries...destroyed by fire rebuilt...Alexandria: Substantial losses were incurred in the fires of 64 (*Nero* 38.2) and 80 (*Titus* 8) and the civil war of 69. Libraries likely to have suffered include the one in the Portico of Octavia (destroyed in 80; Dio 66.24.2), those established by Augustus in the temple of Apollo on the Palatine, by Asinius Pollio in the Hall of Liberty and by Tiberius in the temple of Augustus.

copies...sought from everywhere: Unusual if he was really the philistine suggested above.

never gave any attention to history...poetry: Presumably, the phrase 'from the beginning of his time as emperor' is to be understood.

Memoirs and Acts of Tiberius Caesar: Tiberius' Acts (*Acta*) are his enactments, his edicts, decrees, injunctions and rescripts (Millar, 1977: 260-1). Apart from Tiberius (*Tib*. 61.1), other eminent Romans who wrote their memoirs include Caesar (*Iul*. 56.1), Augustus (*Aug*. 85.1) and Vespasian (Josephus, *Vita* 342). Domitian's admiration of Tiberius went beyond his reading matter, according to Sauron (1991: 39-42) who believes that it was based on superstition: both were born under Scorpio, both became Caesar under Cancer and both became emperor under Virgo. Therefore, he argues, it was far from coincidental that these signs of Zodiac were found in Tiberius' cave at Sperlonga and in Domitian's at Alba, for this so-called 'Ninfeo Bergantino' was, almost certainly, modelled on Tiberius' cave.

letters...somebody's talent: The authorship of these is discussed by Millar, 1977: 203-28. Even if Suetonius' observation were correct, Domitian would not have been the only emperor who had someone else prepare his speeches. Tacitus is scathing about Nero's 'speech composed by Seneca' (*Ann*. 13.3); Trajan's speeches were written by Licinius Sura (Julian, *Caes*. 327 A-B) and, after Sura's death, by Hadrian (*HA, Hadr*. 3.11). Furthermore, Suetonius is hardly consistent, for he previously criticised the way in which Domitian began a letter (*Dom*. 13).

noteworthy sayings: An emperor's noteworthy sayings were a standard feature of Suetonius' Lives. The Domitian pictured here seems somewhat different from the philistine of *Dom*. 2. In a work less hurried (and longer), these inconsistencies might perhaps have been smoothed over.

Maecius: Senatorial Maecii of this period include Maecius Celer (consul 101); Roscius Maecius Celer (consul 100); Maecius Postumus (consul 98); Maecius Postumus (Arval Brother in 80) and Maecius Rufus (consul under Vespasian).

snow sprinkled with honeyed wine: The recipe for mead has changed but little – mix new Attic honey and old Falernian (Macrobius, *Sat*. 7.12.9). Perhaps Domitian was thinking of the practice of cooling wine and mead with snow – sometimes, the wine was strained through a linen cloth covered with snow (Martial 8.45.3, 9.22.8, 14.103-4). Here, presumably, the reference is to someone with more grey than red in his hair, reminiscent of the colours of Sulla's face (Plutarch *Sulla* 3).

21 *[pages 40-1]*

lot...most wretched: Marcus Aurelius assigned the remark to Hadrian (*HA Avid. Cass*. 2.6); but it was not completely original. Dio attributes a less concise version to Augustus (54.15.2).

dice: For other 'sinners', see *Aug*. 70.2, 71.1; *Calig*. 41.2; *Claud* 5, 33.2;

Nero 30.3 and *Vit.* 4. Though forbidden by law (Cicero, *Phil.* 2.56), it was prevalent at the Saturnalia (Martial 5.84.5, 4.14.7-9, 14.1.3) and elsewhere (Juvenal 1.88-90; 8.10; 11.176 and 14.4). Centuries later, gambling was still being attacked by Ambrose (*De Tobia* 11, 38) and Cyprian (*De Aleat.* 5-11). See further Balsdon, 1969: 154-9.

even on working days: So did Augustus (*Aug.* 71.1).

bathe during the day: In this section, Suetonius portrays Domitian's behaviour as perfectly normal. On the usual time for bathing, see *Vesp.* 21.

lunch to satiety: The usual time for the midday meal was the sixth hour (*Aug.* 78.1).

not take anything at dinner time: It was regularly taken at the ninth hour (Cicero, *Ad Fam.* 9.26.1). Domitian's behaviour is described quite differently, but more vividly in the *Panegyricus*, where he is accused of 'belching from a full stomach, throwing food at his guests, (then)...indulging in secret gluttony and private excesses' (49.6).

Matian apple: C. Matius (*PIR*2 M 369), after whom this apple was named (*NH* 15.49), must be distinguished from the C. Matius (presumably his father) who is attested as a friend of Cicero (*ad Fam.* 11.27, 28) and Caesar (*Iul.* 5.2.). Mooney (1930: 602) and Galli (1991: 100) wrongly identify them. The younger Matius wrote three books on cookery and developed the species of apple that bore his name.

modest drink: Both Martial (4.8.10) and Statius (5.1.123) refer to Domitian's temperate drinking habits.

drinking party: It followed the evening meal and lasted as long as the participants wished – Nero's went from midday to midnight' (*Nero* 27.2). In this chapter, Suetonius' hostility to the emperor is evident, for Domitian's rejection of such behaviour has been excluded from his commendable deeds and relegated to the end of the *Life*. Usually, participation in it is linked to and explains imperial vices (*Nero* 26-7; *Vit.* 13.1; *Titus* 7). Domitian's refusal to participate is not portrayed as commendable but, rather is an indication of his anti-social behaviour and suspicious nature. See *Dom.* 3 and below.

nothing except walk...by himself: References to Domitian's fondness for solitude usually contain malicious overtones (*Dom.* 3). Pliny's interpretation was openly hostile: Domitian avoided his subjects and lived a life of solitude behind locked doors (*Pan.* 49.2), whereas Trajan worked and ate in public (49.4-5).

22 *[page 41]*

excessively lustful: Most of the charges levelled at Domitian are comparatively minor, apart from the claim that the emperor was guilty of incest with his niece and of causing her death by forcing an abortion on her (see below). Other sources provide no substantial details. Like the stock tyrant,

Domitian is guilty of lust, cruelty (*Dom.* 10) and greed (*Dom.* 9), but the evidence Suetonius provides in support of the first charge is superficial in the extreme (next item).

bed wrestling: Domitian's remark (reported by Aurelius Victor 11.5 and the epitomator 11.7) could be compared, in tone, with the phrase 'horizontal jogging' coined in 'Yes Prime Minister' (Lynn and Jay, 1986: 40). Once again, Suetonius has included amidst Domitian's non-commendable deeds an item that could well have been used to indicate the sense of humour (see *Dom.* 13) to be expected in a son of Vespasian. Where would Suetonius have placed a similar item in his *Vesp.*?

brother's daughter: Domitian's niece Julia was born on 10 August (Jones, 1984: 209) in the early sixties, daughter of Titus and his first wife Arrecina Tertulla (Castritius, 1969: 492-4). The traditional view (Martinet, 1981: 29-33) is that Julia' mother was Marcia Furnilla (*Titus* 4.2). But Titus had more than one daughter (Philostratus, *V. Apoll.* 7.7) and Arrecina Tertulla (unlike Marcia) had close relatives named Julius and Julia (*AJ* 19.191). See further Vinson, 1989: 431-50 and Jones, 1992: 38-42.

Domitia: See *Dom.* 1, 3 and 13.

offered...in marriage...loved...openly: Julia had married her cousin Sabinus (*Dom.* 10) late in Vespasian's reign, but Domitian seduced her before his accession to the throne; then, after the death of Titus and Sabinus, he lived with her openly (even after his wife's return: Dio 67.3.2). Philostratus believes that he married her (*V. Apoll.* 7.7). Finally, he forced her to have an abortion which killed her (see below). Most of this based on unsupported rumour and nothing else – see Vinson, 1989: 431-50.

compelled...abortion: This charge is repeated by Pliny (*Ep.* 4.11.6) and Juvenal (*Sat.* 2.32-3), but the 'evidence' is not convincing. In an epigram (6.3) written in 90, not long after Julia's death and deification, Martial expresses the hope that Domitia will produce a son, implies that the baby's name will be Julius (6.3.1) and states that (the now deified) Julia will be able to watch over him (6.3.5). But if there had been an affair between Domitian and Julia, he would hardly have written those lines; had her recent death been caused by an abortion forced on her by Domitian, Martial would not have dared to humiliate Domitia publicly by urging her to become pregnant, to give the child a name reminiscent of her husband's mistress and finally to remember that the same mistress, now dead and deified (thanks to her husband), would be able to protect the child. See Garthwaite, 1990: 15-16; and, on abortion in the Greco-Roman world, Nardi, 1980: 366-85.

23 *[page 41]*

that he had been slain: Suetonius uses the same Latin words in *Dom.* 16 and 17, linking the formal death notice to the later description of the reaction to the emperor's assassination.

soldiers took it very badly: The soldiers' attitude was not unexpected in view of their substantial increase in pay (*Dom.* 7) and the veterans' privileges that he granted (*MW* 404). Aurelius Victor describes the hostile reaction of the praetorians (11.9, 11) as does the epitomator (12.7).

immediately tried to have him called 'The Deified': Only the Senate could confer this title, though its members always bowed to imperial pressure, as happened when they were 'urged' to deify Hadrian.

ready to avenge him, had not leaders been lacking: Suetonius refers to the praetorian guard. Their prefects' involvement in Domitian' murder would explain why they were not prepared to avenge him. Dio merely states that 'the plot was not unknown to Norbanus...nor to Petronius Secundus, at least this is the tradition' (67.15.1).

they did...later: In 97, Nerva spoke in vain against the praetorians' demand and was even forced to thank them publicly (*Epit. de Caes.* 12.7-8).

Senate...so overjoyed: So, too, Pliny (*Pan.* 52.4-5). But their attitude towards him had been determined by his refusal to take the oath not to execute any senator (Dio 67.2.4).

shields: These were votive shields adorned with Domitian's image. In the Empire, shields with the portraits of emperors (Augustus, *RG* 34.2; Caligula, *Calig.* 16.4) or of their relatives (Germanicus, *Ann.* 2.83) were placed in the Senate or in a temple.

statues of him: Only one survived, according to Procopius (17.3); see also *Dom.* 13.

inscriptions...erased: So, too, Aurelius Victor 11.8, the epitomator 11.13, Macrobius 1.12.37, Eusebius, *Hist. Eccl.* 3.20 and Lactantius (*De Mort. Pers.* 3.3). On Martin's calculation, Domitian's name was erased in more than 40% of surviving inscriptions (1987: 197-202). Pailler and Sablayrolles' detailed examination (1994: 1-55) has yielded a similar overall figure, but the percentages vary widely from area to area (76% in Asia, 33% in Lusitania but only 18% in Rome and Italy).

memory...abolished: Domitian's memory was abolished (*abolitio memoriae*) but not condemned (*damnatio memoriae*). It seems that, whereas *abolitio* is voted on and passed by the Senate, *damnatio* requires a regular judicial procedure against the deceased under a charge of treason. With Domitian, there is some evidence for the former and none for the latter. So his name was erased from inscriptions and his images destroyed. Describing the Senate's reaction, Pliny claimed that 'it was our delight to dash those proud faces to the ground, to smite them with the sword and savage them with the axe...that baleful, fearsome visage (was) cast into the fire' (*Pan.* 52.4-5). See further Pailler/ Sablayrolles, 1994: 11-55.

a crow spoke: Crows were supposed to be able to mimic human speech (Ovid *Met.* 2.547-50; *NH* 10.124).

Tarpeian roof: Criminals convicted of capital offences were thrown to their deaths from the precipitious cliffs (the 'Tarpeian Rock') on the south-western slope of the Capitoline Hill.

moderation of succeeding emperors: This theme was repeated by Tacitus (*Hist.* 1.1; *Agr.* 3.1]), Aurelius Victor (12.1), the epitomator (11.15), Philostratus (*V. Apoll.* 7.8) and Eutropius (8.1). But, in many ways, Domitian's policies were continued by his successors, and most obviously by Trajan. Autocracy and centralisation increased, Domitian's appointees to imperial provinces continued in their posts and innovations such as the rapid promotion of senators from the Greek East east were maintained. See Waters, 1969: 385-405 and Jones, 1992: 170-3).

Bibliography

Alföldy, A., *Die Monarchische Repräsentation im Römischen Kaiserreiche* (Wissenschaftliche Buchgesellschaft Darmstadt, 1970).

Alston, R., 'Roman Military Pay from Caesar to Diocletian' *JRS* 84 (1994) 113-23.

Anderson, J.C., 'Domitian, the Argiletum, and the Temple of Peace' *AJA* 86 (1982) 101-40.

——'A Topographical Tradition in the Fourth Century Chronicles. Domitian's Building Programme' *Historia* 32 (1983) 93-105.

Arnaud, P., 'L' Affaire Mettius Pompusianus ou le Crime de Cartographie' *MEFR* 95 (1983) 677-99.

Auguet, R., *Cruelty and Civilization: The Roman Games* (1972: repr. Routledge, 1994).

Baldwin, B., *Suetonius* (Hakkert, 1983).

Balsdon, J.P.V.D., *Life and Leisure in Ancient Rome* (McGraw-Hill, 1969).

Barrett, A.A., *Caligula: The Corruption of Power* (Batsford, 1989).

——*Agrippina: Mother of Nero* (Batsford, 1996).

Bastomsky, S.J., 'The Death of the Emperor Titus: A tentative Suggestion' *Apeiron* 1 (1967) 22-3.

Bates, R.L. and Jackson, J.A., *Glossary of Geology* 3rd edn (American Geological Institute, 1987).

Bauman, R.A., 'Some Remarks on the Structure and Survival of the *Quaestio de Adulteriis*' *Antichthon* 2 (1968) 68-93.

——*Impietas in Principem* (Beck, 1974).

——'The Resumé of Legislation in Suetonius' *ZRG* 99 (1982) 81-127.

Beard, M., 'The Sexual Status of Vestal Virgins' *JRS* 70 (1980) 12-27.

Benediktson, D.T., 'A Survey of Suetonius Scholarship, 1938-1987' *CW* 86 (1993) 377-447.

Bennett, J., *Trajan Optimus Princeps: A Life and Times* (Routledge, 1997).

Berchem, D. van, 'Un Banquier chez les Helvètes' *Ktèma* 3 (1978) 267-74.

——'Une Inscription Flavienne du Musée d'Antioche' *MH* 40 (1983) 185-96.

——'Le Port de Séleucie de Piérie et l' Infrastructure Logistique des Guerres parthiques' *BJ* 185 (1985) 47-87.

Birley, A.R., *The Fasti of Roman Britain* (Clarendon Press, 1981).

——*Hadrian: The Restless Emperor* (Routledge, 1997: repr. 1998).

Blake, M.E., *Roman Construction in Italy from Tiberius through the Flavians* (Carnegie Institute of Washington, 1959).

Bosworth, A.B.,'Vespasian's Reorganisation of the North-East Frontier' *Antichthon* 10 (1976) 63-78.

Bowman, A., 'Papyri and Roman History' *JRS* 66 (1976) 153-73.
Bradley, K.R., 'The Chronology of Nero's Visit to Greece' *Latomus* 37 (1978) 61-72.
——*Suetonius' 'Life of Nero': An Historical Commentary* (*Collection Latomus* 157, 1978a).
——'Nero's Retinue in Greece, AD 66/67' *Illinois Class. Stud.* 4 (1979) 152-7.
——'The Significance of the *Spectacula* in Suetonius' *Caesares*' *RSA* 11 (1981). 129-37.
Braithwaite, A.W., *C. Suetonii Tranquilli Divus Vespasianus with an Introduction and Commentary* (Clarendon Press, 1927).
Braund, D.C., *Rome and the Friendly King : The Character of Client Kingship* (St Martin's Press, 1984).
Brind'Amour, P., 'Problèmes Astrologiques et Astronomiques soulevés par le Récit de la Mort de Domitien chez Suétone' *Phoenix* 35 (1981) 338-44.
Brunt, P.A., 'Charges of Provincial Maladministration under the Early Principate' *Historia* 10 (1961) 189-227.
——*Italian Manpower: 225 BC-AD 14* (Clarendon Press, 1971).
——'The *Lex de Imperio Vespasiani*' *JRS* 67 (1977) 95-116.
——'Free Labour and Public Works at Rome' *JRS* 70 (1980) 81-98.
Buttrey, T.V., 'Vespasian's *Consecratio* and the Numismatic Evidence' *Historia* 25 (1976) 449-57.
——*Documentary Evidence for the Chronology of the Flavian Titulature* (*Beiträge zur Klassischen Philologie* 112, 1980).
Cameron, A., *Circus Factions: Greens and Blues at Rome and Byzantium* (Clarendon Press, 1976).
Campbell, B., *The Emperor and the Roman Army: 31 BC-AD 235* (Clarendon Press, 1984).
Carradice, I.A., 'A Denarius of AD 92' *ZPE* 28 (1978) 159-60.
——*Coinage and Finances in the Reign of Domitian, AD 81-96* (*BAR* 178, 1983).
Casson, L., 'Unemployment, the Building Trade and Suetonius *Vesp.* 18' *BASP* 15 (1978) 43-51.
Castagnoli, F., 'Politica Urbanistica di Vespasiano in Roma' *Atti* (1981) 261-73.
Castritius, H., 'Zu den Frauen der Flavier' *Historia* 18 (1969) 492-502.
Champlin, E., '*Figlinae Marcianae*' *Athenaeum* 61 (1983) 257-64.
Chastagnol, A., 'Le Laticlave de Vespasien' *Historia* 25 (1976) 253-6.
Chilver, G.E.F., *A historical Commentary on Tacitus' Histories I and II* (Clarendon Press, 1979).
Chilver, G.E.F., and Townend, G., *An historical Commentary on Tacitus' Histories IV and V* (Clarendon Press, 1985).
Clark, A.M., *Hey's Mineral Index: Mineral Species, Varieties and Synonyms* 3rd edn (Chapman and Hall, 1993).

Clarke, G.W., 'The Date of the *Consecratio* of Vespasian' *Historia* 15 (1966) 318-27.

Cohen, S.J.D., *Josephus in Galilee and Rome: His Vita and Development as a Historian* (Brill, 1979).

Coleman, K.M., 'The Emperor Domitian and Literature' *ANRW* 2.32.5 (1986) 3087-115.

——'Fatal Charades: Roman Executions staged as Mythological Enactments' *JRS* 80 (1990) 44-73.

——'Launching into History: Aquatic Displays in the early Empire' *JRS* 83 (1993) 48-74.

Couissin, J., 'Suétone Physiognomoniste dans les *Vies Des XII Césars*' *REL* 31 (1953) 234-56.

Crawford, M.H., *Roman Statutes* (*BICS Suppl.* 64, 1996).

Crook, J., 'Titus and Berenice' *AJPh* 72 (1951) 162-75.

Dabrowa, E., 'Le Limes Anatolien et la Frontière Caucasienne au Temps des Flaviens' *Klio* 62 (1980) 379-88.

——'Les Rapports entre Rome et les Parthes sous Vespasien' *Syria* 58 (1981) 187-204.

Daltrop, G., Hausmann, U. and Wegner, M., *Die Flavier* (Mann, 1966).

Darwall-Smith, R., 'Albanum and the Villas of Domitian' *Pallas* 40 (1994) 145-65.

Devreker, J., 'La Continuité dans le *Consilium Principis* sous les Flaviens' *Anc. Soc.* 8 (1977) 223-43.

——'L' *Adlectio in Senatum* de Vespasien' *Latomus* 39 (1980) 70-87.

——'La Composition du Sénat Romain sous les Flaviens' *Studien zur antiken Sozialgeschichte* (ed. by W. Eck *et al.*: Kölner Hist. Abh. 28, 1980a) 257-68.

Dilke, O.A.W., *The Roman Land Surveyors: An Introduction to the Agrimensores* (David and Charles, 1971).

Duncan-Jones, R., *The Economy of the Roman Empire* (Cambridge University Press, 1974).

Eck, W., *Senatoren von Vespasian bis Hadrian* (Beck, 1970).

——'Jahres-und Provinzialfasten der Senatorischen Statthalter von 69/70 bis 138/139 (I)' *Chiron* 12 (1982) 281-362.

Eck, W., et al. *Das Senatus Consultum de Cn. Pisone Patre* (Beck, 1996).

Evans, E.C., 'Roman Descriptions of Personal Appearance in History and Biography' *HSCPh* 46 (1935) 43-84.

——'Physiognomics in the Ancient World' *Transactions of the American Philosophical Society* 59 (1969) 1-101.

Fishwick, D., *The Imperial Cult in the Latin West. Studies in the Ruler Cult of the Western Provinces of the Roman Empire* (Brill, 1987).

Frere, S., *Britannia: A History of Roman Britain* 3rd edn (Pimlico, 1991).

Friedländer, L., *Darstellungen aus der Sittengeschichte Roms in der Zeit von*

Augustus bis zum Ausgang der Antonine (7 th edn) English tr. *Roman Life and Manners under the Early Empire* by L. A. Magnus (George Routledge and Sons, 1907: repr. Routledge and Kegan Paul, 1968).

Galli, F., *Suetonio: Vita di Domiziano. Introduzione, Traduzione e Commento* (Edizioni dell' Ateneo, 1991).

Gallivan, P.A., 'The Fasti for AD 70-96' *CQ* 31 (1981) 186-220.

Garthwaite, J., *Domitian and the Court Poets Martial and Statius* (Diss. Cornell, 1978).

——'Martial, Book 6, on Domitian's Moral Censorship' *Prudentia* 22 (1990) 13-22.

Garzetti, A., *From Tiberius to the Antonines: A History of the Roman Empire, AD 14-192* tr. J.R. Foster (Methuen, 1974).

Gascou, J., *Suétone Historien* (École Française de Rome, 1984).

Goodman, M., *The Ruling Class of Judaea: The Origins of the Jewish Revolt against Rome AD 66-70* (Cambridge University Press, 1987: repr., Paperback, 1995).

Gorringe, C.F., *A Study of the Death-Narratives in Suetonius' De Vita Caesarum*' (Diss. Queensland, 1993).

Graves, R., *Suetonius: The Twelve Caesars* (Harmondsworth, 1957).

Griffin, M., 'The Flavians' *CAH* XI 2nd edn (Cambridge University Press, 2000).

Gwatkin, W.E. Jr., 'Cappadocia as a Roman Procuratorial Province' *University of Missouri Studies 5* (University of Missouri Press, 1930).

Hammond, M., *The Antonine Monarchy* (American Academy in Rome, 1959).

Hannestad, N., *Roman Art and Imperial Policy* (Aarhus University Press, 1986).

Hardie, A., *Statius and the Silvae. Poets, Patrons and Epideixis in the Graeco-Roman World* (Francis Cairns, 1983).

Henderson, B.W., *Five Roman Emperors* (Cambridge University Press, 1927).

Henrichs, A., 'Vespasian's Visit to Alexandria' *ZPE* 3 (1968) 51-80.

Hind, J.G.F., 'The Invasion of Britain in AD 43 – An alternative Strategy for Aulus Plautius' *Britannia* 20 (1989) 1-21.

Hopkins, K., *Conquerors and Slaves: Sociological Studies in Roman History 1* (Cambridge University Press, 1978).

——*Death and Renewal: Sociological Studies in Roman History 2* (Cambridge University Press, 1983).

Howell, P., 'The Colossus of Nero' *Athenaeum* 46 (1968) 292-9.

Hudson-Williams, A., 'Suetonius, *Vesp.* 22' *CR* 2 (1952) 72-3.

Isaac, B., 'Vespasian's Titulature in AD 69' *ZPE* 55 (1984) 143-4.

Jones, A.H.M., *The Cities of the Eastern Roman Provinces* 2nd edn (Clarendon Press, 1971).

Jones, B.W., *The Emperor Titus* (Croom Helm, 1984).

——'Agrippina and Vespasian' *Latomus* 43 (1984a) 581-3.

Jones, B.W., *The Emperor Domitian* (Routledge, 1992).

——*Suetonius Domitian: Edited with Introduction, Commentary and Bibliography* (Bristol Classical Press, 1996).

——*Suetonius Vespasian: Edited wuth Introduction, Commentary and Bibliography* (Bristol Classical Press, 2000).

Jones, C.P., Egypt and Judaea under Vespasian' *Historia* 46 (1997) 249-53.

Keaveney, A., 'Vespasian's Gesture (Suet. *Vesp*. 8.5 and Dio 65.10.2)' *GIF* 39 (1987) 213-16.

Keresztes, P., 'The Imperial Roman Government and the Christian Church I' *ANRW* 2.21.3 (1979) 247-315.

Kienast, D., 'Diva Domitilla' *ZPE* 76 (1989) 141-7.

Kleiner, F.S., 'A Vespasianic Monument to the Senate and Roman People' *SNR* 68 (1989) 85-91.

Kleiner, F.S, 'The Arches of Vespasian in Rome' *MDAIR* 97 (1990) 127-36.

Kokkinos, N.K, *Antonia Augusta: Portrait of a Great Roman Lady* (Routledge, 1992).

Last, H., 'On the Flavian Reliefs from the Palazzo della Cancellaria' *JRS* 38 (1948) 9-14.

Le Glay, M., 'Les *Censitores Provinciae Thraciae*' *ZPE* 42 (1981) 175-84.

Levick, B., 'Domitian and the Provinces' *Latomus* 41 (1982) 50-73.

——*Vespasian* (Routledge, 1999).

Liebeschuetz, J.H.W.G., *Continuity and Change in Roman Religion* (Clarendon Press, 1979).

Lindsay, H.M., *Suetonius Caligula: Edited with Introduction, Commentary and Bibliography* (Bristol Classical Press, 1993).

Magie, D., *Roman Rule in Asia Minor to the End of the Third Century after Christ* (Princeton University Press, 1950: repr. Arno Press, 1975).

Marrou, H.I. *Histoire de l'Éducation dans l' Antiquité* 3rd edn, tr. G. Lamb (Sheed and Ward, 1956).

MacDonald, W.L., *The Architecture of the Roman Empire I. An Introductory Study* (Yale University Press, 1982).

MacMullen, R., *Enemies of the Roman Order: Treason, Unrest and Alienation in the Empire* (Harvard University Press, 1966).

Martin, A., *La Titulature Epigraphique de Domitien* (Beiträge für Klassischen Philologie 181, 1987).

Martinet, H., *C. Suetonius Tranquillus, Divus Titus: Kommentar* (Hain, 1981).

Maxfield, V.A., *The military Decorations of the Roman Army* (Batsford, 1981).

McAlindon, D., 'Senatorial Advancement in the Age of Claudius' *Latomus* 16 (1957) 252-62.

McGuire, M.E., *A Historical Commentary on Suetonius' Life of Titus* (Diss. Johns Hopkins, 1980).

Millar, F., *The Emperor in the Roman World (31 BC-AD 337)* (Duckworth, 1977).

Millar, F., *The Roman Near East 31 BC-AD 337* (Harvard University Press, 1993).

Mitford, Terence B., 'Roman Rough Cilicia' *ANRW* 2.7.2 (1980) 1230-61.

Mommsen, Th., *The Provinces of the Roman Empire from Caesar to Diocletian* (1885: tr. W. Dickson, Ares, 1974).

Montevecchi, O., 'Vespasiano Acclamato dagli Alessandrini' *Atti* (1981) 483-496.

Mooney, G.W., *C. Suetonii Tranquilli De Vita Caesarum. Libri VII-VIII* (Longmans, Green and Co., 1930).

Morgan, M.G., 'Vespasian and the Omens in Tacitus, *Histories* 2.78' *Phoenix* 50 (1996) 41-55.

Murison, C.L., 'The Revolt of Saturninus in Upper Germany, AD 89' *ECM* 29 (1985) 31-49.

——*Suetonius: Galba, Otho, Vitellius: Edited with Introduction and Notes* (Bristol Classical Press, 1992).

Nardi, E., 'Aborto Omicidio nela Civiltà Classica' *ANRW* 2.13 (1981) 366-85.

Nicols, J., *Vespasian and the Partes Flavianae* (*Historia Einzelschriften* 28, 1978).

Osborne, C., *The Complete Operas of Mozart: A Critical Guide* (London, 1978).

Pailler, J.-M. and Sablayrolles, R., '*Damnatio Memoriae*: Une Vraie Perpétuité' *Pallas* 40 (1994) 11-550.

Patterson, J.R., 'Crisis: What Crisis? Rural Change and Urban Development in Imperial Appennine Italy' *PBSR* 55 (1987) 115-46.

Pergola, P.,'La Condamnation des Flaviens "Chrétiens" sous Domitien: Persécution Religieuse ou Répression à Caractère Politique?' *MEFRA* 90 (1978) 407-23.

Pigon, J., 'Helvidius Priscus, Eprius Marcellus and *Iudicium Senatus*' *CQ* 42 (1992) 235-46.

Platner, S.B. and Ashby, T., *A Topographical Dictionary of Ancient Rome* (Oxford University Press, 1929).

Price, J.J., *Jerusalem under Siege: The Collapse of the Jewish State 66-70 C.E.* (Brill, 1992).

Prigent, P., 'Au Temps de l'Apocalypse I: Domitien' *RHPhR* 54 (1974) 455-83.

Purcell, N., 'The *Apparitores*: A Study in Social History' *PBSR* 51 (1983) 125-173.

Rajak, T., *Josephus: The Historian and His Society* (Duckworth, 1983).

Richardson, L. Jr., *A New Topographical Dictionary of Ancient Rome* (Johns Hopkins University Press, 1992).

Ritter, H.W., 'Zur Lebensgeschichte der Flavia Domitilla, der Frau Vespasians' *Historia* 21 (1972) 759-61.

Rogers, P.M., 'Titus, Berenice and Mucianus' *Historia* 29 (1980) 86-95.
Roxan, M.M., 'An Emperor Rewards his Supporters: the Earliest Extant Diploma Issued by Vespasian' *JRA* 9 (1996) 248-56.
Sablayrolles, R., 'Domitien, l'Auguste Ridicule' *Pallas* 40 (1994) 113-44.
Salway, P., *The Oxford Illustrated History of Roman Britain* (Oxford University Press, 1993).
Schmidt, M.G., 'Claudius und Vespasian. Eine Neue Interpretation des Wortes "vae, puto, deus fio" (Suet., *Vesp.* 23.4)' *Chiron* 18 (1988) 83-9.
Scott, K., *The Imperial Cult under the Flavians* (Kohlhammer, 1936: repr. Arno Press, 1975).
Scullard, H.H., *Festivals and Ceremonies of the Roman Republic* (Thames and Hudson, 1981).
Sherk, R.K., 'Roman Galatia: the Governors from 25 BC to AD 114' *ANRW* 2.7.2 (1980) 954-1052.
Sherwin-White, A.N., *The Letters of Pliny. A Historical and Social Commentary* (Clarendon Press, 1966).
Simpson, C.J., 'The "Conspiracy" of AD 39' *Collection Latomus* 168 (1980) 347-66.
Smallwood, E.M., 'Domitian's Attitude to the Jews and Judaism' *CPh* 51 (1956) 1-13.
——*Documents illustrating the Principates of Gaius, Claudius and Nero* (Cambridge University Press, 1967).
Sordi, M., *The Christians and the Roman Empire* tr. A. Bedini (Editoriale Jaca Book Sp A, 1983: repr. Routledge, 1994).
Souris, G.A., 'The Size of Provincial Embassies to the Emperor under the Principate' *ZPE* 48 (1982) 235-44.
Southern, P., *Domitian: Tragic Tyrant* (Routledge, 1997).
Speidel, M.A., 'Roman Army Pay Scales' *JRS* 82 (1992) 87-106.
Steinby, E.M. (ed.), *Lexicon Topographicum Urbis Romae* (Quasar, 1993 [I] and 1996 [III]).
Strobel, K., 'Ein neues Zeugnis für die Statthalterschaft des M. Hirrius Fronto Neratius Pansa in Lycia-Pamphylia aus Oinoanda?' *ZPE* 61 (1985) 1773-80.
——*Die Donaukriege Domitians* (Habelt, 1989).
Sutherland, C.H.V., 'The State of the Imperial Treasury at the Death of Domitian' *JRS* 25 (1935) 150-62.
Syme, R., Review of Scott, 1936 *CR* 51 (1937) 32-3.
——*Tacitus* (Clarendon Press, 1958).
——*Roman Papers* Vols 1-2 ed. E. Badian; 3-7 ed. A.R. Birley (Clarendon Press, 1977-1991).
——*Anatolica: Studies in Strabo* ed. A.R. Birley (Clarendon Press, 1995).
Takacs, S.A., *Isis and Sarapis in the Roman World* (Brill, 1995).
Talbert, R.J.A., *The Senate of Imperial Rome* (Princeton University Press, 1984).

Thompson, L., 'Domitian and the Jewish Tax' *Historia* 31 (1982) 329-42.

Townend, G.B., 'Some Flavian Connections' *JRS* 51 (1961) 54-62.

——'The Restoration of the Capitol in AD 70' *Historia* 36 (1987) 243-8.

Toynbee, J.M.C., *Death and Burial in the Roman World* (Thames and Hudson, 1971).

Turner, E.G., 'Tiberius Julius Alexander' *JRS* 44 (1954) 54-64.

Vinson, M.P., 'Domitia Longina, Julia Titi, and the Literary Tradition' *Historia* 38 (1989) 431-50.

Wallace, K.G., 'The Flavii Sabini in Tacitus' *Historia* 36 (1987) 343-58.

Wallace-Hadrill, A., *Suetonius: The Scholar and His Caesars* (Duckworth, 1983: 2nd edn, Bristol Classical Press, 1995).

——'The Imperial Court' in *CAH* XI, 2nd edn (Cambridge University Press, 1996).

Wardle, D., 'Vespasian, Helvidius Priscus and the Restoration of the Capitol' *Historia* 45 (1996) 208-22.

Waters, K.H., 'The Character of Domitian' *Phoenix* 18 (1964) 49-77.

——'*Traianus Domitiani Continuator*' *AJP* 90 (1969) 385-405.

Watkins, T.H., 'Vespasian and the Italic Right' *CJ* 84 (1988/89) 117-36.

Weaver, P.R.C., 'Where Have all the Junian Latins Gone? Nomenclature and Status in the Early Empire' *Chiron* 20 (1990) 275-305.

——'Epaphroditus, Josephus and Epictetus' *CQ* 44 (1994) 468-79.

Wellesley, K., 'Three historical puzzles in Tacitus *Histories III*: (3) the escape of Domitian from the Capitol' *CQ* 6 (1956) 211-4.

——*The Long Year AD 69* (Elek, 1975).

——'What Happened on the Capitol in December AD 69' *AJAH* 6 (1981) 166-90.

Wiedemann, T.E.J., *Emperors and Gladiators* (Routledge, 1992).

Williams, M.H., 'Domitian, the Jews and the "Judaizers" – A Simple Matter of *cupiditas* and *maiestas*?' *Historia* 39 (1990) 196-211.

Wilkes, J.J., 'Romans, Dacians and Sarmatians in the First and Early Second Centuries' in B. Hartley and J. Wacher (eds) *Rome and her Northern Provinces* (Alan Sutton, 1983).

Wiseman, T.P., 'Flavians on the Capitol' *AJAH* 3 (1978) 163-78.

Young, M.R., *The Later Herodians and Rome (AD 23-93): A Study of the imperial-client Relationship between the Jewish Rulers Agrippa I, Agrippa II, Berenice II and the Roman Emperors from Tiberius to Domitian* (Diss. Sydney, 1999).

Young, M.R., 'Quintilian's Legal Representation of Queen Berenice' *Historia* 50 (2001) forthcoming.

Zinn, T.L., 'To Keeping Vespasian a Virgin' *CR* 1 (1951) 10.

Appendix

SUETONIAN BIBLIOGRAPHY

Since the discovery of the Hippo inscription more than forty years ago, a number of books and monographs have been devoted to Suetonius, including.

Anna, G.d', *Le Idee Letterarie di Suetonio* (La Nuova Italia, 1954).

Baldwin, B., *Suetonius* (Hakkert, 1983).

Benediktson, D.T., 'A Survey of Suetonius Scholarship, 1938-1987' *CW* 86 (1993) 377-447.

Bradley, K.R., 'The Imperial Ideal in Suetonius' *Caesares*' *ANRW* 2.33.5 (1991) 3701-32.

Bradley, K.R., *Suetonius Volume I* (Introduction): with an English Translation by J.C. Rolfe (Harvard University Press, 1998).

Cizek, E., *Structures et Idéologie dans 'Les Vies des Douze Césars' de Suétone* (Les Belles Lettres, 1977).

Coninck, L. de, *Suetonius en de Archivalia* (Paleis der Academien, 1983).

Coninck, L. de, 'Les Sources Documentaires de Suétone, "Les XII Césars": 1900-1990' *ANRW* 2.33.5 (1991) 3675-700.

Corte, F. della, *Suetonio: Eques Romanus* 2nd edn (La Nuova Italia, 1967) and Administration' *ANRW* 2.1 (1974) 392-434.

Duff, J.W., *A Literary History of Rome in the Silver Age* 3rd edn (Benn, 1964).

Galand-Hallyn, P., 'Bibliographie Suétonienne (Les "Vies des XII Césars") 1950-1988. Vers Une Réhabilitation' *ANRW* 2.33.5 (1991) 3576-622.

Gascou, J., *Suétone Historien* (École Française de Rome, 1984).

Gugel, H., *Studien zur Biographischen Technik Suetons* (Wein Böhlau, 1977).

Lewis, R.G., 'Suetonius' "Caesares" and their Literary Antecedents' *ANRW* 2.33.5 (1991) 3623-74.

Lounsbury, R.C., *The Arts of Suetonius – An Introduction* (American University Studies 17, Vol. 3: Lang, 1987).

Mouchova, B., *Studie zu Kaiserbiographien Suetons* (Praha Universita Karlova, 1968).

Murphy, J.P., 'The Anecdote in Suetonius' Flavian "Lives"' *ANRW* 2.33.5 (1991) 3780-793.

Townend, G.B., 'The Date of Composition of Suetonius' *Caesares*' *CQ* 9 (1959) 285-93.

Townend, G.B., 'The Hippo Inscription and the Career of Suetonius' *Historia* 10 (1961) 99-109.

Vacher, M.-C., *Suétone: Grammariens et Rhéteurs* (Les Belles Lettres, 1993).

Wallace-Hadrill, A., *Suetonius: The Scholar and His Caesars* (Duckworth, 1983: 2nd edn, Bristol Classical Press, 1995).

COMMENTARIES ON THE FLAVIAN LIVES

There are a number of commentaries on Suetonius' *Lives* of the Flavian emperors, i.e.

Life of Vespasian: A.W. Braithwaite, 1927; G.W. Mooney, 1930: H.R. Graf, 1937 and B.W. Jones, 2000.
Life of Titus: H. Price, 1919; G.W. Mooney, 1930; M.Martinet, 1981 and M.E. McGuire, 1980.
Life of Domitian: J.C. Janssen, 1919; R.F.C.Gephardt, 1922; G.W. Mooney, 1930; F.Galli, 1991 and B.W. Jones, 1996.

SOME FLAVIAN OFFICIALS

Studies devoted to senior Flavian officials (senators, equestrians and imperial freedmen) include.

Senators

M. Acilius Glabrio: P.A. Gallivan, *Historia* 27 (1978) 621-5.
L. Antistius Rusticus: R. Syme, *Historia* 32 (1983) 359-84.
L. Antonius Saturninus: G. Walser, *Provincialia* 40 (1968) 497-507; B.W. Jones, *Latomus* 33 (1974) 529-35; C.L. Murison, *ECM* 29 (1985) 31-49 and K. Strobel, *Tyche* 1 (1986) 203-20.
M. Aponius Saturninus: R.D. Milns, *Historia* 22 (1973) 284-94.
M. Arrecinus Clemens: B.W. Jones, *P del P* 146 (1972) 320-1; B.W. Jones and R. Develin, *Antichthon* 10 (1976) 79-83 and G. Mennella, *Athenaeum* 59 (1981) 205-8.
[?L. Caesennius] Sospes: H.G. Pflaum, *Historia* 2 (1953) 431-50 and R. Syme, *JRS* 67 (1977) 38-49.
P. Calvisius Ruso: B. Rémy, *MEFR* 95 (1983) 163-82; E. Birley, *ZPE* 51 (1983) 263-9 and R. Syme, *ZPE* 56 (1984) 173-92.
C. Cilnius Proculus: H. Halfmann, *ZPE 61* (1985) 239-50.
M. Cornelius Nigrinus: G. Alföldy and H. Halfmann, *Chiron* 3 (1973) 331-73.
L. Domitius Apollinaris: R. Syme, *RP* 7: 588-602.
P. Egnatius Celer: J.K. Evans, *CQ* 29 (1979) 198-202.
A. Fabricius Veiento: W.C. McDermott, *AJPh* 91 (1970) 124-48.
T. Flavius Clemens: P. Pergola, *MEFRA* 90 (1978) 407-23.
T. Flavius Sabinus: K.G. Wallace, *Historia* 36 (1987) 343-56.

L. Flavius Silva: W.C. McDermott, *CW* 66 (1973) 335-51.

L. Funisulanus Vettonianus: J. K. Evans, *Historia* 27 (1978) 102-28 (*passim*).

C. Helvidius Priscus: J. Malitz, *Hermes* 113 (1985) 231-46; J. Pigon, *CQ* 42 (1992) 235-46 and D. Wardle, *Historia* 45 (1996) 208-22.

M. Hirrius Fronto Neratius Pansa: M. Torelli, *JRS* 58 (1968) 170-5; M. Heil, *Chiron* 19 (1979) 165-84 and K. Strobel, *ZPE* 61 (1985) 173-80.

Cn. Julius Agricola: A.R. Birley, *The Ancient Historian and His Materials* (1978) 139-54; B. Dobson, *Scot. Arch. Forum* 12 (1981) 1-13 and D.B. Campbell, *ZPE* 63 (1986) 197-200.

Sex. Julius Frontinus: W.C. McDermott, *Anc Soc* 7 (1976) 229-61.

A. Lappius Maximus: J. Assa, *Akten des IV. internat. Kongr. für gr. und lat. Epigr.* (1962) 31-9.

C. Licinius Mucianus: R. Syme, *Antichthon* 11 (1977) 78-92 and P.M. Rogers, *Historia* 29 (1980) 86-95.

L. Licinius Sura: C.P. Jones, *JRS* 60 (1970) 98-104.

A. Marius Celsus: C.B. Rüger, *BJ* 179 (1979) 187-200.

Mettius Pompusianus: P. Arnaud, *MEFR* 95 (1983) 677-99.

L. Neratius Marcellus: L. Vidman, *ZPE* 43 (1981) 377-84.

L. Neratius Priscus: R. Syme, *Hermes* 85 (1957) 480-93 and G. Camodeca, *AAN* 87 (1976) 19-38.

Q. Petillius Cerialis: A. R. Birley, *Britannia* 4 (1973) 179-90.

[C. Petillius] Firmus: A. B. Bosworth, *ZPE* 39 (1980) 267-77 and M. Dondin-Payre, *ZPE* 52 (1983) 236-40.

Ti. Plautius Silvanus: P. Conole and R. D. Milns, *Historia* 32 (1983) 183-200.

[?Plo]tius Pegasus: E. Champlin, *ZPE* 32 (1978) 269-78.

M. Pompeius Silvanus: W. Eck, *ZPE* 9 (1972) 259-76.

C. Rutilius Gallicus: R. Syme, *Arctos* 18 (1984) 149-56 and W. Eck, *AJP* 106 (1985) 475-84.

Sallustius Lucullus: B.W. Jones and P. Conole, *Latomus* 42 (1983) 629-33.

C. Salvius Liberalis: W.C. McDermott, *CW* 66 (1973) 335-51.

Ti. Silius Italicus: W.C. McDermott and A. Orentzel, *AJP* 98 (1977) 23-34.

Q. Sosius Senecio: C.P. Jones, *JRS* 70 (1970) 98-104.

D. Terentius Scaurianus: W. Eck, *ZPE* 52 (1983) 151-6.

P. Valerius Patruinus: B. Kreiler, *Chiron* 4 (1974) 451-2.

C. Vettulenus Civica Cerialis: B.W. Jones, *Athenaeum* 61 (1983) 516-21.

Equestrians

M. Arruntius Claudianus: A. Suceveanu, *Anc Soc* 22 (1991) 255-76.

Cornelius Fuscus: J. Colin, *Latomus* 15 (1956) 57-82.

Ti. Julius Alexander: E.G. Turner, *JRS* 44 (1954) 54-64.

C. Minicius Italus: V.A. Maxfield, *ES* 9 (1972) 243-5.

Plotius Grypus: F. Bérard, *MEFR* 96 (1984) 259-324.

C. Velius Rufus: D. Kennedy, *Britannia* 14 (1983) 183-96 and K. Strobel, *ZPE* 64 (1986) 265-86.
Crispinus: P. White, *AJP* 95 (1974) 377-82; W.C. McDermott, *RSA* 8 (1978) 117-22; B. Baldwin, *AC* 22 (1979) 109-14 and A. Vassileiou, *Latomus* 43 (1984) 27-68.

Imperial Freedmen

Ti. Claudius Classicus: P.R.C. Weaver, *Antichthon* 14 (1980) 143-56; G. Boulvert, *ZPE* 43 (1981) 31-41 and Chr. Bruun, *ZPE* 82 (1990) 271-85.
[?Ti. Claudius] Epaphroditus: W. Eck, *Historia* 25 (1976) 381-4 and P.R.C. Weaver, *CQ* 44 (1994) 468-79.
Ti. Claudius Zosimus: L. Schumacher, *ES* 11 (1976) 131-41 and G. Walser, *Chiron* 19 (1989) 449-56.
Ti. Julius (father of Claudius Etruscus): P.R.C. Weaver, *CQ* 15 (1965) 145-54; I. A. Carradice, *LCM* 4 (1978) 101-3 and J.K. Evans, *Historia* 27 (1978) 102-28.
Earinus: C. Henriksén, *Mnemosyne* 50 (1997) 281-94.

Index of Proper Names

V Vespasian
T Titus
D Domitian